The Pianist's Touch

The Pianist's Touch

Method and Theory of

PAUL PICHIER

edited by

WALTER KRAUSE

with the assistance of

Elisabeth Hesse and Waltraut Osborne

translated by

Martha Ideler and Peter R. Wilson

Perelen Publishers

Design and production coordination by
Theo Jung
Palo Alto, California

Dedicated to the memory of Elisabeth Hesse

Contents

From the Foreword to the German Edition

When Professor Paul PICHIER died on September 5th, 1955, the task of making his writings public was left to me, as his student and colleague of many decades. The difficulty of the task lay in the complexity of the personality whose last wish I had to fulfil.

There were so many facets in the personality of this man, Viennese by choice, born in East Prussia with a French name. In fact, the name was not his only inheritance from his Huguenot forefathers: He also possessed the critical French mind which doubts everything and has no respect for traditional ways of thinking. This scepticism was one pole in Pichier's personality; his enthusiastic devotion to the arts was the other. An all-embracing intellectual interest was joined with the ability to deal with a highly specialized subject in its minutest details. The results of his detailed investigations are set down for posterity in this book. But first let me say something about his wide-ranging interests and his life.

Pichier was born on January 18th, 1873, the son of a pastor in Nordenburg, East Prussia. To begin with he studied law and after receiving his degree in this subject, he joined the Prussian civil service. But soon his devotion to the muses began to rule his life, although at first in a direction that later proved to be a digression from his real destination. He took up photography and became a pioneer in the field of colour photography. His efforts in this field did not cease even when he had found the way to his real life's task, music. His interest in the visual arts remained with him throughout his life; his later studies at Vienna University were devoted not only to the history of music but also that of art, and even in his last years, despite failing eyesight, he was an enthusiastic collector and connoisseur of old paintings.

The decisive turning point in Pichier's life was his meeting with Theodore LESCHETIZKY in 1901 in Vienna. Unapproachable as this world-renowned master was, in the case of Pichier he reacted differently. He trained him as an assistant, and for twelve years Pichier had the privilege of observing Leschetizky's teaching and of absorbing the artistic and technical directions given to pianists at all stages of development. Through his capacity to observe and his critical faculty, he was able to enlarge upon what he had learned from the master. Thus he found his life's task, which was to fathom the connection between the mechanics of making a tone and musical expression. For Pichier there was no doubt that there existed a fathomable, purely physical connection, since he, sceptical as he was, refused to believe that there was any mystery about genius. He realised that this connection could only be found in the realm of science and zealously threw himself into the study of physics and anatomy. His critical investigations relating to his chosen task extended over decades, in fact until his death.

How true the results of these investigations were, was proven to Pichier continually in dealing with his numerous students from all over the world. His students recognized this, too, if only those few who were devoted to music with the same fanaticism and who were not soon driven away by the great demands he made of them. Among those who found their way to him and stayed with him there was many an accomplished concert pianist who realised that he had come to a point beyond which he could not progress with the methods he had used up to then. Pichier showed them the way to further progress by giving them two things: a technique based on the deepest understanding of the nature of the instrument and of the human body; and an art of phrasing based on the most profound receptivity to each individual musical composition.

Beside the practical teaching in which Pichier imparted elements of his thoughts to his contemporaries, he always found time to write memoranda, through which he wanted to communicate his knowledge to posterity. From this activity heaps of manuscripts resulted.

After his death, I was faced by them — helpless. A first helper was found in one of his youngest students, Waltraut Paulin (Mrs. Osborne). With her assistance I was able to sort the memoranda under different headings. She also drew up a first draft. Although this meant a great deal, she naturally could not handle what we knew was Pichier's first and foremost demand — a clear scientific explanation. We knew that there was only one man who was sufficiently familiar with Pichier's ideas in this field, since he had worked with him for many years — Dr. Walter KRAUSE; but we also knew that these two men who were so different had had many arguments, which had led to a final break some years before

Pichier's death. Nevertheless, we went to Dr. Krause at the Anatomical Department of the University. There we found further
proof that the path Pichier had taken was correct: In spite of the
past differences, Dr. Krause immediately declared himself ready
to collaborate and even took in hand the writing of this book. For
more than three years he devoted himself to it, conferring again
and again with Mrs. Osborne and me about all the problems which
arose. When at last we saw the finished manuscript, we were
agreeably surprised — as any pianist would be — to see that the
anatomist himself used far fewer anatomical expressions than
Pichier had, and that anatomical details took up only as much
space as was absolutely necessary in order to remain true to the
spirit of Pichier.

Dr. Krause chose the form of a pedagogical dialogue similar
to the pattern of the Dialogues of Plato, with Pichier naturally
receiving the role of Socrates. We three who were in charge of his
literary legacy are his speaking partners. Waltraut Osborne, as the
youngest, takes the role of the student. It is in this role that every
reader should place himself in order to understand the methods
that Pichier developed from his own theories.

The words called for graphic illustration, and we are indebted
to Ludwig Schrott for the excellent plates. Karl Nieschlag, the
sculptor, provided most of the grapic illustrations; and Heinz
Lehfuss, M.D., the photographs. Our thanks are due to both of
these gentlemen, who gave their help without payment.

The publication of this book was made possible by subsidies
from the Austrian Ministry of Education, the Cultural Office of
Vienna and the League ("Notring") of Cultural Organisations of
Austria. These and many other donors from the world-wide circle
of Pichier's pupils and friends deserve our heartfelt gratitude.

We especially thank the most famous of Pichier's pupils, Jörg
DEMUS, who gave two piano recitals to help subsidize this work
and allowed his hand to be photographed, a practical acknowledge-
ment of his teacher which he supplemented with the statement
that the foundation of his entire development as a pianist was laid
down by many years of study under Pichier.

If this volume succeeds in passing on to future generations
what Pichier can no longer personally teach to his pupils, then the
efforts of all of us will not have been in vain.

Elisabeth Hesse

Preface to the English Edition

In the preceding foreword Elisabeth HESSE mentioned the services of many people for the publication of this book, but nothing has been said about herself. In fact, it was she who was the very heart and soul of this task. It is no exaggeration to say that from the day she took over the project, she practically lived for this sole purpose. Only by her enthusiasm, her energy and her practical sense was the German edition made possible.

She also conveyed her enthusiasm to a former pupil of Pichier's, Mrs. Martha Ideler. This American lady devoted herself not only to the work of translating the book with my assistance, but also of publishing it in spite of all difficulties. By the mediation of Mrs. Osborne, a British man of letters and amateur musician, Mr. Peter R. Wilson, had the kindness to improve the style.

Destiny prevented Frau Hesse from living to see this work finished. She died on September 3rd, 1966, in the 80th year of her life and yet full of plans concerning this book.

The difficulty of translating the work was increased by the fact that Pichier had invented numerous terms in German, and much thought was required to find adequate English equivalents for these "Pichierisms". Aside from this special problem, every sentence has been discussed thoroughly with me in order to avoid any misunderstandings on the part of the co-translators. Thus the reader may be sure that nothing in the translation is accidental and that any phrase which sounds paradoxical is so intended by the authors.

It is an agreeable duty for me to express our sincerest thanks to Mrs. Ideler and Mr. Wilson. Above all, however, at this moment our thoughts are with Elisabeth Hesse, to whom this English edition is dedicated.

Walter Krause

DIALOGUE 1

The Demands of the Piano

Frau Hesse: I say, Professor, today Waltraut told me that she will not be put off any longer. She absolutely insists on hearing the ins and outs of the matter.

Professor Pichier: What matter?

Waltraut: Your piano technique.

Pichier: How often must I stress the fact that there is no Pichier piano technique? The technique which I practice, which I teach and which I investigate is the technique of Liszt, Chopin, Rubinstein and of my teacher Leschetitzky, and it seems that it can be traced back by way of Beethoven to the Bach family. That means that it is practically as old as the piano. And this is not mere chance, for it is not a technique which I have thought up, but the one which the piano demands.

W.:   How can you know that all those masters have used the same technique as you?

P.:   Some of them, like C.P.E. Bach[1], have left us literary documents concerning the most essential points of their knowledge about keyboard technique. In the case of other masters, we know through their pupils of one or another statement vividly revealing to us what technique was used by them—although only if we are familiar with this technique. I would just mention Liszt's allusion to "freely movable centres"[2], or Chopin's comparison of the movement of the wrist with the taking of breath in singing[3]. Furthermore we must not forget that outstanding personalities such as J. S. Bach attracted attentive observers[4] whose notes can give us important hints about the technique of the master.

[1] C.P.E. Bach: Versuch über die wahre Art, das Clavier zu spielen, 2nd ed. Schwiekert, Leipzig 1780.

[2] H. F. Clark: Liszts Offenbarung, Vieweg, Berlin-Gross Lichterfelde 1907, p. 262 among others.

[3] E. Caland: Das Künstlerische Klavierspiel in seinen psychologischen und physikalischen Vorgängen. Nagel, Stuttgart 1910.

[4] J. N. Forkel: Über J. S. Bachs Leben, Kunst und Kunstwerke. Hoffmeister und Kühnel, Leipzig 1802.

W.:   Does that mean that everything about the technique you use can be found in such books by the great masters or in books about them?

P.:   By no means. Their infrequent but very pertinent hints are given mostly in an aphoristic style and offer only fragmentary glimpses of this technique. They can therefore be understood only by those who know beforehand what is essential.

W.:   So there is no author who has tried to give a coherent account of piano technique?

P.:   As a matter of fact, any number of such accounts exist in all the languages of civilized nations.

Dr. Krause: Therefore, according to the rules of the scientific profession, it would now be your duty to mention all these books, to give short summaries of their contents and to rip them to pieces with criticism.

P.:   I know. I also know that by not doing so, I shall be suspected of not having studied them all, although they are only too familiar to me. I shall not analyse the previous literature, because we want to build something, and adverse criticism is certainly not constructive. On the other hand, it is impossible to use earlier works as a basis for our considerations, because either they do not deal at all with the technique that is demanded by the piano, but with some other technique, or the authors had this technique in mind but misunderstood it at many essential points. That is the reason why I had to start practically from scratch, as you will immediately recognize.

H.:   And yet — or for this very reason — you have achieved a complete, coherent system.

P.:   No, I have not achieved it but am still working on it. For what other reason would an anatomist sit here at my side as my scientific adviser? And don't I acquire new knowledge every day from my hundred-headed teacher — I mean my pupils — which I also have to fit into my system?

H.:   Certainly, Professor, you will go on learning as long as you live. However, don't you constantly apply your knowledge in teaching? Don't you constantly pass it on to your pupils? It must be a complete system by this time, even if here and there some small gap may remain to be filled.

P.:   And what is it that you believe justifies your description of my teaching as a complete, coherent system, in spite of the gaps in it?

H.:   The fact that it gives the answers to the four basic, inseparable questions about piano technique:

1)   How does the right touch come about?
2)   Why is this the only way of accomplishing the right
touch?
3)   What hinders most pianists in accomplishing this touch?
4)   How can these hindrances be overcome?
   P.:   Of those four questions it is the second which governs
the inner unity of my system. But since it begins with "why", it
presents the worst difficulties, not because it is hard for me to give
an answer, but because it is hard to make people listen to the
answer. The "why" has to do with theory, but the pianist is a
practical person. If he wishes to learn something about the principles of piano technique, he generally expects nothing more than
instructions, like those in a cookbook, as to what has to be done,
but nothing as to why it has to be done. Only a very few realise
that a certain amount of insight into theory is indispensable for
truly accomplished execution, because theory and practice nourish
each other.
   W.:   I promise, Professor, that I shall not run away from
theory, as long as it doesn't go beyond my power of comprehen-
sion. But you always talk a lot about physics and anatomy, and I
haven't the slightest idea of them.
   K.:   You don't need to know any more about these subjects
than a schoolboy does. We shall try to explain anything which is a
little more advanced in such a way that you will understand if you
observe these three conditions:
   1)   let nothing escape your attention;
   2)   when we are discussing a movement of the body, make
it yourself and participate in all the experiments;
   3)   in doing so use your senses—look, listen and touch.
   P.:   You can be sure that it is not my intention to fill your
brain with a specialist's scientific knowledge, which I do not
possess myself. I shall only mention what is essential for the understanding of piano technique. I am even less concerned to create
an aura of erudition by using technical terms relating to physics
and anatomy and so to give the impression that I am dealing with
incontestable truths—which have been attested by the highest
competent authorities and for this reason have to be believed
unfalteringly by the pianist, who in this respect is absolutely
ignorant.
   K.:   In fact, no such academic authorisation can be claimed,
because the scientific facts are frequently not presented in the
customary academic manner. Professor Pichier has invented terms
of his own for physical and anatomical phenomena, terms which

are specially adapted to the problems concerning piano playing. Difficult as my cooperation with him became because of this method of his, it will certainly make it much easier for you to understand.

W.:   But why are physics and anatomy necessary at all?

P.:   Because the touching of the key is a physical process, and because the individual doing it has a human body. The result of the process of touching is the tone. If we keep in mind the obvious fact that the effect is dependent upon its cause, we should realise that nothing in the complete piano-playing-system can be irrelevant to the tone.

W.:   By the term "complete piano-playing-system" you mean the piano and the pianist, don't you?

P.:   To be quite exact, I should include a little bit more. It is a continuous, circular chain, some of whose links are animate, the others — inanimate. For the purpose of description, let us say the chain begins with the finger which touches the key. Then come, in order, the hand, the arm, the trunk of the pianist, the top of the chair, its legs, the floor, the legs of the piano, the piano, and finally the key on which the finger is resting, so that the circle of the chain is complete. We shall always have to keep this circular chain in mind. We shall describe some details more precisely and subdivide some of its links into smaller units, but we can omit none of them.

W.:   To be honest, it seems excessive pedantry to mention the chair and the floor in this connection.

P.:   There will be many occasions when you will realise why it is necessary to mention them. For the moment, I just want to ask you whether the distance between piano and chair is irrelevant, in your opinion.

W.:   Of course not. All right, I withdraw my objections and am ready to listen.

P.:   Listen to what?

W.:   Probably a thorough description of that circular chain.

P.:   A description it certainly will be, but not only a description; for we shall never forget that we are practical people and so shall not be satisfied with saying, "It is so", but shall always add the moral, "Therefore we must conduct ourselves like this", or "Therefore we must not conduct ourselves like that". By the way, you are mistaken if you think that you have only to listen to what I tell you. If that were all, I could persuade you to believe any nonsense. No. You yourself are to observe and draw conclusions

The complete
piano-playing-system

from your observations. I shall restrict myself, as far as possible, to acting as the midwife of your thoughts.

H.: So our next task will be to find a beginning in that circular chain.

P.: In the beginning was the piano.

K.: Excuse me, surely man was slightly earlier!

P.: Not the piano-playing man, and it is only he with whom we are concerned. Granted that there were people playing keyed instruments like the organ and harpsichord, but not the "piano-forte". Consider this Italian name of our instrument, which expresses the fact that you can play "piano" and "forte" on it, and that both the "piano" and the "forte" are effected without a register but solely by touch. That is possible owing to the construction of its mechanism, which, accordingly, is peculiar to the piano. This quite specific mechanism of the piano postulates a quite specific way of handling it. For this reason a touch that might be good for the organ or the harpsichord need not be good for the piano.

Mechanism of the piano

W.: Excuse me, you speak of the specific mechanism of the piano, as though there were only one such mechanism. In fact there are several different ones: the English, the Viennese . . . .

P.: . . . . the Steinway mechanism and so on. Granted. And they differ greatly from each other. Yet the fundamental principle we are concerned with is common to them all, and if a mechanism were not in accordance with this principle, it would not be a piano-forte. So, instead of dealing with half-a-dozen mechanisms, we can take one only as an example. By chance the diagram I have at hand shows the Viennese mechanism (Fig. 1). Let us learn what we can from it.

W.: What am I supposed to learn from that simple diagram?

P.: So you think you know everything already? Now explain how my touching finger makes the string vibrate by means of this mechanism.

W.: We see here that the key (K) is a lever resting on a balance rail (BR). So when I move its front end downwards, I lift its back end. This movement is transmitted to the shank (SH) of the hammer (H), the nib of which is held down by the leather (L) or knuckle, and so the hammer is tossed towards the string (S), from which it falls back immediately.

P.: Exactly. If mentally we skip all the intermediate parts of this mechanism, we can say briefly that the tone results from the downward movement of the key. Here is the relationship

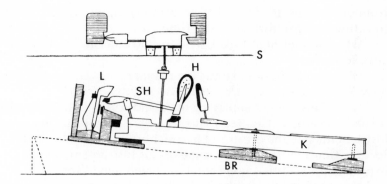

Figure 1. Diagram of the Viennese Mechanism. After Dr. A. Kohn: "Was soll der Klavier spieler vom Bau des Klaviers Wissen?" Musikpadagogische Zeitschrift, Vienna 1925.

Demands concerning the tone

between the two essential factors. The tone is what we want. The downward movement of the key is what we can govern by our volition. Thus we have to analyse both of them thoroughly. First, what qualities must the tone have in order to be in accordance with our conception of the sound?

W.:   It must have the volume and the duration prescribed by the composer.

P.:   Those are the minimum requirements. It is the fateful mistake of many pianists and piano teachers that they consider it enough to satisfy these minimum requirements in the beginning, in the belief that in time things will become better somehow. No, if we ever want to attain the really perfect tone at all, we must aim at it from the very beginning. I mean the kind of tone that makes Mrs. Snob put down her lorgnette and sigh: "What a heavenly man!"

W.:   So you mean the maximum requirements we make of the tone. They would be:

1)   it has to be rich in overtones;

2)   it must not cease abruptly, but it must be possible for it to continue to resound while gradually diminishing in volume—if I may express it graphically, it has to be like this ➤, not like this>;

3)   it has to be free of accidental accompanying noises.

P.:   Very good. So much for the tone. Now let us consider the downward movement of the key. Describe it.

Movement away and vibration

W.:   At first the key is in its highest possible position.

P.:   Let us call it "key-top".

W.: At the end it is in its lowest possible position.

P.: Let us call it "key-bottom".

W.: So my touch moves the key from key-top to key-bottom.

P.: The key moves from one position to another. Is that the only possible kind of movement a body can make?

W.: Certainly, if something moves it comes to another place.

P.: Think of the string when it has been struck. Does it reach another place?

W.: No. Yet it moves; it vibrates.

P.: What is the cause of this vibrating movement?

W.: The force of the hammer which does the striking.

P.: So we learn that a body under the influence of a moving force can either be moved to another place or can vibrate. Under which conditions will the former occur, under which the latter?

W.: If the body — like the string — is fastened, so that it cannot move from its position, it will vibrate.

P.: Only then? I will show you a simple experiment, and I want you to do it yourself to verify the result. Here is an open door. It can swing round on its hinges and so be moved from one position to another. This movement requires so little force that I can do it with my little finger. And now I use all the force of my clenched fist against the same spot which I touched before with my little finger. Did you hear it?

W.: Certainly; it made a lot of noise.

P.: The fact that it made a noise proves that the door vibrated. The fact that the noise was very loud means that it vibrated very strongly. Has it also moved from its position?

W.: Only a little.

P.: From this we see that almost all the power of my fist was used to make the door vibrate, and only a very small part of it remained to move the door from its position.

W.: That's right.

P.: Now apply this to the piano key.

W.: Just as the door can be moved on its hinges, so can the key be moved on its rail. This is the movement which we want to bring about with our touch. Now, however, we have learned that the force of the touch can also cause vibration of the key instead of the desired movement, which of course would mean a waste of power.

Mistakes arising from vibration of the key

P.: Only a waste of power? Just think! If the key vibrates, the vibration will travel through to the hammer shank, with which

24

it is connected. This means that the hammer, besides making the desired single movement towards the string and back, will also vibrate and thus perhaps come into repeated contact with the string.

W.:   Such repeated contact would disturb the vibration of the string caused by the first blow of the hammer. As a result the tone would become muffled, and the full slowly dying sound which we want would be impossible.

P.:   Furthermore, the uncontrolled vibration of the key might toss the hammer up too soon, and so it might touch the string at a moment when the damper had not yet been completely lifted.

W.:   That, too, of course would hinder the string from vibrating freely.

P.:   Apart from this, you have to consider that your touch can naturally only regulate the force of the controlled movement of the hammer, but not the force with which the uncontrolled vibration of the shank throws the hammer against the string. That means that we should not be able to regulate the volume of the tone with the desired precision.

W.:   And finally, the vibration of the key — like the vibration of the door — would make a noise, and so the tone would not be free of accidental accompanying noises.

P.:   So there are four reasons for requiring that the touch should not cause the key to vibrate. Let us list them in order of importance:

1)   in order that the tone be full, slowly dying and not muffled;

2)   in order that the tone be full, slowly dying, and not noises;

3)   in order that it be possible to control the volume accurately;

4)   in order that we do not waste energy.

W.:   How is it possible to avoid vibration of the key?

P.:   We should know that if we know how to produce vibration. We have already met a force that must produce vibration; haven't we?

W.:   Yes, the striking of the hammer against the string.

P.:   So let us analyse that movement of the hammer.

K.:   Looking at our picture, I imagine the sequence of events as follows: The hammer is tossed up with great velocity. Since the retardation caused by the force of gravity is too slight to be

How to avoid
vibration of the key

considered, the hammer will strike the string with practically full velocity. The resistance of the string to the movement of the hammer is so strong that the velocity will immediately fall to zero, and then it will even be reversed by the elasticity of the string. So the hammer will be slammed back, in which movement gravity might play a part.

P.: And didn't something similar happen when my fist struck the door? Here, too, the impetus was great, but because of the resistance of the door, the motion was brought to a standstill.

K.: The difference, though, is that the resistance of the door was due only to inertia, while the hammer of the piano was stopped because the string is fastened at both ends.

P.: That does not matter at the moment. What matters is the difference between that movement we have just discussed and the movement of the door resulting from the pressure of my little finger. What happens in this second case?

K.: The finger approaches the door with very little velocity. It stays with the motionless door a moment, and then together they begin an accelerated motion.

W.: Why accelerated?

K.: At first the door stands still, so its velocity is zero. Later it has a higher velocity; so between these two moments there must be a phase during which the speed increases, and that is what we call acceleration.

P.: So we always find some reciprocal action between the motion of the primary moving and that of the secondary moved body. But this reciprocal action is different when a vibration is caused from the action as the second body is moved from its position. What is this difference?

K.: A vibration is caused if the primary moving body has great impetus before its contact with the second body and transmits this energy to the hitherto motionless body, whereby its own movement is slowed down in proportion to the degree of resistance. If, however, the two bodies simultaneously begin an accelerated movement, this will be a movement away from the position, as far as external fastenings permit.

P.: Then how should the pianist's finger be moved?

W.: In an accelerated motion which begins at key-top.

P.: If, however, the motion should begin above key-top, what then?

W.: The finger would bang the key and so cause it to vibrate.

P.: With this we have come to the first demand of the piano.

Requisite movement
of key and finger

For a full tone, the finger has to come into contact with the key at key-top before beginning the key-moving action.

H.: In other words: the key-moving action of the finger must not begin above key-top, and we must not try to bang the key to key-bottom by approaching key-top with great velocity.

W.: But the finger must impart the necessary acceleration to the key by an accelerated movement which the finger itself begins at key-top.

P.: So the finger and the key begin a joint accelerated movement at key-top. Where does that movement end?

W.: At key-bottom.

P.: Why?

W.: Because there the piano prevents further motion.

P.: Could there be another reason?

W.: If I stopped the motion of my finger.

P.: If you stop the motion, what kind of movement would that be?

W.: A retarded movement.

P.: Haven't we just said that the movement of the finger has to be accelerated? Can a movement be accelerated and retarded at the same time?

K.: Certainly not at the same time. Only it might be possible for it to be accelerated at first and then retarded. If, however, a movement over the short distance between key-top and key-bottom were to be accelerated at first and then retarded, the highest velocity midway would obviously not be very great. I am not the one to decide whether it would be great enough to toss the hammer against the string.

H.: It might do for a "leggiero" touch. But we have decided to speak about the full tone with all the qualities which we have mentioned (p. 22).

W.: In this case we must leave it to the absolute resistance of the piano in key-bottom to stop the motion of the finger, just as it does that of the key.

P.: Therefore the force that moved my finger to key-bottom still exists at the moment when it arrives there. It is only the absolute resistance of the piano at key-bottom which prevents this force from causing a further movement. Let us examine this situation: put your finger on the key in key-bottom and try to move it further down. What do you feel?

W.: Of course I feel a firmness between finger and key.

P.: Why?

The firm key

W.:   Because of the interplay between force and resistance.

P.:   Is there an interplay between force and resistance only
in key-bottom or also while you are moving the key downward?

W.:   I cannot deny there is a certain resistance of the key to
the downward movement, because the key has a spring suspension,
which lifts it back to key-top after it has been touched.

P.:   If the interplay between force and resistance makes the
key feel firm in key-bottom, a firmness of the same kind exists
during the downward movement, though in this phase it will be
much less definite, being based on a lesser degree of resistance.

W.:   That is why my finger already feels a certain firmness
while it moves the key downwards.

P.:   I express this physical fact and this feeling by the term
"firm key". We will often speak of it. But at the moment we are
only interested in the fact that the key, because of its firmness,
can make a firm connection with the touching finger. What is the
nature of this connection?

Adhesion of
finger to key

K.:   To answer this question, let us make an experiment:
first put your fingertip on the front end of a key at key-top in such
a manner that you just touch it, and then move your finger horizontally towards the piano lid. Next make the same pushing motion
on the key in key-bottom and finally on the key when it is half-
depressed.

W.:   At key-top this motion does not meet the least resistance. In key-bottom I feel a very distinct resistance which varies
according to how hard I press the key down. When the key is
half-depressed, the resistance is noticeable, though less than in
key-bottom.

P.:   The resistance to the horizontal sliding of the finger on
the surface of the key may be described as an adhesion of the
finger to the key during the touch.

W.:   But this adhesion is easily surmountable.

P.:   Now make the pushing motion, which overcomes the
adhesion, several times on the half-depressed key. What do you
notice?

W.:   Often, if not always, my finger springs from the key
in the way the tips of our thumbs did when we, as children, slid
them over a shiny table-top to make a noise.

P.:   What happens to the key every time your finger springs
off it?

W.:   There is a jolt that makes the key vibrate, which we
have said must not be allowed in piano technique.

P.:   Therefore, although we can overcome the adhesion of the finger to the key surface in all positions of the key during its downward motion, it may be dangerous for our touch if we do so.

W.:   Which means that the finger must adhere to the surface of the key during the key-moving action.

P.:   In other words: during this action, finger and key make not only a motion in the same direction from key-top to key-bottom, but they make an identical motion, since they are joined by adhesion. .

W.:   That's not surprising.

P.:   No, not a bit. But it had to be said so that we can draw certain important conclusions. Just think, the finger can be moved in many different directions. The motion of the key from key-top to key-bottom, however, has only one possible direction. Which is that?

W.:   Vertically downwards.

P.:   So what direction must your finger take in moving the key?

Direction of gravity

W.:   Vertically downwards.

P.:   Here the question arises whether you have sufficient sense of orientation to direct the motion of your finger accurately in a vertical line.

W.:   I don't know.

P.:   You will know immediately, if you consider that there is a physical force which works in a vertical direction.

W.:   Certainly: the force of gravity.

P.:   And doesn't it affect your body, too? Yield to gravity! Then the force of your key-moving action will take the direction required by the key.

W.:   That's easily said. I would certainly arrive on the keyboard vertically if I jumped down from the fourth floor, but am I supposed to do that each time I want to move a key downwards?

P.:   Your irony is a criticism of the term "free fall" that was used by the school of Deppe and Caland to express their correct realisation that the act of moving the key has to follow the direction of the force of gravity. But only the centre of gravity of a body that is not connected at any point with another motionless body is free to fall vertically, as in the case of your body falling from the fourth floor. My key-moving finger, however, is connected with my trunk, which when I am at the piano, is at rest. So at most what can fall?

W.:   The arm. However, it does not simply fall vertically but around its pivot in the shoulder.

P.:   So you doubt whether I can move my finger downwards in an absolutely vertical line?

W.:   Yes.

P.:   Since the key moves downwards vertically at the same time as my finger is deviating from the vertical, what is going on between my finger and the key?

W.:   Now I ought to know my physics better. I think here we have to deal with the parallelograms of motions or forces, which are both rather mysterious to me.

Parallelogram of motions

K.:   What made them mysterious was probably the fear of a bad mark at school. Now you need not be afraid; so let us look at the matter calmly (Fig. 2). My finger has a tendency to move obliquely from P to X, but the key can follow it only in the vertical direction from P to Y. As a result, besides the joint vertical motion of finger and key, the finger must at the same time slide horizontally on the key from Y to X, and the direction and length of this movement will be equivalent to a movement from P to Z. That completes the parallelogram, which in this case is a rectangle.

W.:   That's really quite simple.

P.:   It would be very simple if the finger could slide on the surface of the key. But we have stated that there is a certain adhesion of the finger to the key during that motion. What results from this?

K.:   In this case we have to consider our diagram, not — as I did just now — as a parallelogram of motions, but as a parallelogram of forces and to interpret it in this way: PX represents the actual force exerted by my finger, and it falls into two components. One (PY) is the vertical key-moving force, the other (PZ) is a horizontal, pushing force which cannot be followed by the key.

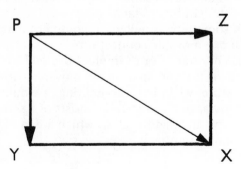

Figure 2.

P.:   You called the horizontal force a "pushing" one. What do you mean by "pushing"?

K.:   Moving an object away from me or trying to do so.

P.:   What do you call it if you move the object towards you?

K.:   "Pulling".

P.:   You referred before to the horizontal component of force that results from an oblique direction of finger movement. Must it be pushing? Couldn't it also be pulling?

K.:   Of course, both are possible. It depends on the direction in which the force of my finger is inclined, whether towards me or away from me.

P.:   Hence the question arises: Is the practical effect the same whether you push or you pull when depressing the key?

W.:   Certainly not. The push is objectionable, because as we have already learned, the finger may jump along over the surface of the key when pushing, but in pulling that does not happen.

P.:   Quite right. Let us take a more general instance of the same principle. Have you ever pulled a small farm-wagon by its shaft?

W.:   Yes.

P.:   And have you ever tried to push it?

W.:   God forbid! No! It would go where it wanted and eventually probably turn over, because the shaft is attached to the front axle, which is movable in relation to the body of the wagon. If I pushed, there would be deflections, and this would cause erratic movements which I could not control.

P.:   Such uncontrollable jumps would probably also occur if we tried to move the key by a pushing motion. What, however, is the immediate effect of pulling? Does the joint between the front axle and the body of the wagon cause trouble then as well?

W.:   Not at all. When something is pulled, all parts arrange themselves in a straight line as far as possible.

P.:   So if something is pulled, it would not matter if it had even more than one movable connection?

W.:   Certainly not. For example, I can pull something with a chain, although it is made up of many movable parts.

P.:   Therefore, when I pull something, it would not be a disadvantage that my arm, like a chain, consists of a series of parts — upper arm, forearm and hand — all of which are in movable connection with one another?

W.:   No.

H.:   So to summarize: The key must not be moved by a pushing, but it can be by a pulling motion.

P.:   This raises the further question: Which movements of my finger are pushing, and which are pulling?

K.:   Before we can answer, we ought to consider what sort of movements the finger can make in general. You just mentioned, quite correctly, that the finger is connected with the trunk by the upper arm, forearm and hand, all of which are in movable connection with one another. For this reason an extraordinary number of different finger movements are possible.

P.:   Let us simplify the idea of the arm and imagine that, instead of my arm, I have a rigid stick, beginning at my shoulder and ending at my fingertip. This stick is movable only around my shoulder. Now if I bring the end of the stick into contact with the key, just as we found it necessary for the fingertip in preparing the key-moving action; then I let the stick fall. What will happen?

The arm as a stick

W.:   If the stick is heavy enough to overcome the spring suspension of the key, it will move the key downwards.

P.:   Will it move it by pulling or by pushing? Or will the motion be exactly vertical?

K.:   Since the motion is caused by the force of gravity, it will certainly take place along a vertical plane, but the end of the stick, just like any other point of it, will move in an arc around its pivot at the shoulder. We shall illustrate this by a diagram (Fig. 3a), in which we take care that the vertical distance of the key (P) from the pivot at the shoulder (O) is much less than the horizontal distance. Because of this, the key-moving part of the circular motion (PX_1) is guided in such a way that its vertical key-moving component (PY_1) is much greater than its horizontal component (PZ_1). Since the latter is directed towards the pivot (O), we must call it "pulling".

P.:   So the stick, as an imaginary body in place of my real arm, would move the key in the way demanded by the key; that is to say, there would be no pushing component in the motion. Furthermore, the vertical, key-moving component would be greater than the horizontal component, which means that the energy would be well utilized.

K.:   So could you play the piano with a stick?

P.:   Yes, although not chords.

W.:   But it would be rather difficult to reach all the keys,

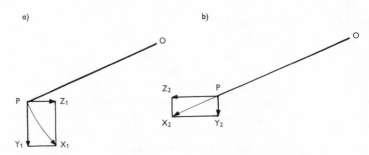

Figure 3. Parallelogram of motions
a) with peripheral movement (PX$_1$)   b) with radial movement (PX$_2$)
of the imaginary Body OP.

PY$_1$: greater vertical, key-moving   PY$_2$: smaller vertical, key-moving
component   component
PZ$_1$: smaller horizontal, pulling   PZ$_2$: greater horizontal, pushing
(directed towards O) component   (directed away from O) component

since they are at different distances from the shoulder and the length of the stick is fixed.

P.:   That's true. Therefore an imaginary straight body could be considered as a valid substitute for my real arm only if it had the additional property of being able to lengthen and shorten itself. What sort of movements would be possible for the free distant end of such an imaginary body in relation to the other end, which we must imagine attached to the trunk at the shoulder?

W.:   Two different types of movement, one of them also possible for the stick of fixed length. In this type of movement the free end would move at a constant distance from the shoulder, as if on the surface of a sphere.

K.:   Let us call that a peripheral movement.

W.:   The other type of movement arises from the fact that the unattached end can approach or retreat from the shoulder at will. In terms of the sphere we have just mentioned, this means that its radius can be reduced or increased respectively.

K.:   Let us describe these as radial movements.

P.:   Are there not also movements that belong to neither of these two pure types?

K.:   Yes, but we can reduce them to peripheral and radial components.

W.:   Well then, let us observe that my actual fingertip can perform the same two types of movement in relation to my shoulder. We have already learned that we can use a peripheral

Peripheral and radial movements

motion along a vertical plane downwards for moving the key. Can
we also use a radial motion for that purpose?

W.:   Certainly. All I have to do is to make contact with the
key and increase the length of the imaginary body, so that the
distant free end becomes more distant from the shoulder.

P.:   How would this radial motion affect the key?

K.:   As we see in Figure 3b, the direction of this movement
(PX_2) is perpendicular to that of the peripheral movement. Therefore, the vertical, key-moving component (PY_2) is much smaller
than the horizontal component (PZ_2), which is lost for the key-
moving action. Since it is directed away from the centre (O), the
horizontal component is pushing.

P.:   So this radial motion is in every respect what we have
to avoid. We can summarize by saying that only peripheral movements may be used for moving the key, but never radial movement
directed away from the player.

H.:   In spite of this, there are many techniques, which apply
the radial movement for the key-moving action and expressly
require this manner of playing.

P.:   We can call them "aiming" techniques, because the act
of aiming generally implies that we cause an object to move away
from us and to a certain target. With this idea in mind, we can
formulate another demand of the piano: We must avoid "aiming"
techniques.

K.:   But if you don't aim, how do you arrive at the right
place with your fingertip?

P.:   Don't forget that we are dealing with the movement
from key-top to key-bottom which begins only after the finger
has made contact with the key at key-top. But you are referring
to how my finger reaches key-top. Of course I must make an aiming motion for this. However, this aiming does not take place
during the key-moving action but before, so that the target is not
key-bottom but key-top. Only after the finger has aimed and
arrived at key-top is the key caught up in a movement in the direction of gravity, which implies, as we have discovered, a component
of pulling. The entire sequence of these movements may be compared to the actions of a boatman who wants to pull his boat to
the shore when there is nobody there to help him. He throws out
his rope, aiming it over the top of a post on the shore, and hopes
that it will fall around the post. Then he can pull the rope and
tauten it. Do you understand the comparison?

W.:   It's quite clear: for us the top of the post is the top of

Separation of the
key-moving action
from its preparation

the key, and only after my arm has sunk onto the key does the real work of moving the key begin, during which the arm—which we compared before with a chain—tautens through being pulled.

H.:   We had better say: "The arm is tautened through being pulled", in order to emphasize that in this action the arm is as passive as the rope and not active like the arm of the boatman. But the question of what forces are active will probably be discussed later. What matters just now is the right sequence of aiming at and moving the key.

P.:   Yes. And now let us suppose I do not keep these two different actions separate.

W.:   Then the aiming radial motion would still be operative during the key-moving action.

P.:   What would be the consequence of this?

W.:   1)   The action that moves the key from key-top to key-bottom would be pushing and so might cause vibration of the key and thereby an impure tone.

2)   The key-moving action would not begin on key-top, but I would have arrived there with great velocity, and this would certainly cause vibration of the key and so an impure tone.

3)   After jumping a large interval, I arrive on the key with greater velocity than after jumping a shorter interval. If I moved the key with the same motion of the hand, the volume of the tone would depend on the size of the preceding interval and would hardly be in accordance with the requirements of the music.

P.:   That's enough! We could add to the list of mistakes arising in this way, but these are enough to show us the importance of the piano's demands which we have laid down thus far:

1)   the key-moving action must begin only at key-top;

2)   it must not involve pushing;

3)   as far as possible we have to follow the direction of the force of gravity in the key-moving action.

H.:   But we have only explained how these demands can be met by an imaginary arm. The next question is: How does all this apply to the real human arm?

P.:   Quite right. That will be the subject of tomorrow's discussion.

DIALOGUE 2

Bones, Joints and Muscles

K.: If I understand correctly, today I must lay before you the most important anatomical facts concerning the arm.

P.: Yes, but don't think you can stop at the arm! Don't forget that besides piano and arm, other parts also belong to the circular chain of our complete piano-playing-system.

K.: Then I must discuss practically the entire skeleton and the muscles related to it.

W.: Skeleton? I remember! We had one at school.

K.: But the skeleton you had at school consisted of dead bones, whereas we are interested in the skeleton of the living body. So we will study it with the help of two illustrations which show it at the piano (Plates A and C). Many pianists sit lower. It is only because you have this skeleton that you are able to play the piano. The skeleton is solid, and you need something solid for the key-moving action. So a snail, which has no skeleton, would not be able to play the piano.

W.: But a stick is solid. That is why we were able to imagine a piano-playing stick.

K.: But our skeleton differs from a stick in that it consists of many parts: separate bones which are movable in relation to each other. The place where one bone is in movable connection with another bone is called a joint. The structures by which we are able to move the bones voluntarily we call muscles. As we are interested in movements, the musculature as the active part is much more essential for us than the purely passive skeleton, just as the motor of the automobile is more essential than the chassis. Yet we shall take the skeleton as the basis of our description, because it is the framework which is reflected in the general architecture of the body. I take it that you are acquainted with this general architecture?

W.: Yes. We have a trunk, neck, head, two arms and two legs.

K.: Through trunk and neck there is an axial support, the spine, which consists of many bones one on top of another, the vertebrae. We differentiate between various sections of the spine according to the regions of the body through which it passes. Each section consists of a certain number of vertebrae. At the top, in the neck are the neck vertebrae (PL. A/2), then in the region of the rib cage, which in Greek is called thorax, the thoracic vertebrae.

W.: Thorax! Thoracic vertebrae! That's what I was afraid of: Greek and Latin names!

K.: Don't worry! We shall use those terms only when it is absolutely impossible to find or create an English name.

W.: Do you mean to say that you will create names of your own?

K.: Yes, names which express in an understandable way where the part is situated. For instance the term "neck vertebrae" is one which we invented for your benefit.

W.: Thank you. I see. After the neck vertebrae and thoracic vertebrae most likely come abdominal vertebrae.

K.: We say "lumbar vertebrae" (PL. A/6). Below them is a large immovable part of the spine, which we call the sacrum (PL. A/8). It is situated between the uppermost parts of the buttocks. To the sacrum the two hip bones (PL. A/7) are joined by very rigid connections which we can consider as practically immovable.

W.: Do the hip bones also belong to the spine?

K.: No. The endpiece of the spine is formed by the coccyx (PL. A/9) which is of no interest at all for us. The two hip bones with the sacrum form a solid ring, called the pelvis. The hip bones are connected with the bones of the legs.

W.: Is that all we have to know about the skeleton of the trunk?

K.: No, we still have to mention the ribs (PL. A/46 and C/21). They are a series of paired curved bones, which originate from the thoracic vertebrae. They are inclined around the organs of the chest, and in front most of them are connected with each other by means of the breast bone (PL. A/41 and C/22). In this way they form a posterior, lateral and anterior wall for the chest cavity. Together they are called the rib cage, which tapers upwards.

W.: How can that be? The trunk is surely broader in the upper part of the chest than in the region of the waist.

K.: Yes, because the shoulder girdle rests upon the upper section of the rib cage.

W.:   This shoulder girdle — is it a girdle that circles all the way round?

K.:   No. The right and left halves are completely independent of each other. On each side we have two bones: the collar bone (PL. A/45 and C/26) and the shoulder blade (PL. A/42). The collar bone forms a distinct projection between chest and throat while the shoulder blade is a flat, more or less triangular bone in a movable position behind the rib cage. The distinctness with which the different parts of this bone can be felt depends upon the thickness of the enveloping muscles. The most noticeable part is its lower corner (PL. A/40), which can often be seen protruding. From here, one edge of the bone that can also be distinctly felt rises parallel to the spine; we shall call it the inner edge. The other edge, rising from the lower corner, is embedded in muscles that project as a distinct fold behind the armpit, called the posterior axillary fold (PL. B/6). From the upper part of the shoulder blade, a very prominent ridge of bone (PL. A/3 and C/25) projects and continues into the shoulder-top (PL. A/44 and C/24).

W.:   Shoulder-top? Do you mean what one usually calls "the shoulder", on which, for instance, a weight may be carried?

K.:   Yes. The shoulder-top forms a movable joint with the collar bone, which extends in the form of a double curve from here to the upper end of the breast bone. The joint between collar bone and breast bone, breastbone-collarbone joint (PL. C/27), is the only connection in the skeleton between shoulder girdle and rib cage.

W.:   Then although the shoulder blade rests on the rib cage, there is no joint between them, is there?

K.:   No, the shoulder blade is embedded in muscles. But it does form a joint with the upper-arm bone (PL. A/39 and C/20), the shoulder joint (PL. A/43 and C/23), which is situated directly under the shoulder-top.

W.:   So there is a continuous skeleton chain from the rib cage to the arm, and the links are in this sequence: breast bone — collar bone — shoulder blade — upper-arm bone.

K.:   That's right. You understand that the shoulder girdle would be classed externally with the trunk, but from the mechanical point of view it belongs more to the arm, since we can fully utilize its mobility for arm movements.

W.:   Now we have arrived at the arm. Here the upper-arm bone reaches from the shoulder joint to the elbow joint (PL. A/38), right?   Bones of the arm

K.:   Yes. However from the elbow there is not just one forearm bone but two, which extend to the wrist joint, one on the side of the thumb and the other on the side of the little finger.

P.:   Here we must use the Latin names: ulna (PL. A/27) for the one on the little-finger side and radius (PL. A/28) for the one on the thumb side.

K.:   The ulna starts with the ulna hook (PL. A/25) on which one rests when leaning on one's elbow. From here one edge of the ulna can be felt for its entire length, up to the small head of the ulna (PL. A/29) which we can see projecting from the back of the wrist on the little-finger side.

W.:   I see it. But it takes only a very small section of the whole breadth of the wrist.

K.:   That's true. The radius is much broader in the region of the wrist, which is sufficient reason for us to say that the hand is carried by the radius only. The following section of the skeleton of the hand consists of eight small bones, the wrist bones (PL. A/26).

W.:   Isn't that funny? When I use the word "wrist", I mainly think of the region immediately above the projecting head of the ulna; but now I learn that the wrist bones are situated beyond that head. Must I know all those eight bones by name?

The five finger-beams

K.:   Not at all. Just keep in mind that they occupy about one-third of the area between the end of the forearm bones and the beginning of the fingers. The rest of this area is what we shall call the middle hand. It has five bones side by side, the middle-hand bones (PL. A/30), from each of which a finger extends. The spaces between the middle-hand bones are filled by soft tissues, mainly by muscles, so that from the outside this part of the hand constitutes a unit.

W.:   But in the hand of a skeleton, where these soft tissues are absent, the fingers appear so strangely long, because the middle-hand bones seem to belong to the fingers, don't they?

K.:   Yes; for each finger together with its middle-hand bone, we shall use the term "finger beam". As you can see, the thumb has two members; the index, middle, ring and little fingers have three each. So the first finger beam is three-membered and the others four-membered.

W.:   Do these members of the fingers have names?

P.:   I call them nail member (PL. A/36 and C/13), middle member (PL. A/34 and C/11) and basal members (PL. A/32 and C/9).

W.:   Then the thumb has only a nail member and a basal member.

K.:   Yes. And the three joints between the four members of each finger beam, which are situated at the three knuckles, we name in the same order: terminal joint (PL. A/35 and C/12), middle joint (PL. A/33 and C/10) and basal joint (PL. A/31 and C/8).

W.:   Then in the thumb the middle joint is missing, or it is one with the terminal joint.

K.:   That ends the first short survey of the arm skeleton, and now we turn to that of the leg, which in many respects is analogous.

Bones of the leg

W.:   Then there must first be a structure which is analogous to the shoulder girdle.

K.:   We know it already: the pelvic girdle, which consists of the two hip bones.

W.:   But you said the joints between the hip bones and the sacrum are rigid, whereas the shoulder girdle is clearly movable.

K.:   That is the essential difference. Everything in the upper limbs and their girdle is constructed for the maximum mobility; in the lower limbs and girdle, on the contrary, for stability. Here the whole weight of the body has to be transferred from the spine by way of the pelvis to the leg, and for this transfer of weight stability is necessary. For this purpose the spine forms one large bone, the sacrum, instead of several vertebrae, and the pelvic girdle, in contrast to the shoulder girdle, consists of only one bone at each side, the hip bone. For the same purpose there are practically immovable joints between the two hip bones in front, in the pubic region, and between them and the sacrum behind, by which a solid pelvic ring is formed.

W.:   I understand. Next is probably a joint between hip bone and thigh bone (PL. A/21).

K.:   That's right. It is the hip joint (PL. A/23), which corresponds to the shoulder joint.

W.:   And in the same way the knee joint (PL. A/19) is analogous to the elbow joint.

K.:   At the knee, however, we find a bone in front, the kneecap (PL. A/20), for which there is no analogy in the arm. Then an anlogy occurs again. Two bones extend from knee to ankle side by side. On the side of the big toe is the shin bone (PL. A/18), while the splinter bone (PL. A/17) on the side of the little toe is much thinner and also uninteresting for us. Both end at the ankle joint (PL. A/12).

W.:   Then I suppose come ankle bones (PL. A/16) corresponding to the wrist bones.

K.:   Yes, except that they are much bigger than the wrist

bones. We are interested only in the heel bone (PL. A/13), part of which projects backwards and downwards from the region of the ankle and forms the bony core of the heel. The region following the ankle bones can be called middle foot. You will guess that it consists of five middle-foot bones (PL. A/14), each of which carries a toe (PL. A/15).

W.:   Now only the skeleton of the head remains to be discussed.

K.:   Here we must consider only two parts which are movable in relation to each other — the lower jaw (PL. A/49) and the other part, all the rest of the skull. Anatomy divides the skull into a number of smaller bones; they, however, are in immovable connection with each other and so are of no interest for us. The lower jaw is connected with the skull on both sides by means of a joint (jaw joint: PL. A/1) in front of each ear. At the back, the skull rests on the uppermost neck vertebra.

W.:   Is that all we have to know about the skeleton?

K.:   There remain a few small parts which form a sort of bridge in the throat hanging from the lower jaw. While all the bones of which we have spoken thus far are connected with each other by joints, these skeletal parts of the throat are suspended only by muscles or ligaments, as they belong to internal organs. First there is a small bone, which you can feel where the forward contour of the throat goes over to the lower contour of the jaw region.

W.:   Oh, yes, I can feel it.

K.:   Because of its intimate relation to the back part of the tongue, it can be called the tongue bone (PL. A/48). Below it are the cartilages of the larynx, the biggest of which is the thyroid cartilage (PL. A/47), easy to feel and, in men, also to see.

W.:   Oh, the Adam's apple!

K.:   We need not mention the rest of the cartilages here.

W.:   And is there anything more to learn about the skeleton?

K.:   Not to learn, but to observe. I mean the movements of the joints. First we have to consider what kinds of movement are possible at all.

W.:   You probably want to emphasize that different joints vary in the extent of their flexibility. I see that I can make very extensive movements in my elbow joint, whereas you have said before that hardly any movement is possible between the sacrum and the hip bones. You anatomists are bound to have a special name for such immovable joints.

Bones and cartilages of head and throat

Extent of movement in joints

K.: Let us call them "rigid joints". But what matters is not so much the extent of flexibility as the question of how many different directions are possible in the movement. In this respect we use the term "degrees of freedom" of a joint, and this can be brought home to you by experiments like the following. With the fingers of your right hand hold a finger of your left hand at the basal member, that is the member on which you may be wearing a ring, and now move the other members of this finger.

Degrees of freedom

W.: I can bend and straighten the finger.

K.: In other words your finger can perform flexion and extension. Can you also move it to the side, so that its tip comes nearer to a neighbouring finger?

W.: Not as long as I hold its basal member fast.

K.: That's right. Only a back-and-forth movement is possible, as with a door on its hinges. That's why we call such a joint a "hinge joint". It is a joint with only one degree of freedom.

W.: I understand. If I had been able to move the finger sideways, that would have been the second degree of freedom.

K.: Quite right. Here is an instance of this: With your right hand hold your left forearm about where you wear your watch, and now make all the possible movements you can with your left hand.

W.: I can make one movement towards the palm of the hand and the opposite movement to the back of the hand. Do we call this flexion and extension again?

K.: We had better say "flexion and overextension", because we can go far beyond the position where forearm and hand form a straight line.

W.: So this flexion and overextension would be one degree of freedom. Besides that I can move the hand sideways towards the thumb or the little-finger side, and that would be the second degree of freedom.

K.: Of course, I can also combine these two possible movements with each other.

W.: Yes. For instance I can make an oblique movement directed towards the thumb and the back of the hand at the same time.

K.: Any other combination is possible. The result is that the tip of my middle finger, let us say, which for the moment I will imagine to be rigidly connected with the hand, can sweep over all joints of a surface which is approximately circumscribed by a circle.

W.:   This surface would of course form part of a spherical surface whose centre is in the wrist joint.

K.:   Quite so. And now, if I move my hand from the extreme thumbward position to extreme overextension and so on all round in such a way that the tip of the middle finger is always at the outermost boundary of the surface described, this motion is called "circumduction".

W.:   And the figure described by the hand is shaped somewhat like a cone.

P.:   Yes, but we shall not call it a conical movement, because a cone has an axis and so only a motion around this axis would be a conical movement. In this case the moving body would always show the same side to the axis, as the moon does to the earth. In circumduction of the hand this does not happen.

K.:   You can make the conical movement of the hand which the professor has in mind if you release your forearm, straighten the elbow, overextend the wrist and rotate the entire arm around its longitudinal axis, keeping it in the same direction.

W.:   I see. Then the hand really does circumscribe a cone, and the palm always faces the surface of the cone.

K.:   But this movement has nothing to do with the wrist joint and its two degrees of freedom. That's why it was possible only after we had released the forearm. Now it is up to me to discuss a joint with three degrees of freedom. Let us choose the shoulder joint. In order to examine its mobility, we shall keep the elbow bent approximately at a right angle and move the upper arm around the shoulder joint as the centre of motion.

W.:   I find two degrees of freedom easily: I can move the upper arm forwards and backwards, and I can move it laterally away from the trunk and towards it.

K.:   So the elbow end of the upper arm can sweep over part of a spherical surface.

W.:   Yes, but where is the third degree of freedom?

K.:   Now point the elbow end of the upper arm in some direction, it does not matter which. Let us say downwards, forward and outwards. Then, while keeping the upper arm in this direction rotate it around its axis of length, so that the angled forearm moves like the hand of a clock between ten o'clock and two o'clock.

W.:   So this rotation of a part of the body around its own longitudinal axis is the third degree of freedom?

K.:   Yes. And any more than these three degrees of freedom in the joints are of no practical importance for us.

W.: Then we know all types of joints now.

K.: No, because so far we have only considered the possibility that rotation is a third degree of freedom added to two others, but it is also possible that rotation is the only degree of freedom.

W.: Where?

K.: In the forearm for instance. To convince yourself let your right upper arm hang down free, then bend the elbow at a right angle. Now keep this position and, while remembering that at the wrist you can move the hand towards the thumb, little finger, palm or back of the hand, but avoiding all these movements, what can you still do with your hand?

W.: I can turn it around its axis of length: I can turn the palm upwards as the beggar does or downwards as the writer does.

K.: The fact that we could not make this movement as long as we held the forearm above the wrist shows that the movement must occur in the region of the forearm. And no doubt it is a movement around the axis of length of the forearm, hence a rotation. Only we use special names here: if we turn the palm up, like the beggar, we call it "supination", if down — "pronation".

W.: In this movement what happens to the two forearm bones which are side by side?

K.: In supination the two bones lie parallel to each other like the two strokes of the Roman number II, in pronation they cross each other like the strokes of an X.

W.: In changing from the II-position to the X-position the wrist ends of the two bones will probably turn around each other.

K.: It is simpler to imagine that the wrist end of the ulna, which we have called its "head", is stationary while around it the wrist end of the radius revolves and takes the hand with it, since we have already found that the radius alone carries the hand.

P.: For this reason, although the radius lies beside the ulna along its whole length, from a functional standpoint it is an intermediate member of the skeleton between ulna and hand. In the elbow joint there is only one degree of freedom between upperarm bone and ulna — flexion and extension. Relative to this upper-arm-ulna system, which in itself cannot rotate, the radius can make the movements of pronation and supination and transmit these rotatory movements to the hand, which is attached to it.

K.: If we look back over our observations concerning the possible movements of the hand, we learn that we can add degrees of freedom to each other. The hand is movable in relation to the radius in two degrees of freedom, and the radius has one —

pronation and supination — in relation to the ulna. Therefore the hand has all three degrees of freedom in relation to the ulna.

W.:   With all due respect to the importance of the degrees of freedom, I would like to come back to the extent of mobility, because I notice a great difference in this, depending upon the particular position. When I hold the arm as we described it just now, with the upper-arm hanging and elbow bent, the pronation ends when the palm is down. If, however, I lift my arm to the horizontal and straighten the elbow completely, I can continue the pronation much further, so that the palm turns outwards and finally even upwards again. While at first we had only about $180°$ of rotatory freedom, I can now achieve $360°$. How is this possible?

K.:   You will be able to answer that yourself, if you put your left hand loosely on the middle of the right upper arm during the movement. What do you notice?

W.:   The upper arm rotates. Now I understand: When the elbow is straight, the axis of length of the upper arm and that of the forearm point in the same direction and so I can now also use the rotation of the upper arm in the shoulder joint for pronation and supination.

K.:   To be quite precise, we are also using the movements in the joints of the shoulder girdle. But it is the shoulder joint which has mainly added to pronation and supination.

P.:   For the time being and for practical purposes, we will not ask in which joints these movements take place and will simply consider the position with the palm turned down as the middle position of rotation. All positions in which the little-finger side of the hand is lower than the thumb side, we shall call positions of supination, although this differs from the preceding anatomical definition of this term, and all positions in which the thumb side is lower than the little-finger side will be our positions of pronation.

W.:   Must we go into all the joints of the body with the same thoroughness that we have employed for the joints between ulna and radius?

K.:   At this stage it may be sufficient that we have basic concepts and general terms to which we can refer when we are discussing movements and postures which are important for the pianist and when we may find it necessary to investigate a particular joint in more detail.

Structure and function of muscle

H.:   I hope we shall take the same moderate attitude to the muscles which we see in Plate B, and not have to learn all their names.

K.: Don't worry! What matters here is of a still more general nature.

W.: I suppose the general problem is: How does a muscle function?

K.: A muscle has two ends, each of which is attached to a part of the skeleton either directly or by means of a tough cord, which we call a tendon.

W.: I know, we can see tendons on the back of the hand for instance.

K.: Yes. The two ends of the muscle are called the origin and the insertion.

W.: Which is which?

K.: In the limbs, the one nearer the trunk is the origin and the farther one the insertion. If I want to make a movement, a nerve stimulus runs to the muscles that can play a part in this movement. Under the influence of this nerve stimulus, a change takes place in the muscle which results in a tendency for it to become thicker and therefore shorter. The tendency to shorten itself obviously means a tendency to bring the insertion nearer the origin, and so it is a force which causes one part of the skeleton to move towards another.

W.: I understand. If a muscle is situated at the flexion side of a joint, its endeavour to become shorter causes a flexion of the joint; if it is at the extension side, it causes an extension; if on the outside, a movement away from the body, and so on.

K.: That is entirely correct. But you would be quite wrong to imagine that each muscle serves a particular movement and each movement is done by a particular muscle. You must understand that what the anatomist describes as an individual muscle, giving it a special name, is a particular mass of muscular tissue which he sees as a unit when dissecting a body. The arrangement of these individual muscles is not at all according to your concept of one at the flexion side, one at the extension side, and so on.

W.: Then how is it?

K.: The simplest way of explaining it is to show how the reality differs from your concept. First, a muscle often surrounds a joint on several sides in such a way that its different parts can have different effects on the joint. It is even possible for two parts of one and the same muscle to have opposite effects on the same joint.

W.: So that one part would be a flexor, the other part an extensor?

K.:   Yes, or one part an inward rotator, the other an out-ward rotator of the same joint.

W.:   Then what is such a muscle good for? It cancels its own effect.

K.:   You must not think that a nerve impulse can stimulate nothing less than the entire muscle. Different parts of a muscle situated side by side are perfectly able to work independently. For instance, the extending part of a muscle can be inactive, while the flexing part of the same muscle is working. The second difference from your concept, which implies an ideal relation between joint and muscle, is that often we have not only one but several muscles capable of causing a certain movement in a particular joint.

W.:   So could there be more than one flexor at the elbow joint, for example?

Muscles passing over one or more joints

K.:   Yes, there are several. And now the third difference is that a muscle does not always pass over one joint only, thus influ-encing this joint alone, but there are numerous muscles which are related to two or even more joints. If, for instance, the biceps of the upper arm (PL. B/27 and C/5), which is known even to lay-men, originates from the shoulder blade and is inserted in the radius, it is obvious that it can influence both the shoulder and elbow joints. I leave it to you to figure out how many joints are influenced by the one group of finger-flexors (PL. B/19 and C/17), whose origin extends to the upper arm, whilst they are inserted in the middle members of the fingers.

W.:   I should say the elbow joint, ulna-radius joint, wrist joint and the basal and middle joints of the finger.

K.:   Pay attention to the fact that the muscle, and the ten-don as its continuation, passes over all those joints one after another. We can illustrate this by a chain with six links, the first and last of which are connected by a stretched rubber band. The minute the rubber band is released and so contracts, it causes a movement in each joint of the chain. In the same way the muscle which is related to several joints is not only able to, but must influ-ence all the joints over which it passes.

W.:   Have we now dealt with all the peculiarities of muscle action?

Movement and state of being

K.:   At least we can hope that, when you have fixed all this in your mind, you will understand which sorts of movement and what states of being can be caused by the muscles.

W.:   What states of being? Until now we have only said that a muscle can cause a movement.

K.:   If the movement is possible.

W.: Why should it not be possible?

K.: Just try to lift a suitcase full of iron or open a locked door!

W.: Of course that's impossible.

K.: But if you try to do it, an activity begins in the muscles which ordinarily would perform the motion of lifting or opening. The muscles will swell, and they will swell even more than they would have, had you been able to perform the action. They will tighten but will be unable to perform the action. They will tighten but will be unable to shorten.

W.: Because an external hindrance prevents this shortening.

K.: Yes, but in other cases the hindrance can be internal, and then it may be one of two kinds. First we must remember that the construction of a joint, e.g. its ligaments, imposes certain limits on the movements it can make. If a movement has been carried through to the limit set by the construction of the joint, the muscle which works in this direction cannot cause further movement, however much it tries.

Firmness by muscle tension

W.: Of course not. But why should it? Why, for example, should I use an extensor muscle when I have already reached extreme extension, or a flexor muscle in extreme flexion?

K.: Just think! We have already mentioned a similar inter-action between force and resistance in discussing the relationship between finger and key. What is the result of this interaction?

W.: A feeling of firmness. So we said on that occasion (p. 27).

K.: And so also here firmness results. If at the end of ex-tension the extensor muscle ceased to be active, the joint in question would be straight, but it would not be firm in this posi-tion. If, however, the muscle continues to be active, there is absolute firmness, as further extension is prevented by the joint, and flexion — by the muscle.

P.: And that's the practical purpose for which — in our piano technique too — we often have to use muscles against the hindrance of ligaments. We must do this whenever it is necessary for a certain part of the body to be firm in itself. Therefore let us keep in mind that muscular action of this sort against hindrances in the skeleton does not always mean a waste of energy, although it does not cause any movement.

K.: In contrast to this, let us now consider the second kind of inner hindrance to muscle action. I mean the situation in which one muscle works against another.

Mutually antagonistic muscle tension

W.: For instance a flexor against an extensor?

K.: Yes, or an inward rotator against an outward rotator, and so on. Such pairs of muscles with opposite functions are called "antagonists".

W.: But who would use such mutually antagonistic muscles simultaneously?

K.: First a very trite example: The he-man who likes to show his well-developed biceps in public. Why does this muscle swell so much? Because simultaneously with the elbow-flexing biceps its antagonist, the extensor muscle of the elbow (PL. B/28 and C/19), is active, and the biceps uses much more effort to tense against this resistance than when it can flex the elbow without any opposition.

W.: But this situation is quite exceptional.

K.: Certainly it is exceptional if we do anything like this consciously. In fact it would be quite exceptional if I were to use any muscle consciously at all.

W.: What do you mean by that?

K.: If, for instance, I reach for a pencil on a table in front of me, I make a forward movement in the shoulder joint, an extension in the elbow joint, a flexion in the finger joints and so forth. At any time I can become conscious of the fact that I am doing all that, but really I am conscious only of the fact that I am reaching for the pencil. The individual movements which bring about this result are a matter of routine, which I have acquired in childhood and practised ever since. I am even less conscious of the muscles which I use for these movements, but I use them unerringly and with success. You notice that there are many individual movements contained in such a simple act, and of course there are many muscles which must co-operate. This co-operation of the muscles for performing a certain movement is called "co-ordination" of the muscles. Now the new question arises: is there only one possible method of co-ordination for a certain movement or are there more?

Co-ordination

W.: I should say there is only one.

K.: Think it over step by step. First we will suppose that, before beginning the movement, my hand had been in a certain position at the edge of the table. At the end of the movement my hand is by the pencil. Is there only one possible route between the original and the final positions, or are there several?

W.: Several, of course. The hand can slide along the table, or it can be lifted to different levels above it.

K.: Well, these different routes require different methods

of co-ordinations. Furthermore, when my hand is beside the pencil, or when I stop it somewhere on the way, at either moment
both the position of my trunk and that of my hand are unequivo-
cally defined. But does this imply that the parts of my body
between trunk and hand have a certain position also? To try it,
put your hand, palm downwards, on the table in front of you at
such a distance that the elbow is moderately flexed. In this situation we can consider the positions of hand and shoulder as
invariable; or can it have different positions?

*Double-conical
movement of the arm*

W.: It can have different positions. I can let it sag vertically
under the line from shoulder to wrist, or I can lift it more or less
outwards from this position. When I move the elbow from one of
these positions to any other, it performs a conical movement, or
more correctly: a double-conical movement, because both the
upper arm and the forearm thereby cover part of a conical surface.
In rising outwards from its deepest position, the elbow describes
an arc which represents part of the periphery of the common base
of the two cones. The points of the cones are shoulder and wrist,
and their axis is the line from shoulder to wrist.

K.: Are you sure that it is a truly conical movement, not a
circumduction?

W.: Definitely conical, because the flexion side of the elbow
always faces the axis of the cones.

P.: How do the cones differ if the hand varies its distance
from the shoulder?

W.: The nearer the hand to the shoulder, the less the height
of the cones and the wider their bases.

P.: You will understand that the varying distances from
shoulder to hand and the corresponding varying heights and basal
diameters of the double cones are interesting to us as pianists, since
we have to reach keys at various distances and consequently, in
piano playing, the distance between the hands and the body is
constantly increasing or decreasing. In each of these many hand
positions the elbow can theoretically be at any point on the periphery of the base of the respective double cone. The question, which
of the possible elbow positions is in accordance with the demands
of the piano, will have to be discussed thoroughly later.

K.: What matters at the moment is only that different
positions of the elbow are possible with an unvarying position of
the hand. And since each of these elbow positions depends on a
different muscle action, we now know a second reason why the
attainment of a special aim is possible by different muscle

co-ordinations. But even if we could assure that the movements of the joints were always the same, we must remember that a given movement of a joint might be caused by different muscles.

W.:   That would be a further reason why co-ordinations can vary.

K.:   Actually these different reasons, which we have discussed independently of each other, are inter-related. Let us start from the fact that a particular movement in a joint can be brought about by two different muscles. It can be that one of these muscles passes over this joint only and so moves only this joint in the direction we want, while the other muscle that could serve the purpose passes over two joints and so changes the position in the other joint also. For instance, the one muscle could be only a flexor of the elbow joint; the other, as well as doing this, might also lift the upper arm in the shoulder joint. Now, if two men were used to bending their elbows in different ways, one preferring the muscle which passes over one joint, the other preferring the muscle which passes over both joints, what would result from this difference in habits?

W.:   In bending their elbows the two men would hold their shoulder joints in different positions.

K.:   If, however, for some reason in the course of a certain action it is necessary for the elbow to be bent while being held low, what must the man who is accustomed to bending his elbow by the muscle which also lifts the upper arm in the shoulder joint, do?

W.:   While bending his elbow, he must at the same time use a muscle which lowers the upper arm in order to counteract the involuntary tendency to lift.

K.:   Here we have a simple example of how muscle works against muscle. From it we can also see that the antagonistic tension could have been avoided, if the man had used the muscle which is only a flexor of the elbow. While we have already learned that there are different co-ordinations for attaining a certain aim, we can now add that they vary in the amount of energy expended. In one co-ordination there is antagonistic muscle tension resulting in a waste of energy, while in another this is avoided.

P.:   However, this squandering of muscle strength is only one of the disadvantages of antagonistic tensions. We must remember that firmness results from forces working against each other. We have mentioned above (p. 47) that the attainment of such firmness is the purpose for which we have a muscle acting against the hindrance of ligaments. Now, however, firmness results as a matter

Co-ordination with and without tension

of chance, simply because an uneconomical co-ordination was used. This involuntary firmness represents an obstacle to a freedom which would otherwise be possible. So we learn that co-ordination which involves mutually antagonistic tensions is not only uneconomical but also impairs freedom of movement, and for that reason we shall speak in this case not about firmness but about fixation.

W.:   And all that depends only on whether I use muscles passing over one or more joints?

K.:   Not at all. Only for the sake of simplicity I started with this example which might be of some slight importance. There are other factors of much more importance. We will keep to the example of movement with upper arm held low. We have learned that, in the case of the man with antagonistic muscle tensions, the low position of the upper arm is caused by the effect of an arm-lowering muscle. Why is the upper arm low in the case of the man with the other type of co-ordination?

Gravity and muscle co-ordinations

W.:   Probably simply because of gravity.

K.:   So we realise that gravity also plays a part in the movements and positions of our body and its different parts.

P.:   As a matter of fact, gravity is the second external influence which we recognize to be important. The first was that of external resistance. Let us keep in mind that we must never base our considerations of body movements on the idea that each of us is a single solid body floating in space without gravity. On the contrary, we must always think of the joint influence of three equally important factors:
1)   gravity,
2)   external resistance, and
3)   our muscles.

I mention the muscles last on purpose, because they are the one factor which can and must adapt to the other two factors, which are invariable.

K.:   Let us first consider gravity. We respond to it to the greatest extent, when we lie down. In this position we need no muscles, because gravity works against the external resistance of our support and determines the position of every part of the body without the co-operation of any of the muscles, as it does with a dead body. But what happens when we sit or stand? Is this possible without muscles, too?

Equilibrium

W.:   Since you have mentioned the dead, I must say, "No", because the dead neither sit nor stand.

P.:   Therefore sitting and standing are not at all passive states but activities and, furthermore, activities which are conditioned by the force of gravity.

K.:   Isn't that surprising? Look at a tin soldier! He has no muscles and yet can stand.

W.:   But he is all in one piece without any joints, and so cannot cave in. We however would cave in and must prevent this by the force of the muscles.

P.:   Thereby you are stressing the importance of the muscular system for creating a firm support for the body.

K.:   We must consider comething else: all parts of the tin soldier are immobile. But now imagine that he has a shoulder joint and lifts his arm forwards, as you do when you play the piano.

W.:   This might bring him out of balance and he might fall forwards.

K.:   Yes, he would lose his balance, which reminds us that the state of equilibrium of the body is continually changing with every movement, since the centre of gravity of the entire body is displaced with the shifting of each part.

W.:   What can we do against this threat to our equilibrium?

K.:   There are two possible means of defence against any sort of threat: on the one hand, the policy of strength, which constantly uses all available means to guarantee security against every possible danger; on the other, the policy of "wait and see" — flexible adaptation, with the minimum effort, to every situation as it arises.

The person comparable with a pedestal

W.:   Are we talking about politics and strategy now, or still about co-ordination?

K.:   Just apply it to co-ordination! With reference to the possible means of defence, how does one person maintain his balance when it is threatened, and how does the other? Here the policy of strength is based on the fact that the smaller the mass which is being moved, and the larger the counteracting mass, the fewer disturbances there will be. So what would you do as a follower of this policy?

P.:   Wherever possible, I would not move my arm, but only my finger. If I had to use my whole arm, I would try to do so without the use of the shoulder girdle, which I would rather keep in firm muscular connection with the trunk. At the same time I would add the weight of my legs to that of my trunk by creating a firm immovable connection between them, and in doing so I would establish such a solid base for support that my trunk practically forms an immovable whole with chair and floor. Now, am I secure from all disturbances of my equilibrium?

W.:   Yes, entirely.

P.:   And do you know whom I have described just now?

W.:   I believe it was me before I became your pupil.

P.:   Don't flatter yourself! I should not have dedicated this study to you alone. But such people populate many concert stages and many teachers' chairs in conservatories. They are the pure finger-technicians.

K.:   But how does all that come about — the connection of the shoulder girdle with the trunk, the trunk with the legs and all the rest? Just think, we have to deal with the fixation of joints in positions which are not extreme positions. How can I make the joint immovable in either direction from such a position?

W.:   If you prevent the movement in either direction by the muscles which have the opposite function, i.e. by antagonistic muscle tension.

K.:   As a result, we have a rigid man whose body is just like a pedestal from which the arms are moved. He consists of mutually antagonistic tensions through and through, so his co-ordinations are certainly not those which save the most energy.

P.:   And his movements are certainly not free, but cramped.

W.:   Now I realise what the other man will do, the one who follows the policy of adapting himself with the minimum effort. He will not be afraid to use his entire arm, including if possible the shoulder girdle, for playing the piano. He will not restrict the movability of his trunk, but he will use it, among other things, for counterbalancing the threats to his equilibrium as they arise.

Co-ordinations through the whole body

P.:   So we recognize that, no matter which type of co-ordination we are dealing with, we must rid ourselves of the idea that the movement of a certain part of the body concerns only that part and only those muscles which directly produce the movement. On the contrary, in both types of co-ordination the entire body and all its muscles may be concerned in the slightest movement of a very small part of the body. The difference between the two types is that one man keeps almost all his muscles tense in anticipation, while the other uses one or the other auxiliary muscles according to the needs of the movement, but these muscles, too, may be situated far away.

K.:   We have to keep in mind, though, that it is not so easy to follow this second policy as to follow the first. It requires a certain experience always to perform the correct counteractions

Learning co-ordinations

against momentary disturbances, also a certain confidence that in each case it will be possible to overcome all disturbances.

H.: That is the reason why, in learning a new activity, one is inclined to work with mutually antagonistic tensions.

K.: That probably refers both to human beings and to animals.

P.: The difference is, however, that the "dumb animals" very quickly find and use the economical, uncramped, free movements. That's why the way an animal moves usually impresses us as being so very elegant. It is the privilege of the master of the universe alone to spend all his life with muscle tensions.

K.: As a matter of fact, it is much more difficult for a two-legged man to keep his balance than it is for his four-legged cousins of the animal kingdom; and what we are faced with here is a problem of balance. Further, we must not wonder that civilized man of today in particular has lost confidence in his own body and in his ability to control natural forces directly without the help of machines.

H.: And since it is a matter of confidence in alien natural forces, it is understandable that in moments of excitement when you are inclined to lose all confidence, for instance when you step onto a concert stage, there is always the special danger that you will fall back into muscular tensions which you had otherwise got rid of.

W.: But how do you get rid of those tensions?

K.: What do we say about the process of learning in general? Some learn right away, some later and some never. It is the same with the learning of co-ordinations, although they have nothing to do with intelligence. We have to imagine the centres of intelligence and of co-ordination in entirely different parts of the brain. So there are real geniuses of co-ordination, who need have no special mental capacities at all, and vice versa. In beginning to learn a new activity and having to acquire new co-ordinations for it, one person aims unerringly at the co-ordination which saves most energy and which allows him the freest movements, while the other person is satisfied, if he manages the activity somehow. Since he knows only the one co-ordination which he has acquired by chance, and since therefore he cannot make any comparison, he will never notice how wasteful of energy his habits are. Most people throughout their lives will perform the simplest actions, such as speaking or writing, with an enormous waste of energy and never notice it. Only when one is faced with an unusual task, e.g.

making long speeches to large audiences, only then does one's voice fail.

W.:   And is there no help?

K.:   Oh, yes. Here the voice specialist comes in. He must eliminate the co-ordinations that have been habitual since early childhood and replace them with new co-ordinations, which are free from mutually antagonistic tensions. Of course, it is much easier, if the wrong co-ordinations are not given a chance to establish themselves, and the teacher of a new activity lays stress on the correct mode of execution right from the beginning. A skiing teacher knows that well enough. But how many elementary-school teachers forget that in teaching handwriting, it is not only important what this or that letter looks like, but just as important is how the pencil or pen is held? This regrettable neglect on the part of many teachers is the reason for the frequency of writers' cramp.

P.:   Exactly the same is true of piano teachers. They also fail in their duty if they just teach pupils to read the notes, find the keys, keep time, acquire a certain fluency and obey expression marks. It is just as essential to teach the correct co-ordinations for piano playing. It is even more important here than in teaching handwriting, because, in the latter case, what matters for the meaning is what is written, not how it is written. It is entirely different in playing the piano, because here we have to deal with a work of art. Here the meaning is completely dependent upon the impression given by the sound. How can the listener experience the liberating effect of the work of art, if the performer himself is the slave of his own mutually antagonistic tensions? Who would endeavour to attain an artistically perfect performance on a piano of defective technical construction? And what about the defective technical construction of the player, his wrong co-ordinations? Can this be innocuous? That's why I consider it my most important task to find the correct co-ordinations, understand their why and wherefore, teach them to my pupils and call upon other teachers to do likewise.

W.:   Can the teacher always convey them to the pupil?

P.:   With the good will of the pupil, almost always. Of course, it will be more difficult in some cases than in others; for instance, if it is a matter not only of building up new co-ordinations but also of eliminating ones which are wrong or inadequate. That is why I asked about our maximum demands for the tone right at the beginning (pp. 21–22), so that we can discuss right away the co-ordinations which are necessary for this ideal sound. Otherwise, if to start with we had aimed at any old tone, afterwards we should have to re-trace our steps very laboriously.

H.: Because of the difficulties in eliminating wrong co-ordinations which have become habituated, it is much easier to teach children than grown-ups, even if the grown-ups have not played the piano before. You see, bad habits which we acquire in one activity affect our other activities also.

W.: That's understandable, since we have found that in fact every activity concerns the entire body.

H.: Therefore the state of the entire body can be changed by one sort of activity. So we can understand how a young man whose legs were paralysed by poliomyelitis learned not only to play the piano, but also to walk, when he became a pupil of our professor.

P.: Because his inability to walk was only partly caused by the organic paralysis; it was also due to mutually antagonistic tensions.

W.: Do I understand that a person is either cramped in his whole body or is completely free of mutually antagonistic tensions?

P.: That is not so. In fact, the completely free state is an ideal, which like every ideal is practically unattainable. In reality, we find people who are more cramped and others who are less cramped. In the former, more systems of mutually antagonistic tensions are active than in the latter.

Tension systems

W.: What do you mean by a "system of mutually antagonistic tensions"?

P.: Experience has taught me that there are typical combinations of mutually antagonistic tensions which appear and disappear together in different parts of the body which are often far away from one another. That's what I call a system of antagonistic tensions. It often runs through the entire body and it is more or less independent of other such systems.

W.: "More or less independent"? So it is not completely independent?

K.: Within a unit such as the human body, complete independence between different systems can hardly be expected.

P.: The practical situation is as follows: If a person has tensions in several such systems, the loosening of a certain muscle can cause the complete disappearance of the tensions in the system to which the muscle belongs. In other systems the tensions will not disappear completely, but relaxation will be facilitated thereby.

W.:   But why should a certain series of muscles which are dispersed all over the body, but are at the same time members of a particular system of antagonistic tensions, have such an intimate functional relation with each other, more intimate than with other muscles which might be closer, but belong to a different system?

P.:   To elucidate this in respect to each system would certainly be an interesting task for our anatomist, but it would lead us too far into theory. We had better keep to the practical side: If we do not loosen single muscles but all muscles together which belong to a certain system, we can attain the greatest possible freedom from mutually antagonistic tensions more easily than if we had not taken the existence of the systems into account.

K.:   Until now, we have been basing our approval of this state of greatest possible freedom from mutually antagonistic tensions on different reasons of a general nature, but we have not yet heard a special reason why the piano demands this freedom in the player.

Demand of the piano concerning co-ordination

P.:   Just recall once again the picture of the person with mutually antagonistic tensions (p. 47) and remember the demands of the piano (p. 34). Then ask yourself whether these demands can be met by the player who is cramped.

W.:   No. The man whose trunk we compared to a pedestal makes his body the fixed centre of his world, and from a fixed centre there can only be radial movements outwards, which we have called "aiming". Such aiming movements, however, are counter to the demands of the piano (p. 34). Furthermore, mutually antagonistic tensions preclude the working of gravity. The key, however, demands the player to work as far as possible in obedience to the force of gravity.

P.:   Right. Of course, we shall have to refer these general considerations to many special instances.

W.:   So the essence of the technique you want to be used does not consist in certain movements, but in the state of being without tensions.

P.:   Mainly in that. But we must not underestimate the importance of movements either, since some of them are absolutely contrary to the demands of the piano.

W.:   Of course: the radially-aiming movements.

P.:   Yes. There are others though. But among those which are in accordance with the demands of the piano, none is better or worse than any other. If hereafter we describe the typical way some of them are made, we must remember that it is almost always possible to change them in their geometrical course, without changing the state of the muscular system which is the determining factor, and therefore without changing the quality of the tone. On the other hand, it can happen that two movements look exactly alike and yet may be executed with the muscular system in two entirely different states. This means that there are infinite possibilities for the wrong execution of a movement which, from a purely geometrical standpoint, would be a correct one. To sum up, there are infinite ways of playing correctly, but since, for each of these ways, there are infinite possibilities of executing them wrongly, the number of wrong ways is infinity multiplied by infinity.

W.: What the innumerable correct ways of playing have in common can be summed up in the words "loosen" or "relax", can't it?

P.: No. We have to say more particularly: "release mutually antagonistic tensions", because muscle tensions which do not work against other muscles but against ligaments, thus ensuring firmness, are often necessary in our technique. Don't forget that I am not an apostle of biogymnastics but a piano teacher.

H.: So although we started today with pure anatomy, we have now arrived at piano playing. Now it is time to sit down at the piano.

P.: That we shall do tomorrow.

DIALOGUE 3

The Playing Apparatus as a Whole

W.:   May I sit at the piano right away?

P.:   Yes. But first we must take heed where we place the chair, as we have already stressed (p. 20).

Position of the chair

W.:   Of course, it must not be too far away, so that the player has no difficulty in reaching the farthest keys.

P.:   Certainly. But it must not be too close either, because as we shall soon see, this would make the elbow angle too small, which would hinder the playing. It is the best to place the chair so that the elbow is at an angle between 120° and 150° when you touch the middle keys. I will postpone our further requirements concerning how to sit until we can understand the reasons for them.

W.:   Now may I strike a note?

P.:   What good would that do? It will be enough to close the chain, piano-floor-chair-player, to a complete circle. And this we can do noiselessly by putting the hand on the edge of the keyboard in such a way that the middle members of the second, third and fourth fingers rest on the edges of the keys. After this has been done, we shall observe this person at the piano.

W.:   We have already done that thoroughly.

P.:   Yes, from an anatomical point of view, from which we saw that he had a trunk, neck, head and four limbs. What does all that mean with regard to piano playing?

Playing apparatus and supporting apparatus

W.:   From that point of view he has above all an arm.

P.:   Why do you mention the arm "above all"?

W.:   Because we use it for playing.

P.:   Therefore let us not say "arm" but "playing apparatus", leaving open for the moment, what parts belong to the complete playing apparatus. And what mechanical function does the rest of the body have?

W.:   It serves as a support for the playing apparatus.

P.:   Then the body of the pianist consists of a playing apparatus and a supporting apparatus. We will again leave open the question which parts of the body belong to neither of these and are therefore superfluous from the point of view of piano playing. Playing apparatus and supporting apparatus are essential, and to an equal degree. I can't be emphatic enough about this, because there is always a tendency to take account of the playing apparatus only. We must remember that we do not float weight-lessly and that for every activity a firm support is necessary, as Archimedes recognized long ago. So also our piano-playing apparatus needs a support.

H.:   Nevertheless, we also are going to start with the playing apparatus.

Length-adjusting, grasping and weight apparatuses

P.:   Yes, but from a functional standpoint, and we know the function in its essential features from the analogy of the boatman's rope (p. 33).

W.:   First we must throw out the hand to key-top.

P.:   We throw it over the distance from the supporting apparatus to the key. This distance is the length of the straight imaginary body which we took (p. 31) as a valid substitute for the real arm or, as we would say now, the real playing apparatus.

W.:   This distance, however, changes with the individual keys, and therefore we concluded that the imaginary body must possess the ability to become longer or shorter.

P.:   So we need an apparatus which adjusts the length of the imaginary body to varying distances. Let us speak of a length-adjusting apparatus.

K.:   Actually, in going from one key to another, the straight imaginary body from the shoulder to the fingertip changes not only its length but also its direction, so the length-adjusting apparatus is also a direction-changing apparatus.

P.:   I grant you that, but since the pianist has scarcely any problems with the changing of direction and a good many with adjusting length, I have chosen the name "length-adjusting apparatus". To continue, but not necessarily following the sequence of events, what must happen when the playing apparatus is thrown out over the keys?

W.:   I must attain a connection between my hand and the key.

P.:   When I lay hold of something in order to unite it with my hand, we describe this as "grasping"; so, in the second place, we need a grasping apparatus.

W.:   Lastly, the key has to be moved in the direction of gravity, and this has to be done by pulling and not by pushing.

P.:   Since there is now a force acting in the direction of gravity, we can speak of a weight apparatus. And that completes the playing apparatus.

W.:   I see: The playing apparatus consists of a length-adjusting, a grasping and a weight apparatus. Now the individual parts of the playing apparatus must be divided up between these three.

P.:   But in doing so, we must not start with the idea that a particular bone or muscle can belong to only one of the three apparatuses. Don't let us forget that adjustment of length precedes the key-moving action. It is quite possible for one and the same part of the body to contribute to both the preparation of the key-moving action, i.e. in the length-adjusting apparatus, and to the action itself, in which case it would function as part of the grasping or weight apparatus.

H.:   Now let us ask ourselves what sorts of movement we can employ to adjust length.

Adjustment of length

W.:   It is a movement which we can liken to that of a man sawing wood. The sawing motion consists chiefly in bending and straightening the elbow joint. Naturally, the other joints of the arm, especially the shoulder joint, also take part.

P.:   Right, but that's not all. Lift your arm forwards and straighten your elbow completely. Now your hand is at a certain distance from the trunk. Then see if you can still increase the distance.

W.:   Yes, quite a bit, by moving my shoulder forwards.

P.:   This pushing forwards of the shoulder is a movement of the shoulder blade in the joints of the shoulder girdle. So already here, in observing the length-adjusting apparatus, we learn that the shoulder girdle, as well as the arm, belongs to the playing apparatus. Therefore, at which joint must we mark the boundary between playing apparatus and supporting apparatus?

W.:   Not at the shoulder joint, as I should have thought, but at the joint between breast bone and collar bone.

P.:   Now a little attention to the question of the muscles in these length-adjusting movements. Which muscles do I need for bending and straightening the elbow?

W.:   The straightening can be left mostly to the weight of the forearm and hand; it is then the business of the elbow-flexing muscles to limit the amount of extension. The bending must of course be done by elbow-flexing muscles. In spite of this I have no feeling of activity in my biceps at all.

P.:   That's good. It proves that the length-adjusting apparatus acts without any antagonistic tensions, in such a way that the elbow-flexors work only against the light weight of forearm and hand. How long must the activity of the elbow-flexors last?

W.:   Since we have learned that the adjustment of length takes place only in preparation for the key-moving action, the function of the elbow-flexors ends when we begin to move the key.

P.:   Of course it must end at this moment for, as you have just stressed, the elbow-flexors work against gravity, whereas the key-moving action must take place in the direction of gravity.

W.:   Then couldn't the key be moved simply by the release of the elbow-flexors?

P.:   No, that would be impossible, because they would release only the weight of the forearm and hand, and that is not enough to overcome the resistance of the spring suspension of the key. In other words, at the moment of coming in contact with the key, I can release my elbow-flexors without necessarily moving the key, because the weight of forearm and hand, which before was carried by the elbow-flexors, is now carried by the buoyancy of the key.

W.:   What weight do I need, then, to overcome this buoyancy?

P.:   Add the upper arm, and it will be enough.

K.:   That's strange! Have you considered that the weight of a man's arm is about ten pounds? This whole weight would be needed to move the key to key-bottom?

The arm as a chain

P.:   No, not the whole ten pounds. Think of this: we are speaking now about the effect of the weight of a chain. Imagine a chain suspended at both ends and hanging heavily in between. Naturally, the weight of such a chain apportions itself to both suspension points. The heavier the whole chain is, the greater is its effect on each of the two end points. As long as we have the two end points on the key and the elbow respectively, the effect of the weight on the key is not enough. Taking the shoulder joint as the end point nearer the body, the effect of the weight is enough, because in this case the total weight of the chain is increased by the weight of the upper arm.

W.:   This condition of the arm, as a heavy hanging chain, would be in absolute accordance with the demands of the piano, because a chain by its nature hangs in the plane of gravity, and at its end point it has a pulling effect in a downward direction, whereby the second and third demands of the piano (p. 34) are met.

P.:   Quite correct. Therefore, it would pay us to look at this chain of the arm more closely. We notice first that the links of the chain are of different sizes and weights, that the heaviest ones are found near the body and that they becomes successively smaller the further they are from the body, all the way to the finger on the key. To make an exaggerated comparison: the chain starts like a ship's anchor chain and ends like a watch chain.

K.:   Would the links of the watch chain by themselves be able to transfer the weight of the anchor chain links to the distant point of support?

W.:   No, they would simply slide off.

K.:   Yes. And in the same way my hand resting here on the edge of the keyboard would slide off. Can you explain this?

W.:   The heavy links of the chain tend to fall backwards in a circle around the point of suspension near the body, thereby pulling the light ones off the further point of support.

K.:   But haven't we observed a certain adhesion between finger and key?

W.:   Yes, but this results from the interaction of imposed weight and key resistance. The finger itself weighs very little and therefore can adhere only very loosely, so that it offers practically no resistance to the backward pull of the heavier parts of the chain.

K.:   Now what must you do to keep it from falling off?

W.:   Increase the adhesion.

K.:   But we have said that the adhesion results from weight. Can you increase the weight of the finger?

W.:   I would have to bring the light-weight parts of the chain into firmer connection with the heavy ones, so that the weight of the latter would also act on the distant point of support.

K.:   How can you do that?

W.:   By muscle action.

K.:   Yes, by the action of the muscles which prevent the movements which would take place between the separate parts if they were to slide off. What sorts of movement are they? It will be easier for you to answer if you imagine the chain to consist of only two parts (Fig. 4). Please don't forget that we are talking about the movements during sliding off, not what happens after one part has slid off completely and falls away.

W.:   The two parts (OG and GP) of a freely hanging chain form an angle which opens upwards. In the course of sliding off, this upper angle would decrease.

K.:   Of course, the same would happen at all the joints of a

chain with many parts. Which muscles can prevent the reduction
of the upper angles at the joints of the chain?

W.:   Muscles on the lower side of the chain.

K.:   Therefore to keep the arm in a condition corresponding
to that of a chain, we need the activity of muscles on the lower
side of the arm. These muscles have the function of transferring
the weight of the heavy parts of the playing apparatus, which are
near the body, to the distant point of support on the key.

W.:   So the playing apparatus could be represented by the
following model (Fig. 5). A series of metal parts are united by
joints at G_1, G_2 and G_3, and on the lower side they are connected
by springs (Sp_1, Sp_2, Sp_3). One of the end parts (OG_1) is suspended in such a way that it can move freely around the end point

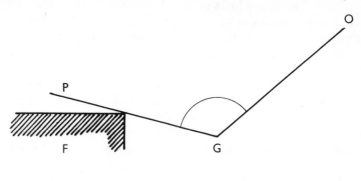

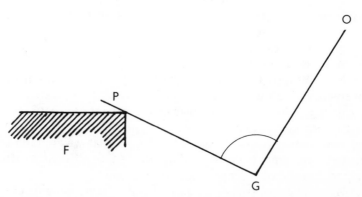

Figure 4.   Two phases in the sliding-off of a chain with two members, one of which
(OG) is movably suspended at the end point O, while the other (GP) rests loosely on
the firm support F. The angle at the joint G decreases between the first and second
phases.

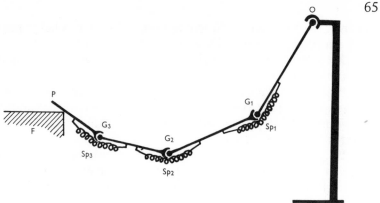

Figure 5.

(O) of the chain, whereas the other end part (G3P) rests on a firm support (F), on which it can glide. The springs will allow a certain sagging, but if they have adequate tension they will prevent the chain from falling away.

   K.:   When you speak of "adequate tension" in reference to the springs or muscles, you probably mean that the tension must not be too slight, or else the chain would fall. But couldn't it also be too great?

   W.:   What harm could that do?

   K.:   We said that the tension of the muscles on the lower side prevents a reduction of the upper angles. If the tension increases what will be the effect?

   W.:   Enlargement of the upper angles.

   K.:   And what would that mean for the whole chain?

   W.:   An increasing distance between its two ends.

   K.:   So, in which direction would the distant end of the chain move?

   W.:   Radially away from the shoulder. However, that is the kind of movement which pushes against the key and so acts against the demands of the piano.

   H.:   So we learn that the tension of the underside muscles has to be just enough to permit the transfer of weight of the heavy parts of the playing apparatus to the key, but not more. We have here a typical example of the precise adjustment of muscle action to gravity.

   P.:   The condition of the arm in which this adjustment is perfect I call "suspension". From everything we have said, we conclude that suspension is a basic requirement we have to make of

Suspension

the arm. We can further conclude that suspension is never possible as long as there are mutually antagonistic tensions.

K.: How can you know whether your pupil is meeting this requirement or not?

P.: First of all by the quality of the tone, for the key is always the best judge of the condition of the playing apparatus. Furthermore I can put myself in the place of the key.

K.: How could you possibly do that?

P.: Remember, we have said that the arm represents a chain in which, by means of the tension of the muscles on the lower side, the weight of the heavy parts near the body is transferred to the distant supporting point. It does not matter whether this distant supporting point is the key or some other object.

K.: All right.

P.: Here I hold my finger horizontally in front of you. Now drop your finger on mine, as you would do in moving the key. If your playing apparatus is in the state of suspension, what should I feel?

K.: The weight of my arm.

P.: Correct, but I don't. Your finger is resting quite lightly on mine. Now, what can I say about the condition of your playing apparatus?

K.: That there are mutually antagonistic tensions in it, preventing it from sagging freely.

P.: On the other hand, the same tensions might cause your finger to press against mine. Of course it requires some experience to distinguish this sensation of pressing from that of natural weight. In any case the matter is clinched if I begin to move my finger and yours with it to any position within your reach. The natural weight-pressure will be practically constant, whereas the strength of the sensation of pressing which results from antagonistic tensions, changes from place to place.

K.: Yes, I feel that myself.

P.: I can make a similar test while the pupil is actually playing. After he has moved the key to key-bottom and when his finger is resting there, I slide my finger under the middle member of his finger and try to lift it, and with it the whole playing apparatus, from the key. Usually I encounter insurmountable opposition, but if the player is in relaxed condition with "suspension" in his playing apparatus, it is easy for me to lift his finger far away from the key. In this case I need to carry only the natural weight of the playing apparatus, even when the preceding movement has produced a fortissimo sound.

H.:   The teacher cannot make these tests with a pupil often enough. Over and over again one finds a tense arm, and one must never tire of repeating, "Let it fall! Relax!", until at last the true weight-pressure comes. Then the pupil himself feels the natural weight of his arm.

P.:   Because of this, I call an arm in that condition a "heavy arm", whereas the arm with mutually antagonistic tensions is a "light arm".

K.:   Of course this does not mean that — physically speaking — the arm in one condition is really heavier than in the other.

P.:   No, I am only expressing the subjective feeling about the weight of my arm.

K.:   This subjective feeling is perfectly understandable. Where so many forces are constantly at work, as in the man with mutually antagonistic tensions, the weight of a particular part of the body will scarcely be noticed among all the other forces at work, and accordingly will hardly be utilized. Let us compare this with a clock of the sort you see on a church tower. Its hands certainly have weight; but in constructing the mechanism, would the clockmaker give any consideration to the weight of the minute hand, in such a way that he would leave it to the weight alone to move the key, or to help to move it, from the full hour to the half-hour? No, among the forces in the mechanism the weight of the hands will be disregarded. For the mechanism, the hand is not heavy, just as the arm of the man with mutually antagonistic tensions is not heavy for him.

P.:   That is so. The arm is heavy only if our muscle actions are adjusted exactly to its weight, as for instance in the condition of suspension. Since this condition of heaviness is associated with freedom from inhibiting tensions, we can say in short: "That which is heavy, is free".

Freedom and repose

W.:   If I recall what I have experienced under your guidance in the last few weeks and months, then I become aware that the condition of relaxation, which I have attained with great effort, gives me in fact a very comfortable feeling of freedom. It is curious that we feel freedom if we submit to a law — the law of gravity.

K.:   It is only subjection to arbitrary rules that we feel to be tyranny, not submission to a universally valid law.

P.:   We can agree with Goethe's words: "It is the law alone that gives us freedom". For us, the law that gives us freedom is the law of gravity; the tyranny from which it liberates us is that of antagonistic tensions.

W.: There is also a feeling of repose that comes with the feeling of freedom.

P.: Everything that obeys gravity as far as it can comes finally to a condition of repose, namely static equilibrium. The chain hanging between its two end points is in this condition. We must now describe it more precisely.

H.: Remember that we are dealing with the arm in the hanging position which it adopts of itself, without mutually antagonistic tensions, when we have put the fingers on the front edges of the keys in the way described above (p. 67)

K.: To begin at the far end, let us ask ourselves first which part of the surface of the fingers is touching the keys.

W.: Originally I had taken it for granted that it would be the palm side, i.e. the flexor side, but on closer inspection I see that the fingers are slightly tilted, so that it is more the side facing the little finger which rests on the keys.

P.: This resting on the side is still more noticeable, if we lift the wrist in such a way that the fingers touch not only the edges of the keys but their surfaces. What do we call this position of the hand, in which the outer surfaces of the fingers are turned down?

W.: Supination (p. 44).

P.: So we observe that when the arm is in the chain condition, the hand of itself adopts the position of supination.

W.: But why?

P.: Go back a moment. How do the forearm bones lie in relation to each other when in supination?

W.: In the region of the wrist, the head of the ulna is distinctly lower than the radius.

P.: And what did we say (p. 43) about these two bones as links in the skeleton chain of the arm?

W.: Since the radius alone carries the hand, it is an intermediate link between hand and ulna. Therefore the sequence of links in the chain is: upper arm — ulna — radius — hand — finger.

P.: This means that the forearm resolves itself into two parts, ulna and radius, which although they are located side by side, yet from the point of view of force and gravity one follows the other. It is the ulna to which the weight of the heavy parts of the playing apparatus is transferred from the upper arm, whereas the radius is held high by the hand at the distant point of support. Can we wonder that the weighted ulna falls under the high-held radius?

W.: No. It is really self-evident. All that simply means supination.

P.: The precondition for this falling of the ulna under the radius is that the force of gravity has a chance to act and that the fall is not prevented by mutually antagonistic muscle tensions, which in this case would limit the freedom of pronation and supination. Therefore this separation of the ulna from the radius by the force of gravity is one of the best criteria of freedom from mutually antagonistic tensions in the arm. The head of the ulna will of itself become the deepest point of the chain only in an arm which really does hang like a chain.

H.: But we must guard against the idea that the mere deep position of the head of the ulna is a sign of a relaxed condition of the arm. Of course it is also possible for me to force my cramped arm into this position.

P.: By saying that the radius is held high by the hand on the key, while the ulna tends to sink with the heavy parts of the arm near the body, we have defined the boundary between the grasping and the weight apparatuses. The weight apparatus consists of the heavy parts tending downwards, while the grasping apparatus comprises the parts which, by grasping, intercept this downward motion. Therefore the ulna belongs to the weight apparatus, the radius — to the grasping apparatus.

K.: Of course the radius belongs to the grasping apparatus, because for a grasp which is free in every direction, we need three degrees of freedom, and we have found (p. 44) that only in conjunction with the radius does the hand possess all three possible degrees of freedom in relation to the ulna.

H.: However, we must not conclude that pronation or supination movements originating in the forearm are ever used for grasping or for any action which is needed to move the key.

P.: That means that we do not require active motions between ulna and radius — at least not while moving the key — but the possibility for free movement between them. More generally, we can say that the grasping apparatus and weight apparatus must be free to rotate relatively to each other.

H.: Now that we understand the importance of the head of the ulna as the deepest point of the chain, because the arm hangs under the influence of gravity, let us go to the other end of the ulna and look at the position of the elbow.

Lateral fall of the elbow

K.: In doing so, we must remember what we said yesterday (p. 49) about the possible positions of the elbow.

W.: We found that with any one position of the hand it is possible for the elbow to be in any number of different places, all of them being on the circumference of the common base of the double-conical segment which the upper arm and forearm can describe around the axis shoulder-wrist.

P.:   In the light of our knowledge about the arm as a sagging chain, are all these elbow positions of equal value?

W.:   Of course not. If the arm sags freely like a chain, the elbow must be in a place which is vertically below the line from shoulder to wrist.

P.:   If it is not there, but is lifted outwards from its deepest possible position, what then?

W.:   Then the arm is no longer in a chain condition; it is no longer heavy. There are bound to be mutually antagonistic tensions in it, and the action of the playing apparatus in the plane of gravity can be disturbed by lateral pushing.

P.:   Yes. Those are the simple undeniable facts which follow from our previous considerations. But it is equally undeniable that every pupil has a tendency to lift the elbow outwards from its lowest position.

K.:   And not only piano players. I noticed the same tendency in myself when I first held a steering wheel, or as a soldier when holding a rifle. In all these activities it became evident that sureness of movement and freedom from fatigue were possible only when the driving or shooting instructor had instilled in me the necessary position in the plane of gravity.

P.:   I can only say: "Happy the driving schools and happy the shooting schools where the instructors impress the correct postures on their pupils!" But we need not go so far from piano-playing to find analogies. For other musical instruments the same law is valid. Notice the posture of a good violinist! We have an ideal example in the caricature of Paganini (Fig. 11, p. 157), which will be instructive also in many other respects. Here too you see the elbows in the deepest possible position.

K.:   I have heard of violin teachers who made their pupils hold a plate under the armpit to keep them from allowing the arm to rise.

H.:   I have my doubts about imitating this method. Haven't we said that it should be gravity which keeps the elbow in its deepest position? If I am afraid of letting the plate drop, I shall actively press my elbow against my side, and so by this very method might be tempted to use mutually antagonistic tensions.

P.:   Anyway it is out of court for piano playing, because in the first place, the plate would be bound to fall to the floor as a result of movements for length adjustment, and secondly, there are also hand postures in which the elbow must leave its deepest position.

W.:   Which are they?

P.:   Try yourself. Hold your hand in pronation.

W.:   What for: Haven't we just found that the position required by the weight of the arm-chain is supination?

Geometrically and dynamically low

P.:   Yes. But sometimes musical expression requires pronation, so we must also consider this possibility. Put your hand in pronation on the key board and observe your elbow.

W.:   It is compelled to rise outwards.

K.:   That is quite understandable, because pronation between ulna and radius can go no farther than to the position in which the palm is facing down. If I continue pronation beyond this position, it must be through a rotatory movement in the shoulder joint, as we already know (p. 44). If the elbow is bent and the hand is to remain in the same place, the shoulder-joint rotation can take place only around the shoulder-wrist axis of the double cone, and that means only by an outward lifting of the elbow.

P.:   Yet what can we require of the elbow in that case?

W.:   That it does not rise higher than is absolutely necessary for the desired hand position, so that the lateral distance from the position of static equilibrium, and therefore the disturbance of this equilibrium, is as small as possible.

P.:   In other words, the elbow shall in every instance fall to the deepest possible position in the double cone, and we shall call this the "lateral fall" of the elbow.

K.:   Meaning, the needed pronation has always to be carried out to the greatest possible extent between the two forearm bones and to the least possible extent in the shoulder joint. Then not only the elbow but the whole ulna will take the deepest position which is possible in the given situation.

P.:   That applies particularly to the head of the ulna in the wrist. We have just stated (p. 68) that it is the deepest point in the arm-chain, but of course for positions of pronation this is no longer true from a geometrical standpoint: the head of the ulna is distinctly higher than the radius at the wrist. Still, it is the distant end of the weight apparatus in an arm in which, according to our requirements, weight and grasping apparatuses are separated mechanically from one another. And if, also in accordance with the demand of the piano (p. 34), the key-moving action is carried out by a purely peripheral movement of the weight apparatus, the

72

tendency for a downward motion around the shoulder manifests itself most distinctly in the head of the ulna, because there the circle centered at the shoulder has the greatest radius. Therefore, however high the head of the ulna may be geometrically, dynamically it must remain the deepest point of the playing apparatus.

W.: But we certainly could not say that it is dynamically deep if one of these requirements is not fulfilled, could we?

P.: Then it would be dynamically high, even if it were the deepest point geometrically, because it would push the grasping apparatus from above against the keys, instead of representing the free end of the weight apparatus whose downward action by-passes the keyboard.

W.: By-passes the keyboard? How is it supposed to move the key then?

P.: Don't forget that we are talking about the head of the ulna. This downward movement of the ulna will be caught up by the grasping apparatus and so transmitted to the key.

W.: And since this downward movement is a peripheral motion around the centre in the shoulder, the end point of the weight apparatus near the body is the shoulder joint, isn't it?

P.: No. You must not forget that in the weight apparatus we are dealing with heavy parts, and the heaviest part belonging to the upper limb is the shoulder girdle. Hence, let us class it with the weight apparatus, which therefore reaches from the head of the ulna to the breastbone-collarbone joint.

H.: Of course, if we consider the playing apparatus as a chain, as we have found it useful to do till now, the shoulder girdle presents a certain problem. A chain sags in a vertical plane; so does the arm between fingers and shoulder joint. But the breastbone-collarbone joint, where the shoulder girdle is joined to the supporting apparatus, is clearly outside this plane. Because of its position on the rib cage, the shoulder girdle cannot sink into the plane of gravity like the rest of the chain. But in common with all the other parts of the chain, it must sink as deep as it can.

W.: Then the weight apparatus includes the shoulder girdle, upper arm and ulna, and the grasping apparatus — the radius, hand and fingers?

P.: Yes. And the distant end point of the playing apparatus belongs to the grasping apparatus, while the end point near the body belongs to the weight apparatus.

W.: Do you mean that the grasping apparatus is suspended at the distant end point and the weight apparatus — at the one near the body?

Weight apparatus: head of ulna to breastbone-collarbone joint

Points A and B

P.:   Not quite that, because we know that the whole chain, and each of its parts, needs two points of suspension. In practice, however, we must not forget that we are not dealing with a chain which is hanging motionless, such as we have considered till now, but with a chain which is being moved. Naturally, this brings up the question of the centres of movements.

W.:   It seems to be beyond question that the ultimate centre of all movements is at the end of the playing apparatus near the body.

P.:   That is true as long as we are referring to movements in which the playing apparatus has no distant point of support, i.e. movements in preparation for the key-moving action. These movements, which we make mainly for length adjustment until we reach the top of the key to be played, can of course be directed only from the end point of the playing apparatus near the body. So this point, which is both end point and point of suspension, becomes also a centre of motion, and in this new function we shall name it briefly "point A".

W.:   During the key-moving action this point A would no longer be the centre of motion?

P.:   Certainly it would, but would it be the only possible one? As soon as the finger has come into firm contact with the key, the chain condition with its two points of suspension is established. Why should only one of them come into question as a centre of motion? Try and see whether the second point of suspension, where the finger rests on the key, cannot become a second centre of motion also.

W.:   Oh, yes. For instance if I bend my wrist joint the wrist is made to rise over the key. In the same way, by bending the basal joint of a finger its basal knuckle is raised over the key. The rest of the arm is pulled forward by these movements.

P.:   That's right. So we learn that the suspension point of the arm-chain on the key can also become a centre of motion, which, to differentiate it from the centre of motion near the body, we shall name "point B".

W.:   That's clear enough.

P.:   Further, we should remember that point A is a joint, no matter for the moment whether it is the shoulder joint or the breastbone-collarbone joint, or, in atypical situations, the elbow joint. Is point B also a joint?

Finger-key joint

W.:   Of course not. I cannot speak of a joint between a part of my body and a part of the piano. Yet I must say that the movability is like that of a joint.

P.:   Therefore, in the mechanical respect, we do have the right to speak of a joint between finger and key, which we find at the boundary between the living and the inanimate parts of our complete piano-playing-system. How many degrees of freedom does this finger-key joint have?

W.:   All the three possible ones, since its movability is in no way restricted.

P.:   What are these three degrees of freedom?

W.:   The first I have already mentioned: the raising of the wrist around point B. The second would be the swinging of the wrist around this point in a horizontal plane.

K.:   Yes, a swinging of the wrist towards and away from the median plane.

W.:   What is the median plane?

K.:   The plane of symmetry which divides the body into a right and a left half.

W.:   I see.

P.:   Remember this word. We shall use it repeatedly. And the third degree of freedom in the finger-key joint?

W.:   Rotation of the finger on the key.

P.:   That's right. Now let us return to the first degree of freedom, which is practically the most important. You have said that by a flexion of the wrist or finger, the wrist or the basal knuckle of the finger respectively are raised over point B. In which part of the playing apparatus do these movements take place?

W.:   In the grasping apparatus, of course. In fact, flexions of the wrist and fingers are the very actions we call "grasping" movements.

P.:   Therefore, just as the centre of motion of the weight apparatus is in point A, so the centre of motion of the grasping apparatus is in point B.

W.:   How can motions around two different centres take place at the same time? That is simply impossible.

P.:   Of course, you are absolutely right: within one system we cannot make two actual extended movements around two different centres at the same time. It is a different matter, however, if we are concerned not so much with the movement itself as with the tendency to motion. Or if we do have to deal with actual extended movements, they cannot be simultaneous. The first possibility again has two sides, a positive and a negative one. The positive one states: What matters is the tendency to motion or

Tautening of the arm-chain

the potential movement. The negative one states: The actual movement does not matter. Let us take the positive statement first. In which direction does the weight apparatus tend to move of itself in the key-moving action?

W.:   Downwards around point A.

P.:   Yes. Now suppose a man loses his grasping apparatus in the act of moving the key without noticing it. What kind of movement would his weight apparatus make then?

W.:   It would move in a circle around the shoulder down and backwards.

P.:   Quite right. That means that the head of the ulna, being the end of the weight apparatus, passes by the keyboard. Both it and the elbow tend to move down and backwards. But now re- member what sort of movement would those parts make as a result of grasping?

W.:   Flexion of the wrist or finger pulls the wrist and elbow forward.

P.:   This means that the potential movements originating from the weight and the grasping apparatus are working in oppo- site directions from each other.

W.:   That results in a pulling and tautening of the chain, which is just what the piano demands.

P.:   So we recognize that for meeting this demand the op- posing tendencies to motion in the weight apparatus around A and in the grasping apparatus around B are important. The actual movements, insofar as they interest us at the moment, would not go beyond the extent which is made possible by the movement of the key from key-top to key-bottom and by the slight changes within the playing apparatus from a slack to a taut condition.

W.:   But in practice we make more extended movements.

P.:   Yes; around A or around B?

W.:   For length-adjustment they would naturally be directed from A, since for that purpose no point B exists.

P.:   That means that from point A we can and do make all sorts of movements. But if we observe the movements of the weight apparatus around A, we find only one movement is effec- tive as giving weight, namely the one you just described as a circu- lar motion down and backwards around the shoulder. This movement has no greater extent than from key-top to key-bottom. Of course, during this the tendency to movement in the grasping apparatus is at work, because otherwise the motion of the weight apparatus would not be transmitted to the key. Would the

How point B originates

tendency to movement in the grasping apparatus at this stage cause an actual movement of any importance around B?

W.:   No; for although we feel the key to be firm, this firmness is too slight to serve as a usable centre of motion. Only when the key has reached key-bottom is it firm enough for a perceptible movement around B to take place.

K.:   To sum up: As long as the finger is not in contact with the key, every movement in the playing apparatus takes place in such a way that the more distant part is moved around the part nearer the body. But as soon as point B is reached, the nearer part can be moved around the distant one. This change of the centre of motion does not happen abruptly but gradually on the way from key-top to key-bottom, by virtue of the fact that the firmness of the key increases on the way.

P.:   We have a similar change of the centre of motion in walking. When we walk the weight of the body is supported by one leg, while the other swings freely forward. As long as a leg is swinging, its distant parts move around the ones nearer the body; as soon as this leg has become the supporting leg, the parts near the body move around the most distant one, which is the sole of the foot on the ground. In walking, the change of centres of motion is brought about by virtue of the fact that the weight of the body creates a firm connection between the sole of the foot and the ground. In just the same way the weight of the playing apparatus connects finger and key to form a finger-key joint and thus creates a new centre of motion, the point B.

W.:   And therefore the precondition for the development of a point B, a true finger-key joint, is the heavy arm.

P.:   In other words, someone who plays with a light arm will be able to reach the key and to move it to key-bottom, but the key will not be involved in the process of motion as a new supporting point and will remain the target of the motion.

H.:   Another point which shows us the negative effect of "aiming".

P.:   In an aiming movement like that, the centre of motion always remains point A, wherever it happens to be. Our point A lies ultimately in the breastbone-collarbone joint, as we already know. The point A of aiming movements can be the shoulder joint, just as well as the basal knuckle of the finger, from which the finger is tossed into the key.

K.:   And that, of course, would mean pushing and not pulling, which explains what has been said about the import of the tendencies to motion in the weight and grasping apparatus (p. 75). Still the question remains concerning actual movements around B which are not simultaneous with those around A.

P.:   If they are not to be simultaneous with those around A, these grasping movements can take place only when the key has reached key-bottom.

W.:   What can be their purpose, since with reaching key-bottom the motion of the key has come to an end? At this moment it is already too late to accomplish any kind of movement which would affect the motion of the key.

K.:   You ask about the purpose of this movement. Must everything have a purpose? Aren't there many events which happen without a purpose, simply because they are the necessary consequence of a given situation?

W.:   And what would be the situation that gives rise to a movement like that after the key has come to key-bottom?

K.:   We have just stated that in the grasping apparatus there is a tendency to motion, which as yet does not cause an actual movement, but intercepts the motion of the weight apparatus. It is in the nature of this tendency to become an actual grasping movement which occurs after the mission of interception is accomplished, i.e. not earlier than in key-bottom.

P.:   Therefore, we can interpret this ensuing movement as a safety valve for forces which are at work during the key-moving action. On account of its causal and temporal relation to the completed movement of the key, I have named this movement of the grasping apparatus the "after-motion". Nevertheless, your question about the purpose of the after-motion is completely justified. For we must not forget that as a rule playing the piano does not mean playing just one note or chord.

W.:   So the purpose of the after-motion would lie in its relation to the playing of the succeeding note?

P.:   Yes, that is one further function of the after-motion, that it brings our playing apparatus into a position from which we can play the next note or chord. Moreover the after-motion is important for all the playing which follows, not only for the immediately succeeding key-moving action. Think of a man who has a fixation between hand and trunk due to mutually antagonistic tensions. He will be able to make movements from point A only. The tensions will prevent him from making point B, which appears and disappears quickly, a shortlived centre of motion too. Consequently the motion around B is a test, which we can repeat as often as we want, to see if there is any kind of tension which would hinder free movability. Furthermore, the motions around B are also good for releasing slight passing tensions which might hinder the length-adjustment apparatus in particular.

K.:   I wonder whether this after-motion which you are now discussing is identical with the one which we described just before as a safety valve for the forces at work during the key-moving action. According to that first definition, it was the tendency to motion which mattered. Now, however, the actual motions seem to be important.

P.:   It is always the tendency to motion which really matters. Just think, the movement is purely a question of geometry; only in speaking of the tendency to motion are we dealing with the causal forces, with dynamics. Let us examine more closely from this viewpoint the movement of the wrist over the resting finger. We took it for granted that this movement is brought about entirely by a tendency to flexion in the wrist joint, whose proper function would be to move the hand with the finger downwards. But since the key hinders the finger in this downward motion, the wrist rises around the tip of the finger, whereby the finger-key joint becomes the dynamic centre, point B.

W.:   Yes. And was this a false supposition?

P.:   Only insofar as we failed to notice that the very same movement can also be carried out in an entirely different way. I can also direct it from the shoulder and elbow joints, i.e. from point A, in which case the wrist would also be flexed, but without the wrist-flexor muscles being the motivating force of the whole complex motion of the playing apparatus. As you can easily convince yourself, in this instance the finger rests only loosely on the key, which guarantees only that its point of contact with the key is the geometrical centre of the circle described by the wrist. In no way has a true finger-key joint, a point B, been formed, since this by definition must be a dynamic centre.

H.:   The difference between these two procedures, which is important for the pianist, is as follows: If I make the movement from point B, the weight of the upper arm and forearm, which tend to fall back, engenders a pulling in the finger-key joint. On the other hand, if I make the movement from point A, the wrist is pushed away from me. I would not be able to neutralize completely the effect of this pushing on the key by means of wrist flexion, as in general one can never neutralize by means of antagonistic movements if one has gone astray from the natural movements which follow gravity.

Geometric and
dynamic centre

K.: Since you have stated that the two movements are geometrically alike, you as a teacher probably cannot distinguish whether the pupil has made the movement from point A or point B, can you?

P.: Sure, I can! I can tell by the general posture of the pupil, by the freedom and speed with which he moves and by the sound he produces. Don't say that the sound cannot be influenced by a movement which succeeds the motion of the key, but remember that this after-motion has been executed by means of antagonistic movements because the playing apparatus was full of mutually antagonistic tensions beforehand.

H.: Now all the questions which arose concerning the relationship between movement and tendency to motion (p. 74) have been answered.

P.: And with this we conclude our general observations on the playing apparatus and call it a day.

The Grasping Apparatus

H.:   Which part of the playing apparatus shall we analyse today?

P.:   We'll begin with the grasping apparatus. What do we already know about it?

W.:   It consists of finger, hand and radius; and it serves for the grasping movements.

Large and small grasping units

P.:   What grasping movements have we mentioned so far?

W.:   Flexion of the wrist and flexion of the finger.

P.:   We know that flexion of the wrist is a movement of the hand relative to the radius. Since the hand has its supporting point on a finger, or several fingers in the case of a chord, this movement concerns every part of the grasping apparatus. The flexion of the finger, however, is the business of finger and hand only; the radius is not directly involved. Accordingly, we can distinguish a large grasping unit that involves the entire grasping apparatus, when grasping by wrist flexion, from a small grasping unit for grasping by finger flexion.

K.:   In discussing finger flexion, we must remember that this movement can concern all three finger joints—basal, middle and terminal. What do we know about these joints?

W.:   The middle and terminal joints are hinge joints, where we have only the possibility of bending and straightening. But what about the basal joint?

K.:   The basal joints are ball-and-socket joints, because the ends of the middle-hand bones, whose heads form the basal knuckles, are approximately spherical.

W.:   Now I remember that there are technical constructions that one calls ball-and-socket joints. They have three degrees of freedom. Have the basal joints also three degrees of freedom?

P.:   On this score, we have a private feud with the anatomy books.

W.:   The question can't be so hard to settle. There is no problem about the first degree of freedom: I can bend and straighten, even overextend a little.

K.:   The extent of overextension varies with the individual. What is important is the fact that there is always a certain passive overextension beyond the active one.

W.:   Passive overextension? What's that?

K.:   Stretch your fingers as far as you can. Now, with the palm down, put the middle members of the fingers on the table edge and press down with the hand.

W.:   Oh, yes. Now the resistance causes an overextension much stronger than any I could ever achieve myself.

K.:   That's what we shall call a passive movement. But what about the second degree of freedom in the basal joint?

W.:   I can bring each finger nearer to one or the other adjoining finger.

K.:   Correct. And the third degree that we can require of a ball-and-socket joint is rotation around the longitudinal axis of the finger.

W.:   That would mean that the nail would be turned alternately towards one or the other adjoining finger, instead of remaining on the back of the hand. No, I can't do that.

K.:   Fick said the same thing. And, since he is the high priest of joint mechanics, all the anatomy books take over his statement. Nevertheless, he has conceded that passive rotation is possible.

W.:   Passive? How could that be?

K.:   Well, bend your index finger at the middle joint in a right angle, and hold your hand in such a way that the little-finger edge is lowest—now put the side of the nail member of the index finger on the edge of the table and press down with your hand.

W.:   Oh, yes. There is a twisting in the basal joint.

K.:   To produce the contrary motion we can press the hand upwards against the underside of the table edge. Here we have the contrary rotation.

W.:   Yes, and now, since by passive rotation I have acquired the correct idea of the motion, I can also manage to do it actively— though only with a bent middle joint.

K.:   You have certainly always been able to do it, and everyone who handles delicate instruments uses it.

P.:   But in practice our ability to use rotation as an isolated movement is not as important as the fact that we can combine it with other movements. I hope you remember what circumduction is (cf. p. 42).

W.:   Yes. When I circumduct my index finger in its basal

Passive movements

Conical movement in the basal joint

joint, I start from the extended position. First I move it towards the middle finger and under it; then I bend it as much as possible, move towards the thumb, and finally return to the extended position.

P.: As you just did it, it was pure circumduction, because your fingernail always remained on the side corresponding to the back of the hand. But now, while you bring your index finger towards the middle finger, try to turn the index fingernail towards the middle finger at the same time.

W.: I can, but not all the way.

P.: Who said to turn it 90°? But it is possible. Now make the opposite movement towards the thumb, turning the nail also towards the thumb.

W.: It works. And all that is a conical movement, isn't it?

P.: Of course, we can by no means cover the entire surface of a cone, but that little part which we do cover is of great significance.

H.: And the two terminal positions of this movement are just as significant. When I have reached one of them and am still exerting the muscle force which effected the movement—in other words, when I attempt to pass the limit of this conical movement— an extraordinary lateral firmness is produced in the basal joint of the finger.

W.: What is the point of this firmness? Haven't we stressed that firmness hinders the freedom of movement and therefore has to be avoided?

P.: Yes, but then we were referring only, and expressly, to the firmness or fixation that results from mutually antagonistic muscle tensions. In the present case, however, the firmness results from the activity of a muscle against the opposition of the joint mechanism. And as to the purpose of this lateral firmness of the finger, haven't you observed (p. 24) that with the hand adjusting itself in supination, the playing finger turns its margin downwards? In this way, the load of the weight apparatus works on it laterally. In order for the relatively weak finger to be able to resist the heavy weight, it needs, of course, to be very firm.

W.: And it is by means of the conical grasping movement that we attain this firmness in the basal joint.

P.: Yes, and what about firmness in the other two finger joints?

W.: They are hinge joints. Since the weight works laterally, it works on these joints in a direction in which they have no flexibility at all, a direction in which the fingers are firm in themselves. Now I understand why it is so important that we play with the marginal surface of the fingers and not with the middle of the finger pad as in many techniques.

P.:   No, you cannot understand at all yet, because apart from certain exceptions to the justly emphasized importance of playing with the finger margin, we have not yet discussed the muscles which govern finger movements.

Long and short muscles of the fingers

K.:   Here I should like to differentiate between two main groups. One, that of the short finger muscles, is in the hand: in the thumb ball (PL. B/21), the little-finger ball (PL. B/24 and C/7) and in the middle part of the palm. The other group, that of the long muscles, is in the forearm and extends partly even to the upper arm; they act on the fingers through long sinews, partly as flexors, partly as extensors.

P.:   Which muscles perform the conical movement that is necessary for attaining firmness of the basal finger joint in a lateral direction?

K.:   Only the short muscles can be responsible for that.

P.:   Are you sure?

K.:   Why do you doubt it?

P.:   On the back of my hand, I see cords—which must be the tendons of the long muscles (PL. B/25), aren't they?

K.:   Yes, the tendons of the different extensor muscles, coming from forearm and upper arm.

P.:   When I make a conical movement with my finger, the extensor tendon of the respective finger shifts. It glides laterally off the basal knuckle. We can even say that this lateral gliding is an indication of a true conical movement.

Lateral gliding of extensor tendons

K.:   I can see it on your hand. I myself am unable to do it.

P.:   It requires a certain amount of practice. Now I ask you: If the tendon of the long muscle is displaced by the conical movement, isn't that a sign that the movement was made by this long muscle?

K.:   No, the pull of the long muscle can move its tendon only in the longitudinal, and not a lateral, direction. However, the tendon of the long extensor muscle is connected on the back of the finger with the short muscles, and this connection would be sufficient reason for the lateral displacement of the tendon and its sliding away.

P.:   So we can say that the lateral firmness of the fingers in a conical movement is attained by short muscles that only affect the fingers and ultimately work against the opposition of the joint mechanism. In contrast to this, I would be able to attain firmness in flexion and extension only by mutually antagonistic tension of the long muscles, in which case I have to remember that they influence other joints besides those of the fingers. Can you tell me which other joints?

K.: The wrist joint and the joints between ulna and radius.

P.: This means, then, that by antagonistic tension these muscles hinder the movements in the wrist and the movements of pronation and supination, don't they?

K.: Certainly.

P.: What about the short muscles? Do they affect in any way at all joints other than those of the finger concerned?

K.: In some cases there might be a slight effect on the next finger-beam; but, for the rest, a short muscle certainly affects only its own finger.

P.: This non-interfering short muscle takes the weight of the playing apparatus if I play with the finger margin. If, however, I turn the finger pad downwards, the weight works on a long muscle; and as soon as I use this long muscle against the weight, I also hinder the freedom of my wrist and the pronation and supination of my forearm.

W.: So a person in this condition would make the still necessary motions of pronation and supination by rotation in the shoulder joint with a lateral lift of the elbow on the base of the double cone (p. 71).

H.: In practice, this means that the elbow would be laterally high in supine hand positions, which we have already described as a typical mistake.

P.: So it is. But it is also evident from the fingers themselves that the long muscles cannot be used for producing firmness against strong opposition on the underside. Whereas lateral weight has to be held by the short muscle in one finger joint only, namely, the basal joint, since the middle and terminal joints have no flexibility in this direction, the long muscles would have to control all three finger joints in the case of opposition from the palm side. In coping with all these problems, one or the other joint might easily fold in. Haven't you met people whose terminal joint, for instance, is in extreme passive overextension, while the middle joint rises up at an almost acute angle?

K.: That's the way many people hold their pens or pencils. They are the surest applicants for writer's cramp.

P.: That is the same as saying that it is a matter of mutually antagonistic tensions. We often see such people at the piano, and I can trace the chain of cramps right down through the body to the very feet. It often happens that I can release the cramp in the fingers, if I prevail upon the pupil to relax his big toe.

W.: How does that happen? Do all those cramps originate from the cramped state of the fingers—or do they start in the big toe, if everything can be corrected from there?

K.: As Kant has rightly said, the ruling principle in any organism is interrelation; and so I find it hopeless to try to decide what is cause and what is effect. I believe that in the case of physical cramp there is a vicious circle. In principle, such a circle can be interrupted at any point. The only question is where to approach it best. In this case, the professor has discovered this point to be the big toe.

H.: But even if it were possible to give a complete answer to the question of the relationship between the tensions from muscle to muscle, that would go far beyond our practical interest. By the way, the finger with the folded-in terminal joint is only one of several possible types.

P.: Yes, there is also the nail member that is fixed in a bent position with flattened middle joint, or overextended basal joints with claw-like bent fingers—hands that always remind me of a horseman who has lost the reins and is clutching at the horse's mane. In the same way, these pianists claw into the mane of the piano, the keyboard. No matter which of these finger forms we meet with, they are always the result of a state of cramp; and the consequences never fail to appear. Quite apart from the muted sound, we see how the overworked forearm muscles become so thick that eventually the forearms look like hams. Also the sinews of the long muscles respond to the undue overwork by inflammatory processes in the tendon sheaths at the wrist. Then the doctor is supposed to come to the rescue. In fact, there is need of a piano teacher to instruct these often famous artists in the elementary facts of piano touch.

K.: Are we to conclude then that the long flexors and extensors of the fingers are entirely superfluous for the pianist?

Finger-stepping with long muscles

P.: At present we are only speaking about the encounter of the finger with the mechanical load, which arises during the key-moving action and which is often enormous. This needs firmness above all. On the other hand, we have motion without opposition when our fingers step laterally from key to key. For this we must of necessity use the long muscles.

K.: That's right. When the weight works on the margins of

the fingers, the movements up and down the keyboard take the direction of long-muscle activity.

H.:   Besides, we have only stressed the inability of the long muscles to carry great weight during the key-moving action. They can, however, take up a weight which is not too heavy, or rather they can share in taking it up. Therefore, it depends on the amount of weight working on a particular finger, whether we must move the key with the margin of the finger, or whether we can move it with a part nearer the middle of the finger pad.

P.:   In any case, we shall never use the exact middle of the pad, since we cannot do without the participation of the short muscles whose activity can be regulated more precisely.

H.:   We shall discuss which position of the finger is necessary in a particular case as the opportunity arises. In any case, we shall always strive to apply the weight to the finger as far laterally as possible and not apply it closer to the middle of the pad than is absolutely necessary for the given situation in playing.

P.:   Now we must ask ourselves whether what we have said applies equally to all the fingers.

K.:   No. Of course, the thumb is definitely an exception.

W.:   Probably because it has only two members instead of three.

K.:   That has something to do with it. But look at the whole hand when it is at rest. Note the special position of the thumb.

W.:   Yes, there is an obvious distance between it and the other fingers. And not only that. The back of the hand, which is only slightly arched in the region of the other four middle-hand bones, so that one can almost describe it as flat, falls away entirely toward the thumb edge of the hand. In this way, there is almost a right angle between the plane which runs through the thumbnail and that of the other nails.

P.:   What results from this position of the thumbnail on playing with the thumb as compared to playing with the other fingers?

W.:   Of course, it must play with the margin opposite to that used normally by the other four fingers, because the margin which faces the keyboard is the one which is turned away from the other fingers, whereas with them we use as a rule, i.e., in supination, the margin which is turned away from the thumb.

K.:   And now let us observe the possible movements it can make. What happens when we spread the fingers?

W.:   We see that the movement of the thumb occurs in a

The thumb

place not at all corresponding to that for the other fingers. The spreading of fingers 2–5 takes place in the basal joints, i.e., between middle-hand bones and basal members. With the thumb, however, its middle-hand bone is spread from the rest of the hand, so that here the movement takes place between a wrist bone and the middle-hand bone. The basal joint of the thumb seems to have hardly greater movability than the terminal and middle joints of the other fingers. In view of its movability, one can think of the middle-hand bone of the thumb, even though it is embedded in flesh, as its basal member. Then the thumb would also have a basal, middle and nail member like the other fingers and would be lacking the middle-hand bone.

K.: Plausible as this may seem, we shall keep to the usual way of describing the thumb as consisting of a middle-hand bone and two finger members. Now let us investigate more thoroughly the possible movements of the thumb's middle-hand bone in relation to the wrist.

W.: First, I can move the thumb away from the index finger in a plane which is oblique to that of the back of the hand, and back again to the index finger.

K.: That is the first degree of freedom. What else?

W.: There is another movement, which one might call "flexion"; but it is peculiar in that when performing it, the thumb is also twisted so that its nail turns away from the other fingers even more. It becomes practically opposed to the other fingers.

Opposition and rotation of thumb

K.: For this reason, we call this movement of the thumb "opposition". The contrary movement occurs in returning to the plane of the back of the hand and is called "reposition". Let us compare the opposition movement of the thumb with the movements that are possible for the other fingers.

W.: Since in opposition the thumbnail alters its position in the same way the nails of the other fingers do in rotation, we can say that opposition is an automatic combination of flexion and rotation.

K.: That's right. But now if we observe the thumb as a whole and don't bother with the question in which particular joints the movements are carried out, then we find that rotation does not depend exclusively on opposition. An additional, though slight, rotation is possible in as much that when the thumb is in a certain position determined by a particular degree of spreading and opposition, it may still be turned slightly, so that its nail faces, to a varying degree, away from the other fingers.

P.:   We have the best opportunity to convince ourselves of the freedom of rotation when we have opposed the thumb as much as possible, in such a way that its pad rests in the basal hollow of the fourth finger.

W.:   Yes. First, it is possible that the thumbnail is turned completely away from the rest of the hand, facing down when the hand is placed over the keyboard. Then, it is equally possible that the thumbnail faces obliquely away or even to the side.

K.:   Therefore, the thumb, like the other fingers, has three degrees of freedom, and likewise in accordance with the other fingers, the freedom of rotation is rather slight. If we notice a much greater change in the position of the thumbnail than in any other nail, that is not due to greater freedom of rotation but to the fact that there is a compulsory component of rotation in opposition.

Conical movement of thumb

W.:   As there are so may similarities to the other fingers, we can certainly make a conical movement also with the thumb by combining circumduction and rotation, can't we?

K.:   Quite right. So at first we have to see what circumduction is.

W.:   If I start from the position in which the thumb is laterally pressed to the basal knuckle of the index finger, I can, at first in reposition, spread out the thumb away from the second finger-beam and then, leaving it spread, gradually bring it into opposition so that it will finally come in a great circle to the end position just mentioned, in the basal hollow of the fourth finger.

P.:   During the opposition movement, you required the highest degree of spreading. We must linger here for a while. To begin with, what do we mean by the highest degree of spreading?

W.:   That the basal knuckle of the thumb is always as far as possible from the basal knuckle of the index finger.

P.:   That's right. It is the position of the basal knuckle, not that of the end of the thumb, which matters in this movement of the first middle-hand bone. So we must not try to attain this spreading by overstretching the thumb in the terminal joint.

W.:   That would be the same mistake as the overextension of the terminal joints in the other fingers (cf. p. 84).

P.:   Now to proceed: Why do you require spreading of the thumb during the opposition movement?

W.:   Because we are speaking of circumduction, and this, by definition, means moving along the periphery of the space that is granted by the mechanism of the joint.

P.: But what is the mechanical result of the fact that in this movement muscles hold the bone at the periphery against the joint mechanism?

W.: Firmness, as we said before in discussing the basal joints of the fingers.

P.: So the maximum outspreading of the thumb from the second finger-beam will establish sufficient firmness to intercept the force of the key-moving action of the playing apparatus. But with the other fingers, was it really the movement along the periphery of the circle of circumduction from which we wanted to gain firmness?

W.: No, but from the extreme rotatory position. Naturally, the possibility for firmness by rotation is also at our disposal with the thumb.

P.: But remember that we could rotate the index finger in either of two directions. Is this also true for the thumb?

K.: Anatomically, of course, every movement can be made in both directions. So I can turn the thumbnail as far as possible away from the plane of the rest of the hand or twist it back into line with that plane. This second possibility, however, would mean that we would try to put the pressure on the underside of the pad instead of its margin, which is the very opposite of what we found necessary for the other fingers.

P.: That is not the only reason why we should use only turning-away of the thumbnail. So, when we as pianists speak of "opposition" of the thumb, we mean it more literally than the anatomists. We must think of the combination of the so-called opposition with the highest degree of rotation away from the rest of the hand. When we move the thumb in the large circle of circumduction towards the basal hollow of the fourth finger, the thumbnail must be turned practically horizontally downwards in the final stage of this movement.

W.: In this movement of the thumb in the large circle of circumduction with rotation, we have found two sources of firmness: the highest constant degree of spreading and the same of rotation. Are they both needed? Wouldn't one be enough?

P.: Indeed, very often one of these sources has to suffice. In cases of a narrow grasp in playing, we are not able to retain the spreading, and for this reason we must lay greater stress on continuous rotation. But whenever possible, we will also strive to spread the thumb. For the learner, above all, the greatest degree of spreading is an indispensable aid.

H.:   In effect, so far as it is feasible, we must make all thumb movements at the periphery of the circle of circumduction and not move from one place to another across the area of the circle. Above all, when moving the thumb, we must always be careful to keep the thumbnail turned away from the rest of the hand as much as possible.

Thumb muscles

W.:   Does what we said about long and short muscles also apply to the muscles of the thumb?

K.:   Well, its short muscles, which form the thumb ball, as well as its long ones, are much stronger than those for any other finger.

W.:   And is firmness in it also achieved through the short muscles?

K.:   They only are concerned, especially if we think of the firmness arising from rotation.

W.:   And in the thumb, too, can a fixation caused by long muscles have a disturbing effect on other joints?

P.:   Of course. What is more, antagonistic thumb tensions especially affect the whole body.

W.:   Presumably because the thumb muscles are stronger than those of the other fingers.

K.:   Not only on that account. What matters is also the arrangement of the muscles. Look, for instance, at the long extensor of the thumb (PL. C/16), the sinew of which protrudes clearly when you raise your thumb towards the back of the hand. As you see, this sinew is quite oblique. Although its insertion is at the thumb, the origin of the muscle is essentially at the ulna, i.e., the forearm bone on the little-finger side. It is obvious that tension of this muscle against the long thumb flexor, which would be noticed as a fixation of the terminal joint in the thumb, would also greatly hinder the freedom of the forearm in pronation and supination.

P.:   That becomes especially clear if we think of the positions of extreme opposition which are necessary in putting the thumb under, e.g., in scale playing. As we can well imagine, with the thumb in such a position this sinew will be stretched to the limit. If at the same time, the muscle is tensed, all this has the effect of raising the origin of the muscle at the ulna and with it the elbow in a lateral direction. As we know well enough, this lateral raising of the elbow is contrary to the demand of the piano that the playing apparatus should be in the plane of gravity.

W.:   Seen from the other way round, it means that the long thumb extensor hinders the free putting-under of the thumb, doesn't it?

P.:   It hinders not only that, but also all free movement in the large circle of circumduction with thumb rotation, since it counteracts all the components of movement therein. That is why practising the conical movement of the thumb with the greatest degree of spreading and rotation is such a splendid means of freeing the muscle condition in the whole playing apparatus, because thereby the long thumb extensor is stretched and finally compelled to relax.

K.:   Here I should like to remind you that in speaking of the thumb we have also included the middle-hand bone of the first finger-beam, while in the case of the others we have only taken into consideration the members of the fingers.

P.:   Therefore we must now busy outselves with the possible movements of the middle-hand bones 2–5.

Middle-hand spreading

W.:   But surely these bones can make no movements in relation to each other or to the wrist.

K.:   Let us consider the problem step by step for analogy to the possible movements of the middle-hand bone of the thumb. First of all, what about spreading?

W.:   Haven't we said already that in the case of the finger-beams 2–5 the spreading occurs in the basal joints of the fingers and, therefore, does not concern the middle hand?

K.:   What hinders spreading of the middle-hand bones 2–5 are mainly tough ligaments which connect them in the region of their heads on the palm side of the basal joints of the fingers. If I wished to spread the 5th middle-hand bone from the 4th as far as I can spread the 1st from the 2nd, I would have to tear those ligaments apart.

P.:   Good. But before a ligament is torn, it is tautened.

K.:   Of course.

P.:   And apart from the condition in which it is tautened, there is also a condition in which it is not tautened.

K.:   Granted. But the difference between the position of the middle-hand bones in which the ligaments are not taut and the one in which they are can be only a few degrees, possibly even only a few minutes of a degree.

P.:   But if what matters is not the few degrees difference in the direction of the bones, but the tautening of the ligaments . . . ?

K.:   Then this very slight spreading of the middle-hand bones might be relevant.

W.:   Yes: relevant for the attainment of firmness, because a taut ligament differs from a slack one in that it is firm.

P.:   The whole system to which a taut ligament belongs thereby becomes firm. Let us imagine we have stuck two poles in the ground and connected them with a washline. How shaky the whole thing is at first. But if I brace each of the two poles sideways towards the ground until the washline is quite taut, the whole thing has great firmness.

W.:   I understand. In the hand the middle-hand bones represent the poles, the ligaments between their heads the washline; and the lateral bracing must be brought about by muscle-pull.

K.:   The most essential muscles in this respect are probably those in the little-finger ball, which spread the 5th middle-hand bone, and so, indirectly, the 4th and 3rd also, away from the 2nd. In the opposite direction, this spreading will be completed by the spreading of the thumb away from the 2nd middle-hand bone.

P.:   But as we have mentioned before, if we spread the thumb away, we can do this in different planes, depending on where on the periphery of the circle of circumduction the thumb is at the time.

K.:   So the question arises as to whether or not the spreading of the 5th middle-hand bone can also take place in different planes— in other words, whether or not in its movability we can also find an analogy to the second degree of freedom of the middle-hand bone of the thumb.

Vaulted hand

W.:   That would mean opposition? Indeed I can actively move the head of the middle-hand bone in the 5th knuckle slightly palmwards; but that is certainly no opposition.

K.:   Right. Anyway, it takes a direction which is somewhat symmetrical to the opposition movement of the thumb, and for that reason we call it "opposition" also. Since the heads of the middle-hand bones are bound to each other by ligaments, the 5th takes its neighbour with it a little way by this movement, as we can easily see if we carefully observe the contour of the basal knuckles on the back of the hand.

W.:   Yes, the whole back of the hand, which also before was not entirely flat between the 2nd and 5th finger-beams, becomes more definitely arched as a result of this movement.

P.:   With this we have a new point of view. As long as we considered spreading in one plane only, the hand was two dimensional for us. However, now that we can combine spreading with opposition, we arrive at a three-dimensional, vaulted form. The

five finger-beams are no longer to be compared with five poles for
a washline, but with the five ribs of a globe-shaped Chinese lantern—
to be sure, a lantern whose ribs are not connected by pleated paper,
but by something more solid. If I combine the greatest possible
degree of spreading with the greatest possible degree of opposition
of thumb and 5th finger-beam—and if at the same time my fingers,
being slightly bent at the middle and terminal joints, are brought
to the final position of the conical movement in their basal joints—
then my hand actually encloses a space that is approximately
globe-shaped.

Hand as globe

W.:   Strange, I have a feeling as though an inside pressure
were working on my hand trying to enlarge this globe, just as the
air does in a football.

P.:   If you have this feeling, you may be sure that your hand
is in the right condition. The air pressure against the covering of
the football maintains its firmness. And your hand must be
firm, too.

H.:   Speaking of a globe, aren't we also reminded of the
earth?

P.:   Yes. The five finger-beams, i.e., the middle-hand bones
and fingers, would correspond to meridians; the wrist would be the
North Pole; the middle joints would be situated at the Equator, and
the fingertips would reach for the South Pole without ever attaining it.

W.:   Why can't they attain it?

P.:   Because before attaining it, all the movements leading
to this arrangement of the hand arrive at their absolute limitations
in the joints, not only the spreading and opposition of the middle-
hand bones but also the conical movements of the fingers in the
basal joints. But if we could join our fingertips, and thus believe
that we had reached the South Pole, then we can be sure that this
has happened by virtue of movements other than those described.
Then, to keep to the metaphor, we have dug into the substance of
the globe instead of remaining on its surface. The globe would
have become soft. And since its existence is nothing but its firmness and solidity, the globe would no longer exist.

K.:   But haven't we lost the connection with piano playing?
You do not mean that you can play with this globe-hand?

P.:   Well, usually not, as long as it is the smallest possible
globe. This smallest one is useful, however, because with it we
experience best the feeling of firmness, which then remains with
us when we go over to larger globes. In doing this, we diminish

the curvature by diminishing the degree of opposition but maintaining the spreading.

K.:   Hadn't we better say that with this enlargement the globe becomes a vault, since it opens at the underside?

P.:   The simile of the vault could also be applied to the smallest possible globe because in it, too, there is a slit underneath between the 1st and 5th finger-beams. Because of this slit, I have chosen the simile of the round Chinese lantern, which also has such a slit; and the tendency for a globe to form rests plainly on the tendency to close this gap.

K.:   But the enlarging of the globe, by which the gap is obviously widened, conflicts with this tendency.

P.:   Geometrically, of course, the gap is widened. Nevertheless, as we have found, the tendency towards closing must not be lost—because if it were, we should also lose all firmness in a downward direction, and the lantern, becoming slack, would collapse.

W.:   Aren't you asking the impossible? The tendency for the 1st and 5th finger-beams to come together is supposed to remain operative while they are going apart?

P.:   Just think it over! What kind of movement do the ribs of a Chinese lantern make?

W.:   Since the same side always faces the middle of the lantern, it is a conical movement.

P.:   We have defined this as displacement combined with simultaneous rotation. Now let us consider these two components separately. I must adjust the position of the separate finger-beams of my hand in space to the circumstances arising from the distance of the keys on each occasion . . .

W.:   . . . but the rotatory tendency inherent in the conical movement of the fingers can remain operative.

P.:   Yes. It has to have opposite directions in the two outer finger-beams, i.e., those of thumb and little finger, in such a way that these rotate away from each other at the back of the hand and towards each other in the palm of the hand. The rotation away from each other gives a feeling of tension at the back of the hand, as does the spreading.

K.:   Then ultimately the spreading consists only in this contrary rotation?

P.:   Not exclusively. Just as we have stressed especially for the thumb, we can also say here for all the finger-beams that we must strive for the greatest possible degree of actual spreading; but rotation, too, must always be operative in order to guarantee

Contrary rotation of fingers

firmness of the same nature as that arising from spreading at moments when a narrow grasp does not permit actual spreading.

K.:   Here we see again the advantage of being in the natural position of supination, because in this position the rotation of the thumb and little finger away from each other, and with it the conical movement of each, is aimed downwards and so produces firmness which is also directed downwards, i.e., the direction in which it is needed.

P.:   Considered from the opposite angle, this means that firmness of the hand is not as easily attained in pronation, since then the thumb side of all the fingers faces downwards. Therefore, all the fingers are rotated in the same direction, so that rotation away from each other cannot be used to attain inner firmness of the hand. Inner firmness, however, will still be necessary; and it will be achieved by jerking up the outer fingers that are not for the moment playing, and especially the little finger, as strongly as possible.

K.:   Now you mention rotation of all fingers in the same direction. That is understandable. But if you speak of contrary rotation, that can refer only to two fingers, the thumb and little finger.

P.:   Yes, insofar as we are dealing with a grasp by these two fingers. But what if I take a chord with two other fingers?

W.:   Then these two other fingers must naturally rotate in opposite directions. If, for instance, I use the 2nd and 3rd fingers, I must rotate the 2nd finger thumbwards and the 3rd finger towards the little finger.

P.:   That's right. But what if you use the 3rd and 4th fingers?

W.:   Then the 3rd must be rotated towards the thumb, and the 4th towards the little finger.

P.:   So we see from these two instances that two opposite directions of rotation are necessary for the same finger, in this case the 3rd, depending on which finger acts with it.

W.:   Of course, the same is true for the 2nd and 4th fingers. Only the thumb and little finger have a constant direction of rotation, namely, away from the middle of the hand.

P.:   ... Provided that the hand is in supination.

H.:   Now we have said everything that is essential concerning the condition of the hand; for what we said about single fingers still concerned the condition of the whole hand. The spreading of the middle hand and contrary rotation of the thumb and little finger are essential for firmness in the small grasping unit, so that

Grasping movements in
small grasping unit

it can transmit the force of the weight apparatus to the keys. The changes of curvature are changes in this condition, which are necessary to adjust the hand to the different width of each grasp on the keyboard. However, we have still said nothing about the actual movements of grasping in the small grasping unit.

P.: We only know that they must be made without loss of firmness.

W.: Then we already know the grasping movement of the thumb. It must be along the greatest possible circle of circumduction from the basal knuckle of the index finger towards the basal hollow of the fourth finger, combined with the highest possible degree of rotation. This movement alone fulfills the condition we require (cf. pp. 95–96).

P.: That is so. There only remains the question whether the grasping movement in this circle of circumduction is always aiming towards the basal hollow of the fourth finger, or whether it can go the opposite way.

W.: Of course, it must go the opposite way when the thumb has been put under the hand.

P.: Good. If we analyse the grasping movement of the other four fingers, we know that first we must attain firmness in the basal joints by conical movement, in order then to be able to pull the wrist towards point B by finger-flexion.

K.: Do you mean by "finger-flexion" a flexion in all three joints of the finger?

P.: As you can easily prove to yourself, I would actually have to bend all three joints in order to pull the wrist right up to the finger pad of the grasping finger, but in practice the movement ends earlier. For the degree of finger-grasping movement necessary in practice, I nearly always find the movement in the basal joint enough, while the middle and terminal joints are hardly bent beyond the degree of flexion pertaining to the position of rest.

K.: Whether a flexion in these joints contributes or not, depends upon how close to the key the wrist is to be pulled by the grasping movement, doesn't it?

H.: That is so. But the essential fact in this combined movement of the three finger joints is that the wrist must be drawn to the key as far as possible by flexion in the basal joint and as little as possible by flexion in the other two. That is because it is the wrist which is to be pulled up, and not some point in the hollow of the hand, as would be the case with any marked degree of flexion in the middle and terminal joints.

P.:   Taking account of these facts, where can we set the target of the finger-grasping movement?

W.:   If you speak about a target, you probably mean a target which in practice we never reach, just as we never reach the target of the thumb-grasping movement. The target for the grasping of the four other fingers, second as well as fifth, is, I would say, at the wrist end of the thumb ball.

P.:   Remember, however, that we must not aim for this target over the shortest distance. The shortest way would be by pure flexion, which is practised in many techniques. But if, in beginning the grasping movement, we make the conical movement to attain firmness, that is a lateral deviation along the periphery of the space delimited by the joint mechanism, i.e., something like a circumduction arc.

H.:   We know (p. 96) that this conical movement can be made in both directions, and in which direction it must be made in each particular case. Which was which?

W.:   Since its purpose is to attain downward firmness, it must be made towards the little-finger side as a rule. The exceptions are in playing a single key if the hand is in pronation, and in playing a chord if the thumb does not take part. In chords like this, in spite of the position of supination, the grasping finger nearest the thumb, e.g., the index finger, must make the conical movement thumbwards in order to maintain the spreading of the hand.

P.:   Quite right. So in this case the conical movement of the second finger would not be directed downwards. However, this cannot disturb us in any way, for we have learned (p. 83) that at the end of the conical movement we attain great firmness in both directions, on the one side by muscle tension, on the other by joint inhibition.

K.:   We must still remember that rotation of the finger is contained in its conical movement. From what we have just said, we learn that as a rule the finger is rotated in the same direction as the hand, i.e., it is supinated in a supinated hand and pronated in a pronated hand. But in the special case we have just mentioned, of playing a chord without the thumb, the playing finger near the thumb must be pronated and so make a rotation opposite to the supination of the hand.

Rotation of hand and finger

H.:   That means that in most cases hand rotation and finger rotation would be added to each other, so that the finger would be weighted laterally much more than might be expected if judging by the position of the wrist. In this special case, however, the pronation of the index finger playing in the chord will be subtracted from the supination of the hand, and therefore the finger will be weighted only very slightly sidewards from the middle of the finger pad—a situation which we know is possible (pp. 85–86).

P.:   Naturally, the correct performance of all these grasping movements demands a certain amount of practice. The external indication that we have acquired the correct method, with adequate participation of the conical movement, is the gliding-away of the extensor tendons from the basal knuckles (p. 83) to one or the other side, depending on which of the two circumduction arcs the finger describes.

H.:   We must pay special attention to the fact that the great firmness in the hand, which we have recognized as necessary and for which we must strive, does not impair the freedom of movement of the individual fingers. In contrast to the rigid fixation which often appears against the will of the player, it is the essence of the firmness described in such detail here that it does not hinder the free movement of the fingers, but on the contrary, makes it possible in the proper way, since the long muscles do not contribute at all to this firmness.

P.:   Now the most important facts about grasping movements in the small grasping unit have been stated. In concluding, we shall once again call to mind the purpose of these movements.

W.:   The finger, which in itself is light, rests on the key. The wrist, which is weighted by the weight apparatus, has the tendency to sink below the key. So the key finds itself between finger and wrist. If we now grasp the key, it is caught between the light finger which is above and the heavy wrist hanging below. In this situation the key will at first follow the wrist and so be pulled down until it reaches key-bottom; then by the finger-grasp, the wrist, and with it the whole arm, is pulled reciprocally towards the finger-key joint.

Heavy under light

P.:   That's right. If we now shift the whole situation one stage nearer the body, it becomes a matter of the large grasping unit. While in the small grasping unit, the key was caught between finger and wrist by grasping in the basal joint of the finger, in the large grasping unit it will be caught between finger and elbow by wrist-grasping. In both cases the chain condition of the playing apparatus causes a situation that we can briefly describe by the words "heavy under light", since either the heavy wrist or the heavy elbow sinks under the light finger. In grasping, the heavy part is pulled up to the light finger, since the key lies between them. ·

H.:   The fact that the key lies "in between" is the essential difference from every "aiming" technique; for in aiming the key lies, by definition, in front of the finger.

P.:   So in aiming, the key is depressed by a push from above, but in the technique we have described—by a pull from below.

H.:   In other words: Not only in aiming, but also in grasping techniques, it is, of course, the pressing of a member of a finger that has the immediate effect on the key. But in aiming there is a pressure from above working on that part of the finger, in grasping—a pull from below.

W.:   Now we probably need more anatomical facts about the large grasping unit. We know that the radius belongs to it and that the radius is connected with the hand by a joint with two degrees of freedom, also that this wrist joint is affected by the long muscles of the fingers.

K.:   But, besides those, there are muscles which have the main function to cause movements of the wrist joint. There are two wrist flexors, one on the ulnar side (PL. B/23) and one on the radial side (PL. B/18 and C/18), and three wrist extensors, one on the ulnar side (PL. B/22) and two on the radial side (PL. B/26 and C/6). You understand that we can move the hand in any desired direction by the various possible combinations of those muscles, towards the palm, the back of the hand, the radial and the ulnar side, and, of course, in all directions between these. Wrist muscles

H.:   We should remember that we are interested chiefly in the muscles on the underside. They maintain the arm in the chain condition, and they can motivate grasping movements. Which of the wrist muscles are on the underside?

K.:   That, of course, depends on whether the wrist is in the position of pronation or supination, as you can see for yourself. First let us consider the half-supine position, which we have learned to be the typical hand position, in which the wrist is slanting in such a way that the ulna is lower than the radius. Which muscle · must lie on the underside then?

W.:   Since the flexor side is underneath, it must be a flexor, and since the ulna is lower, it must be a muscle on the ulnar side. Thus it must be the ulnar wrist flexor (PL. B/23).

K.:   Quite right. Its sinew runs underneath the head of the ulna to a small wrist bone, which can be felt at the wrist end of the little-finger ball, the pea bone (PL. B/20).

H.:   We can feel this sinew plainly protruding here when we make a grasping movement in the large grasping unit. But we can also feel it as moderately taut in the motionless chain condition, because the tension of this underside muscle is an essential factor in suspension.

K.:   I need scarcely mention that this muscle is assisted by other muscles according to the degree of supination.

H.:   Think, for instance, of the extreme degree of supination that could be used at all in piano playing, the position in which the little-finger side of the hand is vertically under the thumb side.

K.:   Of course, in this position the ulnar wrist extensor would work with the ulnar wrist flexor with approximately equal force. But in pronation the radial wrist flexor would come into play.

P.:   By the way, with the changing position of pronation or supination, not only the respective underside muscle changes, but also the overall shape of the playing apparatus. These changes arise mainly from the necessity, except in extreme cases, for a hand position in which all the fingers have an equal potential for playing, because even if we are not about to play a chord, we still want to have the possibility of playing one. This cannot be done when the thumb is lying on the keys near the lid of the piano and the little finger is near the front edge of the keyboard, or vice versa. Now describe the position of your hand when your fingers are in positions similar to each other on keys in the middle of the keyboard and when your wrist joint is overextended, once in supination and once in pronation.

Wrist-triangles

W.:   In supination the wrist, in relation to the fingers, is swung towards the median plane of the body, in pronation—away from the median plane.

P.:   That's right. It can be put in another way: If I conceive fingertip, wrist and elbow as the three corners of a triangle with its apex in the wrist, in supination a triangle appears, which in relation to the median plane of the body lies outside of my forearm and hand; it is thus an outer wrist-triange. In pronation it becomes an inner wrist-triangle.

K.:   With a raised wrist, the position is naturally reversed: An inner wrist-triangle comes about in supination, and an outer one in pronation.

P.:   Yes. So we see that the different degrees of freedom in the finger-key joint cannot be used independently of each other, but that in practice a certain position granted by one degree of freedom involves a certain position with another degree of freedom.

H.: In conclusion, we must remember that all we have said about pronation and supination, as well as about wrist-triangles, refers not to the grasping movements in the large grasping unit, but to its position. The grasping movements are exclusively wrist flexions or, more precisely, the actions of the wrist muscles on the underside in the given hand position.

W.: But what's going on in the small grasping unit, while we are using the large one?

P.: What would happen if the small grasping unit should be relaxed?

W.: There would be no firmness to transfer the effect of the weight apparatus and that of the large grasping unit to the key.

P.: That is why we have given first consideration in our discussion to firmness in the small grasping unit, this being a generally valid condition, and dealt with it independently of the movements of the small grasping unit. For we know that firmness of the small grasping unit is always necessary. It must not be incidental, but must be continually present in piano playing. The combination of this ever present condition in the small grasping unit with the force that makes possible the state of suspension in the wrist joint produces a dynamic relationship between finger and elbow, into which the key, lying in between, will be drawn. I describe this dynamic relationship briefly as "clasping-back" of the fingers towards the elbow. This clasping-back involves no action of the fingers in the small grasping unit, but only firmness. If we do the grasping in the large grasping unit, the grasping movements of the fingers in the small one are, of course, superfluous.

W.: When do we make grasping movements in the large unit, and when in the small one?

P.: We'll talk about that later.

W.: Tomorrow?

P.: Not yet. Tomorrow we shall discuss the weight apparatus.

Clasping-back of the fingers towards the elbow

DIALOGUE 5

The Weight Apparatus

H.:   So the weight apparatus is on our programme today.

W.:   We already know that the collar bone, shoulder blade, upper arm and ulna belong to it.

H.:   It should be stated here that the joints that are essential to length adjustment, namely, the shoulder-girdle joints and elbow, belong exclusively within the compass of the weight apparatus, so that during the different phases of movement, the parts you mentioned are used at one time for length adjustment and at another for weighting, while overlapping of the length-adjustment apparatus with the grasping apparatus, which was theoretically possible (p. 61), does not occur.

P.:   Practically, it means that, in discussing the weight apparatus, we must always take into consideration the movements for length adjustment as well, which was not necessary in discussing the grasping apparatus.

H.:   First of all, we must supplement somewhat our anatomical knowledge of the joints and muscles of this region.

K.:   You probably know that the connection of the upper-arm bone with the ulna in the elbow joint is a hinge joint, and that the shoulder joint is a ball-and-socket joint with three degrees of freedom between shoulder blade and upper-arm bone. But we must know more about the shoulder-girdle joints.

Shoulder-girdle joints

W.:   By "shoulder-girdle joints" do you mean the breastbone-collarbone joint and the joint between the collar bone and the top of the shoulder blade?

K.:   Yes; I have intentionally associated these two joints because we almost always use them together.

W.:   How so? Ordinarily I can move each joint separately.

K.:   Yes, if the position of each part of the chain is of essential importance. Whatever activity we are performing, what matters in the shoulder girdle are only the changes in position of the shoulder blade on the rib cage. Accordingly, the bulk of the muscles that perform these movements run from trunk, neck and head directly to the shoulder blade and move it, while the collar bone, as an intermediate part, is just taken along.

W.: How many degrees of freedom do we have for these movements?

K.: To understand this problem we must keep in mind that the essential element in these movements is a gliding of the shoulder blade on the rib cage. Although these two structures are not connected by a joint, yet as long as they maintain organic contact the rules of a joint can be applied to them, so we cannot expect more than three degrees of freedom. On the other hand, each of the two shoulder-girdle joints has of itself three degrees of freedom, thus producing more than the three degrees of freedom which at first we expected in the mobility of the shoulder blade in relation to the rib cage. However, we can conclude with certainty that by movements of the shoulder blade on the rib cage which go beyond three degrees of freedom the broad contact is destroyed. So such movements must be the result of mutually antagonistic tensions, and therefore deserve our interest only as being wrong.

W.: Which would they be?

K.: For instance, if the lower corner of the shoulder blade (PL. A/40) or its whole inner margin protrudes from the back instead of lying on the rib cage. But you yourself can certainly tell me the three degrees of freedom of the shoulder blade in which it retains its broad contact with the rib cage.

W.: First I can raise and drop the shoulder, as one does in shrugging the shoulders to show one does not know the answer to a question.

K.: Yes, except that the extent of mobility is considerably greater than is generally used in shrugging the shoulders.

P.: And which of the two does the piano demand from us: the raised or the sunken shoulder?

W.: Since the sunken shoulder has followed the force of gravity, I must settle for it.

P.: That is surely the primary reason. But we shall find other reasons for it when we discuss the supporting apparatus.

W.: Good. In the second place, I can thrust the shoulder forward and backward.

P.: What happens then to the inner margin of the shoulder blade?

W.: With the forward thrust it withdraws from the spinal column, with the backward thrust it returns towards it. Therefore, the forward movement is also a sideward movement, so we can

Cramped positions of shoulder blade

Shoulder down

Shoulder backwards

use it in the length-adjusting apparatus for reaching the far keys on the keyboard (p. 61).

P.: If we disregard these movements for length adjustment, what position must we require of the shoulder blade as a link in the chain of the playing apparatus? Think of what we have said about pushing and pulling.

W.: I understand. A forward thrust of the shoulder means pushing, and is therefore to be avoided. A backward thrust means pulling, and is, therefore, in accordance with the demands of the piano.

P.: So we find that the position of the shoulder blade demanded by the piano is as far down and back on the rib cage as possible. We shall have to develop this in more detail when we come to the supporting apparatus.

W.: I understand this demand absolutely. However, sometimes it is necessary to move the shoulder forward in the course of length adjustment for reaching certain keys. How can the shoulder blade have a backward and forward position at the same time?

K.: If, when my trunk is in a certain position, I want my finger to reach a certain point far to the side and in front and below my shoulder, as would be the case with a distant key of the piano, then the shoulder blade certainly cannot remain in its position next to the spinal column; there is no doubt about that. On the other hand, we must remember that in this situation only two points are really fixed, namely, the breastbone-collarbone joint and the finger tip, but not the shoulder. As you can easily prove to yourself, it is still possible even with maximum extension of the whole limb in this direction to move the shoulder while the breast bone and finger tip remain motionless. Try it and tell me how you can move the shoulder.

W.: It can rise towards the front and sink towards the back.

P.: There you have the answer to your question: Out of all the shoulder positions that are possible with a particular hand position, we must always choose the one in which the shoulder is farthest back and below.

W.: In principle, it is the same as what we have said about the elbow — that it must always take, out of all the positions possible at the time, the one farthest inwards and downwards.

P.: Since in the case of the shoulder blade we have to deal with a continuously changing "backward downward" position, we learn again that what matters is not a particular geometrical position, but a certain condition. When the shoulder blade is held up and forward, there is no doubt about the condition of our muscles: mutually antagonistic tensions must be at work. How could it get into this position otherwise? It is different when the shoulder blade is in a "backward downward" position. Here freedom from mutually antagonistic tensions is possible, but as we have already repeatedly stressed with regard to the geometrically correct position of other parts of the body, here, too, there is the other possibility that this position is fixed by mutually antagonistic tensions. Because of this second possibility, we must never be satisfied to leave the shoulder blade in a certain position backward and downward, but we should move it continuously along the way necessary for length adjustment.

Arm stretching

W.:   Also if there is no great difference in length to be made up for?

P.:   Yes. Remember that as well as this movement of the shoulder blade sidewards and forward, we also utilize elbow-extension for reaching a distant point. If now I have pushed my shoulder blade sideways as far as possible and fully straightened my elbow, leaving it to the force of gravity to extend it up to the limit set by the joint mechanism — when all this has happened, then, of course, my arm certainly cannot become any longer. That is an objective fact. But subjectively it is quite different, as you can prove to yourself right away. With your arm and shoulder in this position, repeat to yourself: "My arm must become longer". What do you feel now?

W.:   I do have the feeling that my arm really becomes still longer, till I have a sensation not only of the greatest extension, but also of the greatest freedom.

K.:   What really happens is probably that all hidden antagonistic tensions are released. Thereby the pressure of the tensed muscles on the joints vanishes, and so it may be that an elastic lengthening of an immeasurably small fraction of a millimeter really does occur in the joint cartilages.

W.:   In any case, one has the feeling of lengthening, and it is a very comfortable feeling.

P.:   Because of the possibility of releasing tensions in this way, we naturally like to practise this stretching. Now this is possible both with arm held free in the air and also with the fingers in key-bottom.

H.:   That means in the first case — from point A; and in the other case — from point B.

P.: Very true. We have just done the exercise with the freely held arm. As to the piano, even for reaching the farthest keys, full stretching is not necessary — at least not for grown-ups. But if I have already struck the key and now pull my wrist forward from point B, we see that this can lead to practically complete, passive extension of the elbow, even in the case of nearby keys. In the case of moderately distant keys, wrist-flexion can take in tow the shoulder blade as well. In the case of the most distant keys, really complete stretching of the entire limb will result. But also when resting on keys less distant, I can attain complete stretching, if simultaneously with the wrist movement, I tilt my trunk backwards as far as possible. Between the contrary motion of hand and trunk, the chain between them will be tautened to the utmost.

K.: Why would you do that?

P.: Remember, we have said (p. 77) that if from point B we can produce passive movements of parts near the body, this is a sign of freedom from cramp, and extensive passive movements can release accidental cramps. Now you will understand why we continue the movements of length adjustment beyond the extent indicated by the actual distance, by passive movements directed from point B.

H.: In all these movements, however, the shoulder blade always remains as far back and below as at all possible in accordance with the distance to be bridged by the limb. The tensions that are released by these movements are, as far as the shoulder girdle is concerned, those of the very muscles which would lift the shoulder blade up and forward from this position, or would lever it away from the trunk (p. 103).

P.: And which muscles are they?

K.: As far as the upward and forward fixation of the shoulder blade is concerned, they must be the muscles that run from the head and neck to the shoulder girdle, the most important being the upper part of the hood muscle (PL. B/4 and C/1).

Hood muscle

W.: Hood muscle! Does it have the form and position of a hood?

K.: As a matter of fact, the comparison is not bad. The muscle runs from the back of the skull to the lateral part of the collar bone and the shoulder blade, determining the shape of the neck, and from the shoulder blade it passes downwards in a pointed shape to the boundary between the thoracic and lumbar regions of the spinal column.

W.: But it is only the neck part of the muscle which is responsible for raising the shoulder, isn't it?

K.:   Yes. The lower part, on the contrary, which lies on the back (PL. B/5), is essential for the purpose of bringing the shoulder blade into the correct position backward and downward and for keeping it there. But we are still not quite through with the muscles which are responsible for wrong posture.

W.:   Is there another important shoulder-lifter?

K.:   Remember that when the shoulder blade is in the wrong position, it is not only raised but also pulled forward, so that muscles lying in front, in the region of the chest, are also involved.

Breast muscles

P.:   Yes; above all there is a muscle that runs to the arm in a fold in front of the armpit.

K.:   You mean the anterior axillary fold, which is formed by the greater breast muscle (PL. C/4). Since it runs from the trunk and from the collar bone to the upper-arm bone, it has, strictly speaking, only an indirect influence upon the fixation of the shoulder girdle to the trunk. The lesser breast muscle, which is covered by it, can work directly.

P.:   They are both extremely disturbing when cramped. The release of breast-muscle cramp is always an essential step in freeing ourselves for all activities. For this purpose, with an erect trunk, we pull the shoulder blades down and back as far as we can and rotate the arms outward.

K.:   That's right; the greater breast muscle is also an inward rotator of the arm.

P.:   Then finally comes a feeling of relaxation, especially in the anterior axillary fold (PL. C/3), and one has a sensation as though the whole front of the body were unfolding.

H.:   Of course we shall understand all this better when we shall have examined the supporting apparatus in detail. At present we are concerned with the fact that most people are wrongly inclined to fix their shoulder blade antagonistically between the upper part of the hood muscle, which acts from above, and the breast muscles, which act in front from below. This also leads to a certain leverage of the lower corner of the shoulder blade away from the rib cage.

P.:   It would be so simple to let the shoulder blade drop down and back, where it can lie in broad contact with the rib cage and where we can hold it by means of the lower part of the hood muscle, without counter-tensions, in any position suitable to the needs of the moment, i.e., with mobility.

W.:   I believe I now understand everything about the positions that the shoulder blade can take by virtue of the degrees of freedom we have discussed, the ones it is to take and the ones it is

108

Tilting of shoulder
blade

not to take. But according to what we said in the beginning (p. 103) about the number of degrees of freedom, isn't there another one that is possible without relinquishing contact with the rib cage? Which would that be?

K.:   Observe that the up-and-down, as well as the forward-backward movements of the shoulder blade can be made in such a way that its inner margin remains parallel to its former position, and so to the spinal column. But in addition, there is the freedom to tilt this margin from the original position.

W.:   Does one actually do this?

K.:   More often than you would guess. Put your hand on the lower corner and inner margin of my shoulder blade and notice what happens when I lift my arm forward or sideways far above the horizontal.

W.:   The lower corner travels far forward and sideways under the armpit, where it now projects somewhat, and the inner margin runs obliquely from outside down to inside up.

K.:   So you find that a movement which you would have sworn took place in the shoulder joint actually took place to a great extent in the shoulder-girdle joints. The raising of the upper arm above the horizontal is not the only instance where this deception creeps in.

W.:   But how is this deception possible? I would never come to believe, for instance, that an elbow-flexion occurred in the shoulder joint.

K.:   No, because the elbow and shoulder joints are situated at the two opposite ends of the link in the chain which is the upper-arm bone. It is entirely different with the link which is the shoulder blade. Its connection with the preceding link, the collar bone, and the connection with the following one, the upper-arm bone, are in immediate proximity to each other, the one at the shoulder-top, and the other immediately below in the shoulder joint. Then isn't it easy to mistake which of the two joints is used?

Shoulder blade as one
arm of lever

P.:   Seen in this way, the shoulder blade is not an ordinary link in our chain: It does not extend from one joint-end to the other; but the main part of the bone projects out of the chain, so to speak, backwards and inwards from the region of the two joint-ends, which are concentrated in a narrow space, and serves for the insertion of the muscles coming from the trunk and for the origin of the muscles running to the arm. Therefore, the main part of the shoulder blade can be compared to an arm of a lever whose fulcrum is in the region of the joints.

K.: Only by taking into consideration this similarity to a lever, can we understand the lifting of the upper arm properly. When we lift the arm from its free hanging position, we do so at first, of course, in the shoulder joint, especially by the force of a shoulder muscle, called the deltoid (PL. B/29 and C/2), that causes the roundness of the shoulder running from the shoulder girdle to the upper-arm bone. The extent of mobility in the shoulder joint, however, is restricted in such a way that, sooner or later, according to the direction of the movement, but at the latest when it has reached the horizontal, the movement in the shoulder joint finds its absolute limit. But now begins a movement by the force of the muscles running from the trunk to the shoulder blade, by which the shoulder blade is tilted in the way we have just depicted. Since the deltoid muscle is still active and thus keeps the angle between shoulder blade and upper arm unchanged, so that these two bones form an angled lever, the shoulder blade now takes the upper arm with it and so raises it above the horizontal.

The angled lever

P.: Which muscles tilt the shoulder blade this way?

K.: Here again we must mention the lower part of the hood muscle (PL. B/5), the fibers of which ascend from the lower thoracic vertebrae, and the lower part of what we shall call the anterior saw-muscle (PL. B/7), which runs on the side of the rib cage from the middle ribs to the lower corner of the shoulder blade.

W.: But why are we so particularly concerned with raising the arm above the horizontal, when in piano playing we practically remain below the horizontal?

K.: Because from a dynamic standpoint the horizontal position is not at all such a distinct limit as it might seem from my former explanation. This results from the following simple consideration (Fig. 6): As soon as the arm (A) is raised sideways, even by only a few degrees away from the position of free hanging, its own weight will release in it the tendency (AX) to return to vertical hanging. Since, however, it is connected with the shoulder blade by the active deltoid muscle, this tendency is transmitted to the shoulder blade and would have the effect of tilting it in the direction opposite to that which we have already considered; i.e., it would bring the lower corner of the shoulder blade nearer the spine (BY). In order that this does not happen, but that the arm is actually kept lifted sideways, the lower corner of the shoulder blade must be prevented by muscle force from approaching the spine. This happens naturally by means of the same muscles which are capable of moving it away from the spine, and which actually

Carrying

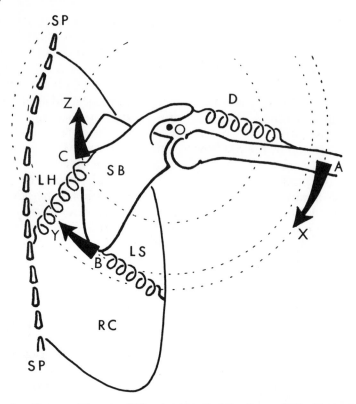

Figure 6. Diagram of the spine (SP) and right half of the rib cage (RC) with the right shoulder blade (SB) resting on it, seen obliquely from the right and from behind. The raised arm (A) is represented by the top part of the upper-arm bone. The weight of the arm tends to move it downwards in the direction A–X. This tendency is transmitted to the shoulder blade by the tensed deltoid muscle (D). Since the axis of the potential shoulder-blade movement runs approximately through O, this tendency is active in the directions indicated by the arrows B–Y and C–Z. As can be seen, the lower part of the anterior saw-muscle (LS) opposes the tendency B–Y, and the lower part of the hood muscle (LH) opposes C–Z.

do this when the arm is lifted above the horizontal, i.e., by means of the lower parts of the hood muscle and the anterior saw-muscle. So we see that even when the arm is only moderately lifted, the same forces must be active which produce the distinct movement of the shoulder blade in lifting above the horizontal.

    P.:   Hence in every position of the arm, the shoulder blade and the arm form a two-armed angled lever. The only thing that changes with the different positions of the arm is the size of the angle in the lever. But in any case, the law valid for any lever, that force-momentum equals weight-momentum, must apply.

W.:   That probably means that the force of the muscles holding the shoulder blade must be just enough to carry the weight of the arm.

P.:   Quite true. That follows from the simplest laws of physics, but experience shows that this requirement is fulfilled in only the rarest cases.

W.:   How is that possible?

P.:   Haven't we explained sufficiently that it is an ideal case of muscle co-ordination, if the muscles do no more than is required by gravity?

W.:   Yes, that is the very difference between the heavy and light arm (p. 66). With the person who has mutually antagonistic tensions, the weight is submerged in all the superfluous muscle activity, and hence the arm feels light. Conversely we feel its exact weight, it is heavy, if we adjust our muscle force accurately to the weight.

P.:   And now we know where we feel the weight of the arm when it is held in the air: in the lower part of the hood muscle deep in the back and in the lower part of the anterior saw-muscle at the side of the rib cage, because those muscles carry the weight of the arm by means of the angled lever. Only when I feel the weight of the arm in these muscles, especially deep in the back, can I speak of carrying the arm.

H.:   Therefore, we cannot practise this carrying too often and endeavour to convey to the pupil what this condition feels like. For this purpose, the shoulder blades must be pulled deep down behind and then the arm be lifted forward approximately to the horizontal, whereat we have to concentrate only on the level to which we bring the wrist, and let everything else fall. Then gradually comes the feeling of carrying low in the back. It is there that we feel the weight of the arm.

P.:   The terms "heavy arm", "carrying" and "angled lever" belong together; indeed, they express the same fact seen from different viewpoints. The opposite concept is the "light arm" of the person with mutually antagonistic tensions.

H.:   Now we know how to carry our arm when it is lifted freely forward. In piano playing, the problem is how to move it down in this condition.

Lowering the arm to key-top

W.:   We already know that. Haven't we always spoken of the effect of gravity? Isn't it simply a case of a free fall?

P.:   Your conclusion is a little previous. We shall recognize right away that neither in preparing the key-moving action by moving the hand downwards from a chosen height to contact between finger and key, nor in the act of moving the key from key-top to key-bottom, can it be a free fall.

W.:   And why not?

P.:   What kind of motion is a free fall?

K.:   An accelerated motion.

P.:   Meaning, it becomes ever faster. If I hold my hand two feet above the keyboard, and then let it fall, at what speed does it reach the keyboard?

K.:   That's easy. The end speed would be about 11 feet a second.

P.:   How many miles an hour is that?

K.:   About seven.

P.:   That you! You can imagine that at this speed the hand would slap the keyboard with considerable momentum, which would certainly be enough to move the key immediately to key-bottom. This means we would move the key straight away, but it would be a movement in which the finger arrives with great velocity at key-top, i.e., the kind that causes vibration of the key, as we have said before. So we would produce undesired accidental noises. What is required, however, is that the finger should stand still before beginning the key-moving action, so that it begins the movement simultaneously with the key. Therefore, if the finger is lowered from above onto the key, this movement must be retarded before key-top is reached, and finally it must stop. It must not be accelerated, as in the free fall. You agree?

K.:   Doubtless. It follows that the downward movement of the hand to key-top must be controlled, a fall which is checked. We can certainly use the weight as a motor for this. But in order that the movement does not become a free fall, we must not allow the arm-lifting muscles, which had held the arm before the beginning of the downward movement, suddenly to relax completely, but we must release them gradually in a controlled manner.

P.:   Very true; only I would not say that we can make use of the weight as a motor for this movement, but that we must do so. For if we used muscles which pull the arm down, mutually antagonistic tensions would result, since at the same time we would not have entirely released the muscles which hold it up.

W.:   I go along with you so far. But what about the key-moving action?

P.:   One question: Does the weight of my arm vary from tone to tone?

W.:   Why should it?

P.:   If it remains the same, then also the weight-pressure of the arm on the key remains the same. And if the weight-pressure is constant, then also the force with which the hammer hits the string is constant. How would we be able to play "piano" and "forte" with this constant arm-weight?

K.:   Theoretically, it would be possible to achieve different momentum for the key-moving action by free fall, if we came to the key from different heights; but we have just precluded that possibility. Therefore, the playing-force must be increased or decreased by muscles, which work with or against gravity respectively.

P.:   We shall first consider the increase of the playing-force by means of muscles that work with gravity. Naturally, this concerns muscles that pull the moderately forward-lifted arm downwards.

Latissimus

K.:   There are several such muscles.

P.:   Notice that if, after sliding off the key, I follow this muscle force, it takes my arm backwards, passing close by the trunk.

K.:   That would correspond exactly to the function of the broadest back-muscle, in Latin "musculus latissimus dorsi" (PL. B/8).

P.:   We shall call it "latissimus" for the sake of brevity. Where does it lie?

K.:   It has an extremely broad origin in the lower back through the agency of a large flat tendinous tissue from the spine and the hip bone, and it also has some muscular slips from the lowest ribs. It runs to the uppermost part of the upper-arm bone; and on its way from trunk to arm it forms a fold, which we call the posterior axillary fold (PL. B/6), since it bounds the armpit at the back.

W.:   If I reach across to this fold with my hand, I can actually feel it tighten when I try to make a downward movement of the arm against a resistance such as that of the key.

P.:   During the key-moving action, this resistance comes from the buoyancy of the key's spring suspension. But what happens if I let the latissimus work on after I reach key-bottom?

K.:   We have established in general that the only motion a muscle can make is that of bringing its two end points towards each other. Therefore, the latissimus is trying to lessen the distance between its insertion in the upper-arm bone and its origin in the lower back. As long as the distant end of the arm is moving freely, it moves downwards around the centre which is in the shoulder joint. Now if the distant end becomes immovable, then inversely this end, which is point B, becomes the centre of motion, around which the end of the arm near the body, the shoulder, moves downwards and somewhat to the rear. This appears clearly and simply in the sketch (Fig. 7), in which I have shown the arm — retaining your analogy to the stick — as an immovable whole, since we can imagine that tension of the muscles on the underside is preventing the joints of the arm from giving way.

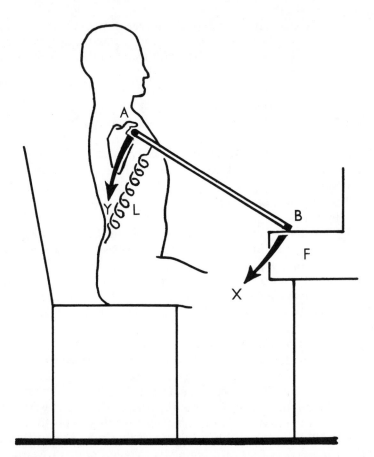

Figure 7. The force of the latissimus (L) works on the imaginary body (A–B). It causes a circular movement around point A with a tendency of point B to move in the direction B–X. But if B meets a firm resistance (F) the force of the latissimus produces a circular movement around point B with a tendency for point A to move in the direction A–Y.

P.:   Quite right. This means that although I hold my shoulder permanently as far down and back as possible, the playing of a "forte" or accented note will cause a slight further descent of the shoulder backwards and downwards. That is a decisive reason why it is impossible to consider the shoulder joint as the centre of motion, as point A, and why we must locate this centre in the breastbone-collarbone joint, around which the descent of the shoulder takes place.

H.:   Unfortunately, by no means all pianists allow their shoulders to sink when playing accents. On the contrary, we very often see an actual raising of the shoulder just at the accents, and not only with our pupils. How is this possible?

Pushing the shoulder up

K.:   Certainly the latissimus cannot be made responsible. There is a clear explanation in the activity of the elbow-extensor muscle (PL. B/28 and C/19), which, of course, can also cause a strong downward movement of the hand. When an absolute hindrance to further movement is met with at key-bottom, continued activity of this stretching muscle will naturally push the shoulder away from the key, which means — upwards.

P.:   To mention pushing is the same as saying that the technique with rising shoulder on an accent is incompatible with the demands of the piano.

W.:   Then are we never allowed to use the eblow-extensor in playing?

K.:   I would not go so far as to say that. Don't forget that the elbow-extensor is at the underside of the arm-chain and all underside muscles are indispensable for the condition of suspension. It is their task to transfer the force of the weight apparatus — or, as we can say now, the force of the latissimus — to the finger. The stronger the force exerted by the latissimus is at the time, the more must all the underside muscles be tensed.

W.:   Does this mean that suspension is a variable quantity?

P.:   Of course, the more force I append to the arm, the stronger must be the suspension in the arm. Therefore, the strength of suspension can be used as a criterion for the force of the key-moving action, but only if the action is properly executed, of course.

K.:   This applies most directly to the elbow-extensor, which is the first muscle to transfer the force of the latissimus. Therefore, in accented notes great activity is necessary in the elbow-extensor. If, however, its effect is greater than the latissimus requires, because one wants to get the force for moving the key not so much from the latissimus as from the elbow-extensor and in doing so transfers point A to the elbow, there results a push and a rise of the shoulder.

H.:   Whereas, as we just found, in the correct playing of accents with increased suspension, the shoulder blade will be pulled deeper.

P.:   But let us return once again to the activity of the latissimus. It has brought the key to key-bottom; it has also pulled the shoulder to the deepest possible point, and it still does not cease to be active. What happens now?

W.:   Now it is simply tensed. Haven't we spoken about the possibility of a muscle working against an absolute outer obstacle? This absolute obstacle need not always be a trunk full of heavy iron. Here it is the key in key-bottom.

P.:   Has it really met an absolute obstacle? Remember, the force of the muscle is striving to bring the two ends of the muscle toward each other. Until now, we have assumed that the insertion comes nearer to the origin. If that is no longer possible, what happens according to the principle of relativity?

W.:   Then the origin comes nearer to the insertion.

P.:   In this case, it means that the deep part of the back is raised forward towards the arm. If I accent with both hands, then the force of both latissimi is enough to release the placement of my supporting apparatus on the chair and to push my pelvis forward between the two arms and towards the piano. This movement, or at least the tendency towards it, will always occur as a consequence of the strong accent. The fact that it does occur is the best proof that the source of energy for the key-moving action was the latissimus and not the elbow-extensor or any other muscle which performs a radial playing movement.

K.:   So there is the possibility that sitting becomes standing, even if it is only potential standing. Probably we shall have to keep this in mind when discussing how the player sits.

H.:   Strictly speaking, it is a four-legged stance, since we use the hands, too, for support.

P.:   But we also learn from all this that there is a limit to the force of the key-moving action. The most I can append to the movement of the key is the weight of my body. This holds for every vertical downward-working force. In other directions a strong man has any amount of force at his disposal, but if, for instance, a load is to be lifted by a rope slung over a pulley, then all his strength does not help him if the weight is heavier than he is.

The same applies to the key-moving action. A player who aims at the key by oblique radial force can mishandle the key as much as his strength allows him; he can even break the hammer. If, however, I play with the downward-working force of the latissimus, I cannot apply more than the weight of my body to both hands together, and so not more than half the weight to one hand.

K.:   This shows us that the division of the body into a playing and a supporting apparatus, which seemed so obvious, has only a conditional validity. In playing accented notes, the supporting apparatus is included in the weight apparatus and becomes the heaviest load in the playing apparatus.

W.:   Our discussion has taken a very roundabout route. Who would not in the beginning have taken it as obvious that everything happens from point A? Then we discovered that an additional supporting point appears, point B. Now point A can indeed vanish completely when everything is carried from B.

P.:   Of course, we must keep in mind that it is an exceptional situation when the weight of the supporting apparatus is absorbed completely into the playing apparatus, but it indicates that in every key-moving action a greater or lesser unloading of the supporting apparatus takes place, since part of the weight is absorbed by point B. In playing "piano", it is only part of the weight of the playing apparatus that is taken from the supporting apparatus; but the more forceful the key-moving action, the more weight will be taken from the supporting apparatus to point B.

K.:   This proves that every key-moving action is ultimately the result of weight: not of the unchanging weight of the playing apparatus, but of a varying weight, since the varying play of muscles can make different parts of the body work by their gravity.

P.:   This varying effect of weight is the most essential factor for attaining a certain volume of tone, but we must not forget the importance of the speed of the key-moving action. It is true that when the key-moving action takes place only around point A, the regulation of speed is practically identical with the regulation of the appended weight. That is to say, if I append a larger part of the body, the speed of the key-moving action will be increased thereby.

W.:   Is there also the contrary possibility that the downward-working mass becomes less than the weight of the playing apparatus and that the speed becomes less than the one determined by acceleration through gravity?

P.:   It must be so. How otherwise could we play "pianissimo"?

You will immediately understand what must take place then if you remember what we said before (p. 111) about the controlled dropping of the playing apparatus to key-top.

W.: That means that also in "pianissimo" playing we must not let the weight of the playing apparatus be freely active downwards, but must reduce it by carrying part of the weight with muscles which would lift the arm in the shoulder joint but must now yield under control.

P.: If in "pianissimo" playing, there is a partial carrying by muscles which raise the upper arm, it must never make us think of an actual lifting of the upper arm around the shoulder and certainly not of a lifting of the shoulder around the breastbone-collarbone joint. On the contrary, in "pianissimo" playing, an especially strong pull downwards of the shoulder blade is necessary in order to counter the temptation to lift it.

H.: Since we have now come to the end of the discussion of the playing apparatus, it will be worthwhile to look back at the most important concepts which we have evolved in the course of it. These are conical grasping of the fingers, spreading of the middle hand, backward clasping towards the elbow, freedom to rotate, sideward fall of the elbow, carrying and suspension.

K.: It is clear that some of these terms describe a condition which must constantly exist during piano playing, e.g., middle-hand spreading or elbow-falling. Others can have only a passing application, depending on the mechanical situation of the playing apparatus. Thus, strictly speaking, it makes sense to talk of "carrying" only as long as the playing apparatus has no distant suspension point B, i.e., as long as it is held above key-top. On the other hand, the term "suspension" makes sense only as long as point B exists, i.e., as long as we are dealing with the movement from key-top to key-bottom or the stay in key-bottom. So suspension and carrying alternate.

P.: But what is important is that the playing apparatus should be in a condition in which the transition from suspension to carrying, and vice versa, can take place without any disturbance, i.e., that the arm should be heavy whether it is being carried or suspended. This heaviness is not a third condition besides carrying and suspension, but is included in them. That means that if my playing apparatus is in the correct condition of carrying, then it can at any time change over to the correct condition of suspension without disturbance, and vice versa. It is the condition in which, by this correct interplay between carrying and suspension, I can

Feeling of constant suspension

govern the nail member of my finger without any mutually antagonistic tensions — and so perfectly that at any time I have the
subjective impression that it is a point B. That is to say, I have the
feeling that my arm is a chain hanging freely between this point B
and the breastbone-collarbone joint, although my nail member
rests on nothing, but is held freely in the air. Of course, I know
that this impression is false, physically speaking, but if you have
this subjective feeling of a point B wandering freely in the air, then
you can be sure that your entire playing apparatus is in the correct
condition. So, since subjectively I have a permanent point B, I
subjectively also have the feeling of constantly being suspended at
this point B. Therefore, I can also recognize the right condition by
the constant feeling of suspension. Objectively, this sensation of
suspension means two things: at one moment — actual suspension;
at the next — the possibility of changing over into suspension
without disturbance. Subjectively, however, these two conditions
are experienced as one. This must be stressed, because the pianist
who wants to follow me will rely above all on his sensations and
not on facts of physics.

    H.:   But facts of physics and anatomy concerning the sup-
porting apparatus will be our subject tomorrow.

    P.:   . . . And we shall also apply them to piano playing.

DIALOGUE 6

The Supporting Apparatus

W.:   Today we are dealing with the supporting apparatus. That is probably the whole body, insofar as it does not belong to the playing apparatus?

P.:   Not at all. Remember what we said in the beginning (p. 20) about the total piano-playing-system. After the pianist's trunk came the top and the legs of the chair, because they take over the load of the supporting body. The legs of the pianist, however, have no function in this system. They are his personal affair, but they will also be mentioned in passing, because they can cause quite a disturbance, and because they are necessary for the use of the pedal. To the supporting apparatus, however, they do not belong, at least not the parts below the knees.

Chair legs and pianist's legs

W.:   Are those parts the only ones which we should not attribute to the supporting apparatus?

P.:   No. Remember that the playing apparatus is connected with the supporting apparatus in the breastbone-collarbone joint and that the breast bone is connected, by the ribs, with only the thoracic region of the spine. Consequently, everything that is above the topmost thoracic vertebra is entirely superfluous for the support of the playing apparatus. What's more, if we consider what we said about possible fixations of the shoulder girdle up-wards (p. 106), we recognize that the head and neck, beyond being superfluous, can even be detrimental.

Head and neck superfluous

K.:   Of course, you are thinking only of the mechanical importance of these parts. As the carrier of the higher sense-organs and the container for the brain, the head can probably be used by pianists, too.

P.:   Let us hope so.

K.:   So there remain, as parts of the supporting apparatus, the thoracic vertebrae with ribs and breast bone, the lumbar verte-brae, the sacrum, hip bones and thighs.

P.:   Quite so. And what do we require of this supporting apparatus?

W.:   Firmness.

P.:   Yes, that is the first requirement. But is it the only one? Would your ideal pianist be a man of stone? Stone is certainly firm and solid enough.

W.:   A certain movability of the supporting apparatus is indeed necessary, too, if for no other reason than that the borderline between the weight apparatus and the supporting apparatus is not distinct, as we said yesterday, so that immovability of the supporting apparatus would imply immovability of the playing apparatus too. But if we require firmness from the supporting apparatus on the one hand and movability on the other, aren't we asking for two qualities which exclude each other?

P.:   Is a wheel movable?

W.:   Yes.

P.:   And must it not be firm within itself?

W.:   Naturally. Now I remember that we had a similar situation in the hand, where by means of middle-hand spreading we attained very great firmness against the mechanical stress of the weight apparatus, without diminishing the mobility of hand and fingers in relation to the keys.

P.:   The same holds for the supporting apparatus. It must offer a firm buttress to the weight apparatus and must not be restricted in its movability in relation to the chair top. How can we attain all this?

K.:   Probably, above all, by virtue of the fact that the spinal column is in no way what we usually think of as a column. This word makes us think of an object which is 1) inflexible and 2) perfectly straight.

W.:   Of course, the spinal column is not inflexible, since it consists of many bones, the individual vertebrae, and not of one single bone, as implied by the name "backbone".

K.:   To be sure you must beware of applying the concepts which we have used in speaking of the limbs to the possible movements in the spinal column. With the skeleton of the limbs we can always locate the movements we observe at definite spots, the joints, where clearly observable changes occur in the angle between the connected bones. It is entirely different with the vertebrae, which are not separated from each other by clefts at the joints but are connected with one another by broad discs. As you can easily imagine, there is no great change of position possible between two successive vertebrae, and thanks to the small vertical dimension of the separate vertebrae — in contrast to the length of the separate

122

bones in the limbs — changes in the relative position of two neigh-bouring bones are not essential. What matters here is that vertebrae which are far away from each other can change their relative posi-tions. This change in position takes place by means of compounding the possible motions in all the discs lying between them. What results is essentially not a change in the angle between two adjoin-ing vertebrae, but a change in the curve of a certain section of the spine. It can become more or less curved, it can be curved in a new direction, e.g., laterally, or it can be twisted in itself.

W.: The mention of curves brings us to the second differ-ence between the spinal column and a true column, namely, that it is not straight.

K.: Quite so. Now there is a certain regularity about these curves. As you can easily see in any person, the thoracic section of the spine is convex towards the back. We call a curve like that "kyphosis". The cervical and lumbar sections, however, are con-cave towards the back; they have, as we express it, a "lordosis". Would you please consider all these facts and names, when you answer such a question as what happens when I straighten up?

Straightening-up

W.: In straightening-up, the lumbar lordosis increases and the thoracic kyphosis decreases. If, however, I bend forward, there is an increase in the thoracic kyphosis and a reduction in the lumbar lordosis.

P.: Right and wrong.

W.: What's wrong about it?

P.: That you described bending forward and straightening-up as opposites.

W.: Then what is the opposite of straightening-up?

P.: You will realise yourself, if you consider what is straight-ened up.

W.: The supporting apparatus.

P.: Yes. The trunk can fulfill its function as a support only if it has a tendency to stretch away from its inanimate underpin-ning, the chair. This stretching tendency is the straightening-up. It does not matter in which direction this tendency to stretch away from the chair is active, whether vertically upwards or obliquely; it does not matter in which direction it is tilted, nor to what degree. The fact that the supporting apparatus is straightened up, in other words, that it is a supporting apparatus, is one thing; what direction it takes, is another. The one relates to its firmness, the other — to its movability. Between the living supporting appa-ratus and its inanimate underpinning, there are, so to say, three

The three degrees of freedom of supporting apparatus

degrees of freedom: I can bend the supporting apparatus forward or backwards; I can bend it to the right or to the left; and I can, by twisting it, turn it right or left. But in all the movements allowed by the three degrees of freedom, it must remain a support, i.e., it must remain straightened up. Now you will know what the reverse of straightening-up is.

W.: When the supporting apparatus ceases to support, when it sags.

P.: Yes, sagging of the supporting apparatus, which means that the person slumps on the chair. What, however, is the reverse of bending forward?

W.: Bending backwards.

P.: Very good.

W.: But anatomically, what is the difference between sagging and bending forward, and between straightening-up and bending backwards?

K.: The answer I shall now give simplifies the full facts, so we shall have to correct it later somewhat. You have just described straightening-up as a motion in the spine, in which the upper end of the spine is stretched away from its base in the pelvic ring. When this has happened, the spine and the pelvis together have a certain form. Can't you imagine that the spine and pelvis remain unchanged in this form, while the pelvis, and naturally the spine with it, moves forward or backwards relative to its underpinning, the top of the chair and the thigh?

W.: Then that would be forward and backward bending, whereas sagging would be losing the form that the spine has attained.

K.: So we can attribute the motion in bending the support forward and backwards to the region below the pelvis, whereas we can consider the straightening-up and sagging as occurring exclusively within the spine, although this must be corrected later (p. 130).

P.: Among the changes in the form of the spine that result from straightening-up, we will pay special attention to the flattening of the thoracic kyphosis, i.e., the disappearing of the hump that one has in a sloppy posture. That means the upper thoracic section of the spine, which before was bent forward, will become more vertical; and the middle thoracic section, which before protruded at the back, moves forward. Now let us ask ourselves how this relates to the shoulder blade, which we require to be moved down on the rib cage in the direction of gravity.

Supporting apparatus and shoulder girdle

W.: If the rib cage were sagging, the downward movement

would also be forward and so push onto the keyboard. Contrariwise, if the rib cage is straightened up, the shoulder blade moves backwards spontaneously on being lowered, so to say, into the space that was occupied by the vanishing hump. The backward movement of the sinking shoulder blade, which we require to tauten the playing apparatus, is thus also a necessary consequence of its relationship to the supporting apparatus.

P.:   While the shoulder blade sinks at the back, the straightening-up supporting apparatus rises in front of it. A person who makes this reciprocal movement between rising support and sinking shoulder blade acquires thereby a sort of ever-lengthening neck. If the movement is continued as far as the connection of the two apparatuses in each of the two breastbone-collarbone joints permits, an extraordinary firmness results, as indeed always happens when a movement is carried out to the absolute limit imposed by the joint mechanism. It is only when this firmness is established that the supporting apparatus becomes a usable prop for the playing apparatus. What would be the use of a supporting apparatus without firmness?

H.:   It is the same with the lengthening of the neck as with that of the arm (p. 105). Here, also, after the full stretching of the supporting apparatus, it is useful to tell ourselves: "I want to become still taller". Then we have the feeling that we can actually stretch even further.

P.:   Of course, the purpose of this exercise is the relaxation of all the muscles that interfere with the stretching of the supporting apparatus and that hinder a lengthening of the neck by fixation of the shoulder blade to the head.

W.:   We know already that the fixation of the shoulder blade to the head is caused by the upper part of the hood muscle. Which muslces hinder the stretching of the supporting apparatus?

K.:   Before this question can be answered clearly, we must say something more about the rib cage, since the thoracic section of the spine, because of its close connection with the ribs, has a reciprocal mechanical relationship with them, too.

W.:   I understand. The ribs and breast bone are sort of intermediate links between the thoracic section of the spine and the playing apparatus, since the latter is connected in the breastbone-collarbone joint with only the breast bone, which is connected by the ribs with the thoracic section of the spine.

K.:   The ribs are connected with the vertebrae by joints and so are movable in relation to the vertebrae. The possible movements

Neck stretching

Ribs

are a raising and lowering of the front ends of the ribs. We do this in breathing: raising the front ends of the ribs creates a widening of the rib cage, i.e., it causes inhalation; lowering creates a narrowing of the rib cage, i.e., it effects exhalation.

P.: These continuous breathing motions naturally represent a certain risk to the suitability of the trunk as a motionless support. Since they take place at the front of the rib cage, we understand that also from this standpoint the shoulder blade, as the carrier of the playing apparatus, has its proper place at the back of the rib cage, where it is least disturbed by these motions.

K.: As a matter of fact, for normal breathing the whole extent of motion, from the deepest lowering to the highest raising, is in no way necessary. We can make shallow breathing motions around any basic position of the ribs, i.e., this basic position can be a raised as well as a lowered one.

P.: Since, as we said, the rib cage becomes smaller by a lowering of the ribs, the required lowering of the shoulder girdle along the surface of the rib cage will be more complete with the ribs lowered than when they are raised.

W.: That means the ribs, and with them the breast bone, must sink just as the shoulder girdle does.

P.: Yes, but since they are so closely connected with the thoracic section of the spine, they also rise with it. Therefore, the ribs and the breast bone, and with them the location of the breastbone-collarbone joint, make two motions concurrently: 1) in straightening-up, they rise with the thoracic section of the spine; and 2) in a lowering of the ribs, they fall away from it. Since, however, the extent of the first movement is greater than that of the second, the result is a rising. And for this reason, I attribute the whole rib cage to the supporting apparatus, although I know that the ribs are actually an intermediate link between the supporting and the weight apparatuses.

K.: We have to take this intermediate role of the ribs into consideration not only with respect to their basic position, but also to certain movements. I am now thinking especially of the latissimus, which we learned yesterday was the most important muscle for moving the playing and supporting apparatuses relative to each other. This same muscle can also cause movements of the rib cage. Since it runs from the lower part of the back to the beginning of the upper arm, it is able to lower not only the arm and with it the shoulder girdle (cf. p. 113), but also the front rib-ends with the breast bone where the collar bone is attached; that

126

means it is a strong exhalation muscle, for which reason it is interesting from a medical standpoint as the muscle used for coughing.

W.:   Then every accent in which we make use of the latissimus must be accompanied by a sudden exhalation.

P.:   That actually happens, and it explains a bad habit that we observe sometimes precisely in players with a correct technique — namely, a light grunt, which the player makes with each accent. It happens because, exactly as in coughing, the strong exhalation does not find free passage through the larynx. I must confess that I myself often give in to this temptation. The reason why this involuntary grunt occurs only with players who possess a free technique is obvious, since only such players use the latissimus correctly, and only with them does it have the opportunity to pull the front rib-ends freely downwards; with cramped players the rib cage is antagonistically fixed in itself.

K.:   Since the ribs are in front of the spine, this antagonistic fixation of the rib cage in itself is due essentially to tensions at the front of the supporting apparatus. In this we must also consider that the muscles which affect the ribs not only move them in relation to the spine, but because of the close relationship between these parts, also bring about a change of form in the spine. In the back, it is true, there are muscles which affect the vertebrae directly; but from the front, and especially in the thoracic region, the essential influence on the spine comes from muscles inserted at the ribs.

W.:   That answers my question about the muscles that work against straightening-up. Where are these muscles?

P.:   For once, let us observe the trunk of the human body in its entirety. We know that the support in the stricter sense, the spine, runs the whole length of the back. From this support the skeleton extends forward only in three regions: above — the skull; in the middle — the rib cage; and below — the pelvis. Thus, between them the skeleton has two wide forward gaps, where the soft parts are unprotected. The upper gap is the throat, the lower the abdomen. But these gaps in the skeleton are spanned by muscles, aren't they?

K.:   Yes, the abdomen has a complete muscular wall, and at the throat we also find quite a number of muscles.

P.:   If we speak about muscles which work against straightening-up, we refer to those very muscles. The abdominal muscles pull the ribs down to the pelvis; the throat muscles pull them up towards the head. Together they cause fixation of the rib cage, and together they make the support sag forward.

Tension of the front

K.:   That is undoubtedly true, but it's not all. This cramp in front could never happen, unless the back muscles were straining against it also; for instance, the throat muscles could never pull the rib cage upwards, but instead would pull the head down towards the rib cage, unless the back and nape muscles held the head high at the same time.

P.:   Yes: from this results the paradoxical fact that with a person in a slumping posture, the muscles of the back usually have to do much more work than with one in a straightened-up posture. The straightened-up person has followed his back muscles to a posture in which they have to make only a slight effort to keep him in equilibrium. With the slumping person, however, these back muscles, to which he never actually yields, continuously strain against the front muscles and also have to work against the weight that is causing a tendency to fall forward. That is why I can feel in different places of the back a swelling of the muscles in a slump- ing person and a disappearance of the swelling when he straightens up. This happens especially in the lumbar (PL. B/9) and nape regions (PL. B/2).

K.:   In this way, straightening-up is not only a change in the form of the spine, but also a change in the condition of the muscles. For a completely straightened-up posture there must be the greatest possible loosening of the muscles in front. Contrarily, with people who slump, the front muscles are tensed against the back muscles, and the separate parts of the front musculature tighten against each other. Thereby the rib cage, as well as the shoulder girdle, becomes fixed in an intermediate position between the opposing pulls working on it from above and below, whereas, as we said before, in the straightened-up person, the rib cage rises freely with the spine and falls freely from the spine. The fact that it rises freely means that it is not held down by the muscles of the abdomen; the fact that it falls freely means that it is not held up by the throat muscles.

P.:   Where is the origin of the throat muscles that cause an upward fixation of the rib cage?

Fixation of lower jaw

K.:   Some originate from the neck section of the spine (rib- supporters: PL. C/28), some directly from the skull, from the region behind the ears (head-turner: PL. B/3 and C/29), some from a complicated bridge at the very front of the throat. Remember that here in the front of the head is the lower jaw. It is connected with the main part of the skull by the chewing muscles (PL. B/1), in the other direction with the tongue bone by muscles forming the floor of the mouth cavity (PL. B/31). The tongue bone is connected with breast bone, collar bone and shoulder blade partly by direct muscles and partly by muscles with an intermediate insertion on the thyroid cartilage, the strap muscles (PL. B/30 and C/30). So if a person tightens this complex forward muscle-bridge, there must also be fixation of the lower jaw, tongue bone and cartilages of the larynx.

P.:   Yet no one shrinks back from doing it. Cramp of the lower jaw is really a typical condition. Now I hope you have the full picture of the person who crouches over the piano and attacks it with teeth-grinding zeal, clawing into the keys with all ten fingers — and you might expect him at any moment to use his nose as the eleventh finger.

H.:   This picture reminds us of what we said about the intimate relationship between the supporting and the playing apparatus. Not only does collapse of the supporting apparatus rob the playing apparatus of the prop it needs, but furthermore — as we have heard — the same system of tensions in front and at the throat, which makes the spine collapse, also brings about fixation in the weight apparatus.

K.:   And you recommend complete straightening-up as a simple remedy for this, don't you?

P.:   We shall be precise about this. You remember that for the pianist, the supporting apparatus has its top end at the topmost thoracic vertebra, so that is where the actual process of straightening-up terminates. In principle, the head and neck are of no account, and I can hold the head in various positions without affecting the playing apparatus. But if there is an inclination to tighten the throat muscles, the simplest remedy is to stretch them forcibly by throwing the had back. Now look at this picture of Liszt at the piano (Fig. 12, p. 166). How he has thrown back his head! Poetically minded people would say, he is receiving inspiration from heaven. I believe we can merely glean an idea of his technique from it.

K.:   Without wanting to contradict you, I believe that the poetic interpretation of the picture is also right. You are speaking about the contrast between freedom and cramp of the muscles. Are these conditions supposed to be totally unrelated to artistic freedom and artistic cramp? For instance, I can imagine the tensed-up person whom you have just described as an ideal producer of "hot" music.

P.:   Quite so, because "hot" music is a matter of noise. Although we have juxtaposed the two pictures of the teeth-grinding, crouching player and the completely free, relaxed Liszt, I must warn you that they are not the only types, because there are many in between — such as those who are outwardly very erect, but who cannot move their bodies in the three degrees of freedom.

W.:   These three degrees of freedom have already been listed (pp. 122-123). The first, bending forward and backward, takes place only below the pelvis (p. 123). Is the same true for the other two, turning sideways and bending sideways?

P.:   For this we must know a little more about the hip bone, since we are dealing mainly with its movements.

Hip bone

K.:   We already know that the two hip bones with the sacrum form a solid ring. Anatomy divides each hip bone into three parts: the ilium, ischium and pubis.

W.:   How is that? Is the hip bone one or three bones?

K.:   It is one, but fashioned in a complex way, and in this complexity we can see the reason for giving individual names to the separate parts. The large mass of muscles which move the leg relative to the trunk in the hip joint encase this joint completely and cover so much of the hip bone that we can feel it only in a few places. First, there is its upper edge, the so-called iliac crest (PL. A/5), which can be felt along its whole length, in the region that is generally designated as "the hip" — e.g., in physical training, one hears the command: "Hands on hips". You can easily see that this iliac crest is curved. Starting in the back beside the lower lumbar vertebrae, it runs sideways and then forward and ends in a projection, which can easily be felt and which we can call "upper front iliac spur" (PL. A/24). In the area of the groin, which follows inwards and slightly below this spur, the hip bone is covered by soft tissues but can be felt again in the pubic region, where it is joined with the pubis of the other side in an immovable connection.

P.:   The pubis and ilium had to be mentioned only in order to give you a general idea of the position of the hip bone. We are much more interested in its third part, the ischium; you will understand why when I tell you that this name means "sitting bone". Aren't we dealing with a sitting person?

Rocking on sitting knobs

K.:   This bone has a gnarled part which, covered by a cushion of fat, carries the weight of the sitting person. We shall call it the "sitting knob" (PL. A/10). It can be felt on either side through the mass of fat which covers it, at a short distance from the anus. If one examines from the side a sitting knob on a bone specimen, one sees that it is curved from the back towards the front and in such a way that a person sits on the two sitting knobs, just as a rocking chair sits on its two rockers. Thus the pelvis can rock back and forth on the sitting knobs, the front and back parts of which will alternate in carrying the weight.

W.:   Yes, that's clear. When I bend forwards, it is the front part of each sitting knob that carries my weight; in leaning backward, the back parts do it.

K.:   You are thinking of the case when the whole spinal column is rocking with the pelvis. What about the possibility of rocking the pelvis back and forth without moving the upper part of the trunk with it?

W.:   Then the rocking of the pelvis would have to be combined with a change in the form of the spine.

P.:   But we have just learned that forward and backward changes in the form of the spine mean sagging and straightening-up respectively. Sit in a vertical posture and completely straighten up in your chair. Now which part of your sitting knobs carries your weight?

W.:   The front part.

P.:   Now without tilting your whole trunk backwards, rock your pelvis so that the back parts of the sitting knobs take more and more of the weight. What happens?

W.:   I slump, because the sacro-lumbar boundary moves backwards and does not take with it the thoracic section of the spine; i.e., the lumbar lordosis decreases while the thoracic kyphosis increases. We have shown all this to be characteristic of slumping.

K.:   So depending upon whether the spine, while unchanged in itself, is tilted with the rocking of the pelvis, or whether the spine makes a contrary motion in itself, the backward rocking of the pelvis will mean backward bending or slumping respectively. Contrarily, forward rocking of the pelvis will mean forward bending or straightening-up respectively.

P.:   Of primary interest to us, of course, is the rocking of the pelvis for straightening-up and slumping.

K.:   By the way, the extent of pelvis-rocking in these changes of posture is much greater than in forward and backward bending.

W.:   Why?

K.:   Consider this: a limit is set to backward bending by the back of the chair. If the back of the chair were not there, we would lose our balance by leaning further back, and to avoid this we have to discontinue the movement. Slumping, on the contrary, has no limit. How often we sit in such a way that not only the hindmost parts of the sitting knobs are resting on the chair, but also the coccyx and even the lower end of the sacrum. If I sit slumping in this way and then lean forward, it is still the back parts of the sitting knobs which are in contact with the chair. Therefore, we can say that the degree of straightening-up or slumping determines a certain basic position of the pelvis, around which, in bending backward and forward, the pelvis and with it the spine can rock back and forth.

W.: But since our supporting apparatus must always be straightened up, we always choose a forward-rocked basic position of the pelvis, in which the weight is taken by the front parts of the sitting knobs.

P.: That is, insofar as they are weighted at all.

W.: Oh, surely you are thinking now of the standing position.

P.: No, I am still thinking of sitting, but of the way the pianist sits, which is somewhat different from what we have said about the way Mr. Everyman sits.

K.: To clarify this difference, we shall start from the comparison with the rocking chair. How extensive is the area of contact of a rocking chair with the floor?

W.: There is no area of contact at all, but only a point of contact between the lowest point of each rocker and what is under it at the time.

K.: Correct. Is that equally true of the relationship between anyone sitting on a chair and the top of the chair? Is the contact here limited to the lowest points of the two sitting knobs, which we compared to the rockers of the rocking chair?

W.: No, the buttocks and part of the thighs are in broad contact with the top of the chair.

K.: Can you tell me the limits of the area of contact?

W.: In front, the boundary is fixed by the edge of the chair. Behind, it is somewhat beyond the points where the sitting knobs are resting on the chair at the time.

K.: So, unlike the rocking chair, the parts of the sitting knobs which are lowest at the time are not the only points of contact with the support, but from a place near them a broad area of contact extends forward to the edge of the chair; is that so?

W.: Yes.

K.: Let me ask you further to remember a little of the most simple school physics. You know that for the sake of simplicity a physicist thinks of the whole weight of an extended body as being concentrated at one point which he calls the centre of gravity.

W.: Yes, this centre of gravity is about the middle of the body.

Supporting area and
line of gravity

132

K.:   So we can imagine the entire gravity of a body as working from the centre of gravity in a straight line vertically downwards. We can call it the "line of gravity".

W.:   Yes, but what bearing does that have here?

K.:   Of course, my trunk also has a centre of gravity, and from this centre I can imagine a line of gravity running vertically downwards.

W.:   Where does the centre of gravity of the trunk lie?

K.:   The exact spot does not matter in this case. Let me repeat your words: it lies about the middle. What matters is how the centre of gravity changes its position relative to the chair top with the rocking of the pelvis.

W.:   That's clear. If, for example, in straightening-up, the pelvis rocks forward, then the middle part of the trunk shifts forward and the centre of gravity must also move forward. Contrarily, if in slumping, the pelvis rocks backwards, then the centre of gravity moves back.

K.:   And with the centre of gravity, the line of gravity naturally moves forward and back. That means if I am straightened up, the line of gravity will run in front of the sitting knobs and through the broad area of contact of my body with the chair. Thereby my weight will be distributed over the whole area of contact, which thus becomes a broad area of support in which no single point is heavily burdened. It is quite different when I sit slumping. Then the line of gravity runs between the sitting knobs or even behind them, so that the whole area of contact in front of them will carry no weight, and the sitting knobs will therefore carry the entire weight of the body.

P.:   For this reason the sagging condition of the body can also be recognized by the fact that in this condition the sitting knobs are pressing against the chair top, whereas in the straightened-up condition they are almost completely unburdened.

W.:   But the area of contact where the body weight is carried in the straightened-up position belongs, at least in part, to the thighs. So doesn't the position of the thighs also play a part?

P.:   Perhaps even more than you think.

K.:   As you know the thigh bone extends from the hip joint to the knee joint. However, it does not run in a straight line between the two; but from the hip joint, which is deeply embedded in the hip muscles, first it runs sideways in such a way that about a hand's breadth below the iliac crest, it is situated directly under the skin.

Pressure of sitting knobs

Thigh and hip joint

W.:   Yes, one can easily feel it there.

K.:   You need not remember that this part of the thigh bone is called the "greater trochanter" (PL. A/11). The part between the hip joint and trochanter is the thigh neck (PL. A/22), and from the trochanter to the knee joint runs the shaft of the bone. You will not be surprised to learn that the hip joint, like the shoulder joint, has three degrees of freedom. Can you tell me what they are?

W.:   First, I can flex and extend the thigh.

K.:   What does that mean in sitting?

W.:   Flexion means raising the knee, extension means lowering it.

K.:   But if instead the thigh bone remains at rest and the trunk moves, what then?

W.:   In that case, flexion becomes what we have already described (pp. 129–130) as rocking the pelvis forward, extension — rocking it backwards. So flexion in both hip joints occurs in bending forward and also in straightening-up. Extension occurs in leaning back and in slumping.

K.:   Good. That much about the first degree of freedom. Now what about the second?

W.:   I can move the thigh away from the median plane and back towards it. For someone who is seated, the alternative of moving the trunk with the thigh at rest hardly comes into question.

Sideways turning

K.:   That is true insofar as in the corresponding movements of the trunk the thighs would not remain at rest but would be shifted somewhat in the direction of their longitudinal axis (Fig. 8), but these movements are possible. They occur when the trunk is turned sideways. As a matter of fact I make these sideward turns chiefly within the trunk itself by twisting the spine in the lower thoracic region. But I can help by making a slight rotation of the whole trunk including the pelvis, relative to the chair top, whereby in turning left, for instance, the right buttock must slide somewhat forward and the left one — somewhat back. This is really no more than a motion of the bones relative to the chair top. Now the soft parts lying between simply yield.

P.:   Naturally, these movements are much easier in the straightened-up posture, because in this condition there is no pressure at any point great enough to hinder them. But now, which movement occurs in the right hip joint and which in the left, if I turn in this way to the left, i.e., to the bass keys?

W.:   In the right hip joint there would be a slight spreading

134

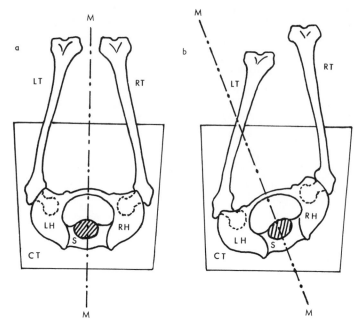

Figure 8. Diagram of the chair top (CT) and the pelvis, i.e., the two hip bones (R.H. and L.H.) with the sacrum (S), and the two thigh bones (R.T. and L.T.) as seen from above. The spinal column would rest on the shaded portion of the surface of the sacrum. The heads of the thigh bones are covered by the hip bones and therefore indicated by dotted lines.

a) Position with the trunk facing straight ahead.

b) Position with the trunk and the pelvis in an exaggeratd turn to the left. As can be seen, when the trunk is turned to the left, the knee end of the right thigh bone is moved forward while that of the left thigh bone is moved backwards. Furthermore the knee end of the right thigh bone is moved a considerable distance from the median plane (M), while the knee end of the left thigh bone is moved so much towards the median plane that it goes far beyond it.

away from the median plane, and in the left — a movement towards it (Fig. 8).

K.: Now what about the third degree of freedom in the hip joint?

W.: This third degree of freedom is, of course, the rotation of the thigh bone around its longitudinal axis.

K.: Let us be more precise: rotation around the straight line from hip joint to knee joint. We know the thigh bone projects considerably from this straight line in such a way that the line, with the shaft and neck of the thigh bone, forms a triangle.

W.:   That means that the thigh bone really makes a conical movement when it rotates around this axis. With inward rotation it rises in the cone, with outward rotation it sinks.

K.:   Quite right. And now what about the corresponding motion of the trunk over the thigh at rest?

W.:   That would be a sideward tilting of the trunk.

Sideways tilting

K.:   Again we must note that the sideward tilting occurs essentially in the spinal column, but a motion of the pelvis relative to the chair top and thigh makes a small contribution as well. If you lean somewhat to the left, the right half of your supporting area is increasingly unburdened; and, accordingly, there will be a slight lift of your right sitting knob and right thigh bone without the soft parts of this area losing contact with the chair top. This slight lift of the right side of the pelvis means, of course, a slight rotation in the left hip joint.

P.:   I would like to stress immediately that this raising of the right side of the pelvis must be as slight as possible, that it must not exceed in the tiniest degree the resiliency of the soft parts. Practically the only right thing to do is to imagine that this movement does not take place at all.

W.:   Why?

K.:   We'll discuss that later. Now let us look back a little. In discussing the possible movements in the hip joint, we have at the same time analysed the degrees of freedom of the supporting apparatus relative to the chair top. As expected, we have found three degrees of freedom. Furthermore, we have come to the conclusion that the movements of the supporting apparatus, in the sense of these three degrees of freedom, occur by no means exclusively beneath the pelvis, as you thought (p. 129). It is true that the forward and backward bending movements occur mainly between the pelvis and entire trunk on the one hand, the thigh and chair top on the other. But we have placed the sideward turning chiefly in the spine itself, and the sideward tilting occurs almost entirely in the spine.

P.:   We must also make another critical examination of the motions of the thigh bone in the hip joint in relation to the trunk at rest. In the three basic movements that you have mentioned — flexion and extension, movements to and from the median plane, and rotation — the whole leg and foot change their positions with the thigh. Practically speaking, however, when I sit at the piano I have my foot at a certain place — on the pedal — and I leave it there. In this position, the knee is bent. Now the question arises:

Double-conical movement of leg

which movements of the leg are still possible when both hip bone and foot remain in their respective places?

W.:   That's the same question we had about the arm: which movements of the upper arm and forearm are possible when the positions of shoulder and wrist remain unchanged? And as with the arm, so here it is a double-conical movement. The axis of the double cone runs from the hip joint approximately to the heel; the common base of the two cones is defined by the arc of the circle that the knee describes; the thigh moves on the surface of one cone, the shank moves on that of the other.

P.:   That's right. Now if the knee moves outwards from its highest position in this conical movement, what sort of movement is made by the thigh?

W.:   It moves away from the median plane. At the same time it is extended in the hip joint, at first moderately, later more. And it also rotates outwards.

P.:   Very true. You have spoken of extension in the hip joint. This means lowering the thigh. But a lowering occurs also in the outward rotation, as we have just (p. 135) said. So if we make this conical motion outward, a forceful lowering of the thigh is included, by means of which the middle of the thigh-bone shaft is pressed against the edge of the chair. However, since the edge of the chair cannot yield to this downward pressure, the pressure must work in reverse as a force that tends to lift the region of the hip joint, i.e., the pelvis, and with it the whole trunk.

K.:   Not in every case. It depends upon where the weight of the trunk is resting. If the line of gravity runs far in the rear, the force you describe — since it works in front — can never raise the trunk, but at most would overthrow it backwards.

P.:   Admitted. But when does the line of gravity run in the rear? When we sit slumping. I am speaking, however, of someone who is sitting straightened up, so that his line of gravity runs in front. Can the force working against the edge of the chair have a lifting effect when the line of gravity is here?

K.:   Yes. But the line will certainly stay behind the edge of the chair, unless we combine a slight bending with straightening-up. However, even if the line comes only near the edge of the chair, the additional pressure directed against this edge changes the entire condition of the supporting area in such a way that the soft parts are pressed back, and this causes a slight raising of the pelvis with the trunk.

P.:   So we learn that, if the trunk is straightened up, the

Balancing on edge of chair

supporting apparatus can be lifted further by virtue of the tendency to outward double-conical motion in the leg. It approximates to a condition in which the weight of the body is balanced on the edge of the chair. Like the beam of a pair of scales, the thigh rests on the edge of the chair and transfers most of the weight of the body onto it. The back part of the beam will be lowered to a measure which depends upon the position of the body at the time, and so a greater or smaller part of the chair top will share in supporting the weight. We act against these movements, which are conditioned by gravity, by the constant tendency to lower the front half of the beam.

　　W.:　　Because of this sinking of the front half, couldn't the shank eventually, instead of the edge of the chair, take the weight (Fig. 9)?

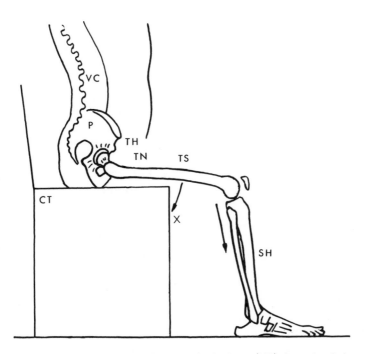

Figure 9. Pelvis (P) and lower part of the vertebral column (VC) above the chair top (CT). Due to the outward rotation of the thigh bone in the hip joint, not only its shaft (TS) but also its head (TH) and its neck (TN) are visible. The downward tendency of the thigh around the hip joint (indicated by the arrow TS-X) effects a pressure of the thigh against the front edge of the chair top, thus transmitting weight to the chair legs, and further it burdens the shank (SH) in its longitudinal direction.

138

P.: That would mean standing, then. Yes, there is always this tendency. Standing is always potentially present in the way we sit at the piano.

W.: Now I remember. Haven't we said that the gradual appending of an increasing part of the body weight to the playing apparatus in the course of the key-moving action continuously implies a potential change from sitting to standing?

P.: But how could the playing apparatus bring about this potential change, if the supporting apparatus were not in a condition of constant readiness? That is the very reason why this way of sitting which we have described is so necessary for the pianist. You notice that the pianist sits as little or as much on his chair as the cyclist does on his saddle. The cyclist, too, is always ready at any time to stand on his pedals. Of course we must not carry the analogy too far and must not ignore the mechanical difference between the way the pianist sits and the way the cyclist does. Where is the chief difference?

W.: In the knees. There is continuous activity in the cyclist's knees, i.e., flexion and extension, whereas our study of sitting (Fig. 9) has shown that the angle of the pianist's knees is not mechanically determined, because the weight does not work on the leg behind the bent knee, but works in the longitudinal direction of the shank, so that the muscles governing the angle of the knee can be quite passive.

H.: . . . . And therefore must be quite passive.

P.: Right. But it is only in the knees and below them that the legs of the pianist are passive and so are mechanically uninteresting to us. Above the knee, the way we sit is no more passive than that of the cyclist. The continuous buoyancy away from the edge of the chair enhances the supporting function of the supporting apparatus. This buoyancy, this activity, I express by saying of the pianist, not as I would of any other person that he sits on the chair, but that he sits away from the chair. I am ready to defend this expression against any grammarian. It is an entirely different matter, though, to how few pianists it can be applied.

W.: But isn't all that directly contrary to the principles which otherwise we have always recognized as valid? Up to now, haven't we always said that everything must be subject to the law of gravity? And now gravity is to be overcome?

K.: What we have always found necessary is a lively reaction to gravity. Hitherto, we have always stressed that this lively reaction is debarred by mutually antagonistic tensions, but it is

"Sitting away from chair"

debarred equally if the body simply collapses without any muscle activity. In short, it is a case where extremes meet. If I sit on an external object in a cramped-up condition as a result of mutually antagonistic muscle tensions, my body forms as immovable a unit with this object as if I were weighing on it like a sack of coal. It has constantly been stressed that the different parts of our body should be "heavy". If I slouch passively on the chair, sagging forward with slack muscles, then my trunk is certainly heavy, but for what? For the chair. If, however, I exercise a tendency away from the chair in the manner we have described, then my trunk is heavy for the muscles that put this tendency into effect. And as long as there are no mutually antagonistic tensions, this heaviness can never be greater than the true weight of the body. This is what is meant by a lively reaction to gravity. It is the same principle that we have found concerning the "heavy arm", where also the weight must be borne by the muscles, which must constantly adjust themselves to the requirements of the moment.

P.: In other words, it is a question of the state of equilibrium in which the supporting apparatus finds itself on the chair. As you know, the science of physics distinguishes three states of equilibrium: labile, stable and constant.

The three states of equilibrium

W.: You must explain that for us a little more precisely.

K.: Labile equilibrium is the condition of a cone which balances on its tip. It is obvious that any slight tilting would end the condition of balance and upset the cone. Stable equilibrium is the condition of a cylinder which is standing on a broad base. Sideward tilting can only come about if one side is lifted against the force of gravity; as soon as the tilting force ceases, the cylinder comes back to its original position. Of course it can also happen that an extreme tilting overturns it. Constant equilibrium is the condition of a sphere which rolls on a level surface. Although it is constantly moving, it always stays in balance. It can pass from one position of balance to another and return to the original one without any appreciable external force, because in every moment the same weight is lifted on one side as sinks on the other.

P.: Which of these states of equilibrium would you say is necessary for us?

W.: Since we require constant mobility of the supporting apparatus, and since its equilibrium must not be lost in these movements, it cannot be labile equilibrium. Since a return to the starting position is supposed to be possible but not obligatory, and since all positions are equal in every respect, it cannot be stable

140

equilibrium.   Therefore, constant equilibrium is the only one left.

P.:   That's the way it is. Naturally, I do not dare to claim that it would really be possible to put ourselves in a condition of constant equilibrium, since a person is not usually a ball. But we must strive to create a condition as though we were in constant equilibrium. Would this be the case if our trunk sat broadly on the surface of the chair, as would be the final situation if we yielded completely to gravity?

W.:   No, because it would be in stable equilibrium like the cylinder. In other words, it would be quite immovable relative to the chair.

P.:   Moreover, we must bear in mind that the human body is a fairly high cylinder, so that even a moderate sideward tilting would result in a change from stable to labile equilibrium and so to upsetting. This is the reason why those very people who sit so firmly and immovably on their stools can often by pushed over very easily by a slight push from the side, sometimes together with the chair with which they have so intimate a mechanical connection.

K.:   And because such a person is aware of this relatively slight stability, he tries, in accordance with the policy of strength of which we spoke the other day (p. 52), to safeguard himself by antagonistic muscle tensions, hindering all movements that might result in a disturbance of equilibrium.

P.:   So we see that in fact anyone who wants to save energy by slouching on his chair, squanders by mutually antagonistic tensions an enormous amount of muscle force in trying to attain stability on the chair. Ultimately one gains nothing in the way of comfort and loses very much in the way of freedom of movement.

W.:   It means that the person and the chair together become an immovable mass.

P.:   That is the extreme case. Let us not forget that between "immovable" and "freely movable" there is also "unfreely movable". This unfree mobility we notice especially in lateral tilting. We will recall what we already know about it.

W.:   We have said (p. 135) that these movements are chiefly in the spine. For instance, if I tilt my trunk to the left, the right half of my supporting surface is increasingly unburdened; and accordingly, the right sitting knob and the right thigh bone are somewhat raised, without the soft parts losing their contact with the chair. And you require that the lifting of the right side of the pelvis should be as slight as possible, so that it does not exceed the degree of resiliency of the soft parts.

Letting fall one side

P.:   What is the significance of this requirement?

K.:   It is really only the logical consequence of the fact that the movement takes place essentially in the spine.

P.:   Now what happens if a person does lift the right buttock higher from the chair?

W.:   That would mean that the movement in the spine is not free.

P.:   And what can hinder the freedom of the movement?

W.:   Lateral trunk-muscles which are antagonistically tensed.

P.:   Yes. Here we get the paradoxical impression that a person is suspending the right side of his pelvis from the spine, while he holds the spine by tensions originating from the left side of the pelvis. I know that my physics might remind one of Baron von Munchhausen, who claimed to have pulled himself out of a swamp by his own pigtail; but the whole thing is a regular Munchhausen affair.

K.:   That may be true; but, unlike Munchhausen, we do have a pivot, namely, the left thigh bone, around which, as we have said (p. 135), the right side of the pelvis can be lifted. The fixation to the left thigh bone would be caused by the lateral hip muscles of the left side, i.e., by muscles lying under the upper front iliac spur and under the iliac crest (PL. B/11).

P.:   Very true. In this region I can always detect a hard swelling of the muscles with pupils who raise a buttock. In addition, of course, the lateral muscles of the trunk are hardened. What can be done to prevent this?

W.:   The lateral trunk muscles (PL. B/10) and the lateral hip muscles (PL. B/11) must relax.

P.:   And what will be the sign of this relaxation?

W.:   The right side will fall.

P.:   And what should happen when I lean to the right side?

W.:   Then the left side must fall.

P.:   In this matter of dropping one side we will take as our model Maestro Paganini, whose spirit we conjured once before (Fig. 11, p. 157). If we look carefully, we see that he is supporting himself on his left leg. From here his supporting apparatus extends upwards to the violin held at the left side. The right side has dropped away from the left to the extent that the right leg has become much too long and is spread away from the left. The dropping of one side is associated with a very distinct outward rotation of both legs in the hip joints, as we can see from the positions of both feet. Just as we have mentioned that the upper half of the body unfolds by means of the outward rotation of the arm,

142

so a similar unfolding of the lower half of the body occurs by
means of the outward rotation of the legs. The violinist stands;
we sit. But we, too, have recognized that a tendency to outward
rotation in the hip joints is necessary. If while standing we try to
imitate this posture of Paganini's, using the right and the left leg
alternately as the supporting leg, and if then we sit down —
keeping the muscles in the condition thus attained — and alternately drop the right and left side in bending to the other side, we
find that we are gradually attaining full freedom in sideward
bending.

    K.:   But only one of the three degrees of freedom of the
supporting apparatus is gained by that.

    P.:   Yes, but it is not irrelevant to the other two. After the
attainment of freedom in sideward bending, certain additional
exercises for sideward turning and for forward and backward
bending will be necessary; but these supplementary exercises are
much more conducive to success if performed on the basis of the
freedom won by the Paganini exercise, since that exercise leads to
a freer condition in the muscles of the entire body. The relevance
of this change in the muscles for the whole body is also evident
from the fact that the condition achieved in standing can also be
applied in sitting, although the joints are in entirely different
positions.

    H.:   Since this condition of the muscles can be achieved in
standing, the pianist must have it also when standing. At least the
moment before he seats himself at the piano, he must have a
posture corresponding to this condition of the muscles, not only
when standing on one supporting leg, as in the Paganini exercise,
but also when standing on two.

Standing at attention and "amuscular" standing

    W.:   In that case it would be like the posture of the soldier
when standing at attention, since this is also surely very
straightened up.

    K.:   No. According to all we have said, there is an enormous
difference. Outwardly the difference is most noticeable in the
position of the shoulder. Whereas the pianist must allow his
shoulder blades to sink — and what's more, must actively pull them
down and back — I remember from my soldiering days a pulling of
the shoulder forward.

    P.:   And you probably also remember the famous "chest
out, stomach in!" which also does not apply to us.

    K.:   Why not? According to all we have said, especially about
the position of the shoulder, the pianist's chest must protrude
freely even more.

P.: Yes, it must protrude freely, but not beyond the abdomen, which the sergeant erroneously calls "stomach". On the contrary, the abdomen must be more forward, and the pelvis must be the farthest forward. From here both my trunk and my legs recede.

K.: That is the posture in which we need the least muscle energy in standing, since in this condition the hip joint is stretched as far as possible, so that the weight of the trunk is suspended on the joint ligaments which run at the front side of the hip joint. We call this posture "amuscular" standing, i.e., standing without muscle force in the hip joint.

P.: So here, also, we are following our general principle of relying on gravity in every possible case, and thereby saving muscle energy. The soldier in his stiff posture, with pelvis and abdomen held back and shoulders pulled forward, has tensed his muscles antagonistically in order to hold these parts of the body in their stipulated places.

K.: Isn't this difference very meaningful if we compare the task of the soldier with that of the artist? In his hostility to his environment, the soldier is continually ready to attack it with concentrated muscle energy, never trusting it. The true artist, on the other hand, must surrender himself trustingly to his environment, must become one with it, even if we are only thinking of the primitive mechanical merging into the mechanical system which he forms together with chair, floor and piano.

P.: This mechanical merging is of course possible only if we are free from disturbing muscle tensions. Our consideration of amuscular standing in the hip joint has taught us that a good part of this disturbing muscle tension is to be sought in the hip muscles, a fact which is perfectly understandable if we remember (p. 133) that backward and forward leaning take place entirely, and the lateral turning to a great extent, in the hip joint.

Hip muscles

K.: Of course, the flexor and extensor muscles of the hip would be responsible for hampering forward and backward bending. I need hardly tell you that the flexors lie in front, in the groin.

P.: In fact, one can often find parcels of hard, swollen muscles here. Relief of the swelling is very important for sitting. As long as these muscles are tensed, the legs are fixed in front to the trunk. Not only is the freedom to lean fack and forward taken away, but also the aforementioned (p. 135) outward and downward conical movement of the thigh is impeded.

K.: It may be worthwhile mentioning that one of the hip-flexor muscles (the straight thigh-muscle: PL. B/17) is also a knee-extensor, since its sinew runs to the kneecap and from there to the shin bone.

P.:   Consequently, in such cases we observe, besides a definite upward tendency in the thigh, a definite fixation of the kneecap; and conversely, we can predicate lack of freedom in movement of the hip from fixation of the kneecap.

W.:   But since the freedom to lean forward and backwards is no doubt impaired by mutually antagonistic tensions, hip-extensors must be involved in this as well as hip-flexors.

K.:   Of course. I want to distinguish two groups of hip-extensors. The one group, which belongs to the buttock muscles in the stricter sense (PL. B/12), runs over the hip joint only and so influences this joint alone. They are not mere extensors but also strong outward rotators.

P.:   So they carry out almost the same sort of movement which we have described as a conical movement of the thigh, where the lowering was also associated with outward rotation. Since we found (p. 136) that this movement can effect a raising of the trunk, if it meets the resistance of the edge of the chair, we now understand that these muscles are active against the weight of the supporting apparatus. Thus the activity of these muscles is not only admissable but necessary for straightening-up, and therefore, they can scarcely be included in the system of mutually antagonistic tensions.

K.:   Then the other group of hip-extensors must be respon-sible for this. These are the so-called hamstring muscles (PL. B/13) which run over two joints, since they originate from the sitting knob and are inserted at the shank just under the knee. We can distinctly see and feel their sinews protruding on both sides of the knee-hollow. Because of their position, they are not only hip-extensors but also knee-flexors.

Tipping the chair forward

P.:   Accordingly, people who tense these muscles have a tendency to scrape the floor backwards with their foot. When this is overdone and the foot is firmly planted on the floor, it has the opposite effect of tipping the chair forward.

K.:   And the influence of these muscles on the hip joint is not perceptible?

P.:   Indeed it is disastrous. Since they originate at the sitting knob, their tension pulls this part of the hip bone forward. If we visualize the whole structure of the pelvis (Fig. 10), we realise that a forward movement of this part situated under the hip joint implies a backward movement of the upper parts of the pelvis, and

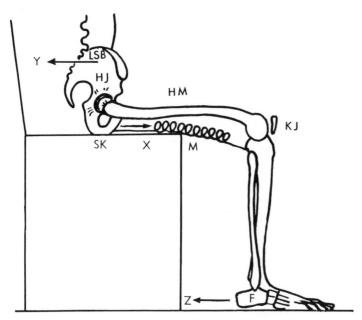

Figure 10. Effect produced by the hamstring muscles (HM) which pass under both the hip joint (HJ) and knee joint (KJ). Since contraction of these muscles tends to bring the two ends closer to each other, its effect on the sitting knob (SK) will be a forward direction (SK–X); since this movement would be centred around the hip joint it would cause a backward movement of those parts of the pelvis which are situated above the hip joint, i.e., especially the boundary between the lowest lumbar vertebra and the sacrum (LSB) in the direction (LSB–Y). This in turn would cause a reduction of the lumbar lordosis. On the other hand the hamstring muscles tend to move the shank backwards around the centre of the knee joint; this would result in a tendency of the foot (F) to scrape backwards in the direction F–Z.

so of the sacro-lumbar boundary. This, as we know (pp. 133–134), means a sagging of the supporting apparatus. Therefore, with people whose supporting apparatus is in this state, we can very often feel the hard distended sinews of the hamstring muscles protruding beside the knee-hollow.

  W.: And naturally the back and forward leaning of the support is hindered.

  P.: Yes, that's where we started. Now about hindrances in turning sideways, insofar as they concern the hip joint.

Pressing the knees together

  K.: According to our description of this process (p. 133), we have to pay attention to the muscles that effect the movement of the leg, when the trunk is at rest, towards and away from the median plane.

P.:   Since the movement away from the median plane is included in the conical movement of the thigh, which we have recognized as necessary, the disturbance will arise mainly from the muscles that can make the movement towards the median plane. After all, they hinder the conical movement, and therefore also hinder complete free straightening-up and free sideward turning. The tendency to press the knees together by the force of these muscles, which one finds in many pianists, especially females, cannot be combatted emphatically enough. I usually meet enormous muscular resistance when I try to prise the knees apart with my hands.

K.:   These muscles form an extremely large mass of flesh on the inner side of the thigh. Because of their position they cannot be seen in our plate.

P.:   When these muscles have finally been relaxed, then we have attained in sitting, too, the condition that we have described as a sort of lateral unfolding of the body when standing.

K.:   Now we have mentioned most of the muscles that influence the hip joint, so we have probably dealt with all the disturbing fixations of the supporting apparatus that are essential.

P.:   Indeed we need not mention any more fixations within the supporting apparatus, since this apparatus ends with the thigh. But there are plenty of fixations that arise from the shank and foot and that affect the supporting apparatus, and, as we know (cf. pp. 84-85), even the playing apparatus. Hard as it may be to understand the connection between cramp in the big toe and tension in the finger muscles, it is easy to see that the supporting apparatus can be influenced by the condition of the shank and foot. Think, for instance, of the lateral shank muscles (PL. B/15), which with the shank at rest would turn the foot onto one of its edges. If the foot remains at rest, however, their tension naturally disturbs the free double-conical movement of the leg and thus destroys the relationship we have described between the supporting apparatus and chair top (p. 136). More important still are the calf muscles (PL. B/16), which open the forward angle between foot and shank; their tension, therefore, raises the shank when the balls of the toes rest on the floor. This, of course, also disturbs the way we sit.

W.:   Since the calf muscles move the foot in this way, they must be the ones which work the pedal; aren't they?

P.:   They would be, if pushing down the pedal were an active movement.

W.:   How could the pedal be pressed down without activity on my part?

Tensions in shank

Pedal

P.:   Try it yourself! First, we must see to it that the right foot is always ready to work the pedal, i.e., the pedal must be under it, best in such a way that the end of the pedal glides under the middle of the foot. Now try to sit correctly with your supporting apparatus in the condition which we have exhaustively described today. Pay special attention that your foot be turned well outward and that the lateral muscles of the left hip be relaxed. Sitting in this condition, put the middle of your right foot over the end of the pedal. If you have no intention of pressing or releasing the pedal, what position would your foot involuntarily take as its basic position?

W.:   It would press the pedal down. Now I understand, it is not the pressing down which requires activity of my muscles, but the release of the pedal.

P.:   Right. Our basic position is "foot deep in pedal". When the pedal rises, this is due to the lifting of the tip of the foot, while the heel remains on the floor. This causes lengthening of the calf muscles, and since this helps to eliminate tension in those muscles it is good for the condition in the whole body.

K.:   When the tip of the foot is lifted around the heel as centre, everything lying in front of the heel is also lifted. So the area of the ankle joint is lifted and with it the whole leg, as you can easily see for yourself.

P.:   Which force produces the lifting?

K.:   Logically, the force of the front shank-muscles (PL. B/14), which are able to reduce the forward angle between shank and foot because their sinews run in front of the ankle joint.

P.:   That is the logical answer. However, since the motion operates not only at the ankle joint in this case, but also causes a lifting of the leg around the hip joint, it is perfectly possible that the movement in the hip joint is caused by a front hip-joint muscle, while the front shank-muscles do nothing but lift the weight of the foot, and not that of the whole leg.

W.:   That is a similar situation to the one which arises in the movement of the playing apparatus around the key as centre (cf. p. 78). There, too, it was possible to make the movement exclusively by the activity of wrist-flexors around point B, or to direct it from point A. In the first case the arm is heavy, in the second — light.

P.:   Thus the leg is heavy if I use only my front shank-muscles, but it is light if the front hip-muscles also are used. The heavy leg will press the pedal down by mere gravity if I relieve just the front shank-muscles. The light leg on the other hand will need the calf muscles for this purpose.

148

H.:	We need hardly mention that the heavy leg is the only correct solution.

P.:	While we are on this subject, we also have to consider that the light leg is fixed to the supporting apparatus by means of the front hip-muscles and thus robs the supporting apparatus of its function as support, as we have already explained (p. 143).

H.:	That means that these legs of ours are not so very unimportant after all. Their positive purpose lies in the use of the pedal; but they also have a considerable negative effect through their tensions.

P.:	Let us keep in mind that no part of our body can be unimportant, since each part influences every other. Nicholas of Cusa, the great philosopher of the late Middle Ages, rightly said on this subject: "The whole of the body is in the eye, eye, and in the hand, hand. The body is represented as a whole in its members through each member. Thus each member is, in the best possible way, what it is. So each member is with complete immediateness in man and thereby the whole of man is with complete immediateness in each part".

H.:	According to that, the playing apparatus also expresses the whole person, and so everything which we have said about freedom in the supporting apparatus is important not only because we actually need flexibility in it and movability of it, but also because it enters into the function of the playing apparatus.

W.:	Now does the ability to move with three degrees of freedom suffice, or must the movements in these three degrees actually be performed?

P.:	When practising, you cannot move your supporting apparatus often enough in different directions in order to make sure of freedom of movement and to relax straightaway any tension which may arise. But if you give a recital, you must remember that the listeners are observers as well, and that continual physical restlessness on your part would be very annoying. So you will restrict your movements considerably, but not to the extent of only just being able to reach all parts of the keyboard.

H.:	Since we have now come to the end of our consideration of all parts of the total piano-playing-system, it would be worthwhile to look back over what we have accomplished. We see that we have as much justification for saying that we have not yet learned anything at all about piano playing, as for saying that we have already learned everything about it. We have learned nothing, because as yet we have become acquainted only with the tools that we want to use for our playing, and nothing has been said about the playing itself. We have learned everything, because we have grasped the general principles of what we are to do: The only thing lacking is the particular application of these general principles.

      P.:   We shall begin with their application next week.

DIALOGUE 7

The Technique of the First Tone and the Chord

H.:   I almost brought a new participant today to our discussions. Yesterday evening we were playing music together at the home of a friend, and when I spoke about our talks, a young pianist there showed great interest.

P.:   Then why didn't you bring him along?

H.:   Because I was able to convince him that he would not profit by it if he were to join us halfway through. I admit it was very hard to make him understand because I had mentioned before that today we were beginning with the practical application of our study. Of course, he deemed that this was the only thing that would interest him anyhow — he could do without the theory, he said.

P.:   Then he will also have to give up any chance of understanding us, because every word that we say about the practical application presupposes a knowledge of our general principles and train of thought.

W.:   Since we know these we can now apply them.

P.:   That's right. Let us use them first for the technique of the first tone.

K.:   What? You simply number the tones?

P.:   No, it is not simply a matter of numbering, but by this method of denoting it I mean to express the temporal relation of the tone to the preceding one and the mechanical relation of its production to that of the preceding one. A tone which is temporally and mechanically separated from the foregoing tone is to be dealt with as though it were the first one, even if many others have preceded it. This is true for all playing which is not legato. In legato, however, every tone within the passage grows out of the preceding one; it follows the one before and is, therefore, a "second tone".

K.:   You define the extent of the application of the first tone by the words "not legato", but that is a purely negative and, therefore, unsatisfactory definition. Can't you express it positively?

First and second tone

P.:   Not in one or two words, because there are very many
different kinds of tones that are not allied with the preceding tone.
Among these there are intense isolated chords, separated from the
preceding one as well as from the following one by pauses; then
there are melody tones, staccato tones and finally the first tone of
a legato passage.

K.:   And you lump them all together?

P.:   By no means. The term "technique of the first tone" is
not supposed to define a certain specific type of key-moving action,
but it is only a basic type which we have to modify greatly in
many different ways for the different musical requirements indicated by the expression marks.

K.:   It means then that, in speaking of the first tone, we shall
not describe the entire course of a certain key-moving action, but
shall just deal with certain facts which are common to numerous
different kinds of touch?

P.:   Substantially, we shall proceed in this way. However,
in order to give you a more direct insight, we shall describe a certain subtype of the first tone in its entire course as an example; but
we must guard against thinking of this subtype as representing the
first tone in general. We shall always have to state whether the
facts mentioned at the time apply to the first tone in general or to
our specific example.

W.:   And which subtype shall we choose as our example?

Intense isolated chord
as paradigm

P.:   I think the most appropriate one is the intense isolated
chord, separated from the neighbouring tones by pauses.

K.:   Are you really going to begin with a chord and not with
a single tone?

P.:   Yes; the piano is a polyphonic instrument, and we must
always be able to employ its polyphony fully. So it would not
make sense to give primary consideration to a position of the hand
in which we can move only one finger, and not several, to key-
bottom. Therefore, in my practical teaching I always start with
the use of at least two fingers, and we will abide by this in our
theoretical discussions, too. It is true, much of what we have to
say in the beginning about the first tone will be applicable to the
single tone as well as to the chord; so we shall have as much right
to speak of the playing finger as of the playing fingers. Later we
will inquire more thoroughly into the special requirements and
possibilities that arise in playing chords.

H.:   What do we know already about the playing of the
first tone?

W.: First of all, I should check the condition of my body to see whether it is free from mutually antagonistic tensions; whether in the supporting apparatus there is the correct tendency for straightening-up; whether the playing apparatus represents a heavy chain with a lateral fall of the elbow in the double cone — and everything else we have learned about the general rules for the condition of the body.

P.: Right. So that we don't have to enumerate all these requirements again, we shall quickly sum up the essentials: support and hand must have firmness in themselves, everything else must be heavy; but both firm and heavy parts must be free.

How to reach key-top

H.: And if we have found our body in the correct condition, what do we do then?

W.: Before I move a key, I must put my finger on key-top. When it has reached there, it must — without exception — be at rest for a while, even if only for an infinitesimal time. Therefore, I cannot gain anything at all for the key-moving action by raising my hand high over the keyboard before playing.

P.: If yet we do sometimes raise the hand high, especially between two intense isolated chords, this movement does not relate to the succeeding key-moving action, but to the preceding. Eventually, we shall have to consider the cause and the purpose of this arm-raising. At the moment, however, the important thing is what we have to do in preparation for the next key-moving action in case the hand is high over the keyboard beforehand. Therefore, the question is how does the lowering of the arm come about? Or — which is perhaps more important — how does it not come about?

W.: It does not come about by means of muscles that lower the upper arm, nor as a free fall, but by means of controlled yielding of the muscles that lift the upper arm. By virtue of the system of the angled lever, the force of the carrying muscles that are inserted at the shoulder blade must be adjusted to this controlled yielding.

P.: You have just described what takes place in the weight apparatus. What is the situation in the grasping apparatus?

W.: It will be simplest to let the hand fall freely in flexion.

P.: Very true; that is the simplest way, because it saves energy, and that's what we always want. But shall we be able to play with this hanging hand, which is bent at the wrist?

W.: Of course not. That would be playing by pressing from above, whereas we want pulling from below — which means that in playing, the wrist must be overextended.

P.:   If you require an overextended wrist to pull from below, then you are choosing the surest way. You want the wrist to be geometrically deep in order for it also to be dynamically deep. But we know (pp. 71–72) that a part of the body which is geometrically high can also be dynamically deep. Therefore, we do not necessarily need an overextended wrist joint for playing; it can be merely extended or even slightly bent, although bent positions scarcely come into question for the special example of the intense chord. In any case, a certain degree of extension will be necessary for the hand to leave the bent position that has resulted from free hanging. How and where does this variable extension of the wrist take place?

W.:   Naturally, we could do it while lowering the hand to key-top. But if we use the force of the wrist-extensors for this, we could just as well have kept the wrist extended from the beginning.

P.:   Is there any possibility of avoiding the use of this force?

W.:   Yes. When the fingers have reached key-top, the weight of fingers and hand will be held up by the resiliency of the key, while the wrist continues to sink below the level of the keys. But the instant we have the desired position of the wrist joint, any further extension will be checked by the tension of the underside muscles, and thus the motion passes over directly into a key-moving action.

H.:   That means that the downward movement of the weight apparatus need not be interrupted before the beginning of the key-moving action. It is only the finger on key-top that has to be at rest before the beginning of the key-moving action. That is enough to avoid vibration of the key.

P.:   So it is. Of course, none of these movements occurs if the arm was not originally raised and if we reach the top of the key to be played by an approximately horizontal movement, i.e., if the hand on its way from other keys slides over the key-tops. That is what we do as a rule.

H.:   Now the preparation for playing is ended, and we can perform the key-moving action itself.

Head of ulna passes by keyboard

P.:   What do we already know about that?

W.:   We should let the weight of the playing apparatus operate by releasing all the muscles on the upper side of the weight apparatus, which have functioned till then. Above all, we should release completely those that lift the upper arm. At the same time, we must tighten the muscles on the underside, using the latissimus as the source of energy and the elbow-extensor for transmitting this energy to the head of the ulna.

H.: Yes. Thereby you are expressing a fundamental truth, which seems so obvious to us, but is overlooked in so many techniques, i.e., that the force for playing must not come from arm, hand or finger, but from the back.

P.: We summed up the downward movement of the weight apparatus, which is brought about in this way, by saying that the head of the ulna passes by the keyboard (p. 72). This by-passing movement must be caught up by the grasping apparatus.

H.: Now the next question arises: what is the position of the grasping apparatus?

W.: Unless we deliberately give it a different position, it will take the position that we have described for the hand at rest on the edge of the keyboard, namely, supination, because this is the position that results simply by the effect of gravity on the chain of the playing apparatus.

P.: Therefore, this is the position that we shall usually take in preference to all others, although we must not forget the positions of pronation, because they, too, are indispensable for the pianist. We shall deal first with playing in positions of supination, because of their greater practical importance.

W.: In this case the playing is done by the outer margins of the fingers, i.e., by the margins which correspond to the little-finger side of the hand.

P.: Does this hold for all the fingers? Also for the thumb?

W.: No, with the thumb it is the other margin.

P.: That is the margin which in the case of the other fingers is used when playing in pronation. As a matter of fact, many pianists are inclined to pronate when playing with the thumb.

H.: Against this, we must stress that in playing with the thumb, the head of the ulna must keep its geometric and dynamic low position relative to the radius.

P.: Nevertheless, its position relative to the keyboard can vary greatly, as we have just emphasized (p. 153). In this respect we will distinguish between three possibilities:

1) at one extreme, the geometrically lowest position with a very over-extended wrist joint;

2) at the other extreme, a geometrically high position with the wrist joint slightly bent; and

Playing in supination

Various heights of wrist

3) as a middle type, a moderately high position with the wrist joint in a straight line or slightly overextended.

W.: And is it left to us which height to choose in each case, or are there any particular rules?

P.: Sometimes it is a matter of choice, as for instance in the case of unaccented tones on white keys.

W.: That is as good as saying which factors particularly affect the height of the wrist. There are above all the black keys, which we can't reach with a geometrically very low wrist. Contrarily, the high positions of the wrist will be eliminated with increasing volume and intensity of the tone, since the greater weight will pull the wrist farther down.

H.: So for our special example of the intense chord only deep and moderately high positions of the wrist come into question, whereas when speaking of staccato we shall have to take into consideration geometrically high wrist positions as well.

P.: What will be the effect of the various wrist positions on the relation of the finger to the key?

W.: With a deep wrist, the only contact is between the middle member of the finger and the front edge of the key; with a high wrist, it is in the region of the fingertip, as a rule next to the outer end of the nail groove; and with a moderately high wrist, the contact will spread the whole way between these two points.

Point of contact between finger and key

P.: So we realise that only with a high wrist does the transmission of force between finger and key take place at the end of the finger. Which part of the finger takes over this task when the wrist is in the other positions?

W.: Since the two joints between the three finger-members are of no account for the key-moving action, it would make no difference which part of the finger was used for it. In practice, however, other than the nail member can be used only in the case of the little finger; if in the case of another finger a member nearer the body were used, the neighbouring fingers would be in the way.

P.: Anyway, we can go as far as the terminal joint with the other fingers, so that with a deep wrist the entire nail member points upwards away from the place of contact. But it would be a mistake to conclude from this that the condition of the nail member, which is thus not included in the mechanical chain of player and piano, is of no interest. On the contrary, it is the tension in the very terminal joint that often causes persistent obstructions to free playing.

H.: In short: no matter what relation the separate members of the finger have to the keyboard, the middle and terminal joints must always be free from flexor tensions.

P.: If the finger joints are in this requisite condition, I speak of a "dead finger".

K.: Now we have said all that is essential concerning the position of the finger on the key, haven't we?

P.: Not yet. Don't forget that the front part of the white keys, where we play, has a width that far exceeds the width of the finger. So we must define the place of contact relative to the width of the key.

K.: Isn't that irrelevant?

P.: Perhaps for the key-moving action itself, but not for the after-motion which as a rule follows it. In order for this to have a support, not only underneath but also at the side, it is necessary to play right next to the neighbouring key, which then furnishes this lateral support.

K.: But from where do you get this lateral support with the black keys?

P.: Then the key which is played must provide it itself. For it to be able to do so, I lay my nail member obliquely over the key, so that the region of the nail groove projects somewhat over the lateral edge of the key and there finds its support.

H.: Important as all these outwardly visible relationships of the hand to the keyboard are, we must not forget that the inner muscular condition is still more important.

W.: We already know that there must be firmness in the small grasping unit and suspension in the large one.

H.: Firmness in the small grasping unit means middle-hand spreading and a tendency for conical movement in the basal finger-joints. Suspension in the large grasping unit means tension of the muscles on the underside, i.e., in half-supination essentially the tension of the ulnar wrist-flexor (PL. B/23).

W.: The combination of these two conditions in the small and large grasping units we have named "clasping back of the fingers towards the elbow", which is most important in the thumb and little finger.

P.: Yes. This is the condition in which our grasping apparatus rests on key-top, and in this condition it is moved to key-bottom by appending the weight apparatus. That is how a first tone is played: The key is moved only by the force of the weight apparatus, while the grasping apparatus acts only as an intermediary.

H.: And when key-bottom has been reached, the grasping

Lateral support for finger

Clasping-back towards the elbow

apparatus, still in the same condition, remains at rest in key-bottom for the period indicated by the note value.

W.:   ... Until the after-motion follows.

P.:   If there is an after-motion.

W.:   What determines whether there is an after-motion or not?

P.:   Let us recall what we said (p. 77) about the function of the after-motion.

W.:   1)   It is the safety valve for the tendencies to motion that were previously active in the grasping apparatus.

2)   It raises the playing apparatus to the position from which the next touch can be made.

3)   It is a test for freedom from tension in the playing apparatus and can relax slight tensions which may have arisen temporarily.

P.:   First we will take point three; it shows the extraordinary importance of the after-motion for a learner, because he must still strive for the right tension-free condition in his playing apparatus.

Figure 11.   Caricature of Paganini by J. P. Lyer. From J. Kapp; Paganini Biographie. Deutsche Verlagsanstalt, Stuttgart-Berling-Leipzig, 1928.

He cannot make the after-motion often enough nor fully enough. If the teacher has his pupil make the after-motion in an exaggerated way after each key-moving action, that is just often enough. For the mature pianist, however, this third point will be relevant only occasionally, when he feels that a slight tension is creeping into his playing apparatus.

W.: Nevertheless, he certainly cannot omit the after-motion, because both of the other two points are still relevant for him. He also needs a safety valve for the tensions active in his grasping apparatus, and he also must raise his playing apparatus to the position required for the next key-moving action.

P.: Don't let us be too categorical about this. The raising to the starting position for the next key-moving action can, in principle, also come from point A, whereas the after-motion is a motion around point B. And as to the safety valve, we must not forget that a steam boiler has its escape valve only for high pressures. So for low pressures or tensions, i.e., if we append less weight, as in "piano" and unaccented tones, there is no need for a release of energy by means of an after-motion. But even when appending great weight, it is possible to release the tension in the grasping apparatus simultaneously with the release of the appended weight, so that it needs no after-motion. If you consider that the Italian word for "to release" is "staccare", then you will understand that we shall be concerned with this possibility in discussing the staccato technique.

W.: It seems, then, that the after-motion is entirely superfluous.

P.: Not at all, because when we want to attain not just a staccato but the full resounding tone, it can only happen by virtue of the after-motion, since only with this motion is the finger disunited from the key in such a way that the string can continue in its vibration. We will analyse the exact course of this movement, using our special example of the intense isolated chord, which offers probably the most striking instance of the indispensability of the after-motion.

H.: Let us call to mind the situation in which this motion begins.

W.: The fingers are resting at key-bottom. They have the tendency to clasp back towards the elbow. They cannot follow this tendency, however, because the head of the ulna is pulled down by the force of the weight apparatus, and the wrist joint is consequently more or less overextended.

P.:   But the after-motion is the transformation of the backward-clasping tendency into an actual motion. What is the prior condition for this motion?

W.:   The force of the weight apparatus, i.e., mainly that of the latissimus, must diminish so that it can be overcome by the force of the grasping apparatus.

P.:   Diminish, but not cease altogether. We do not want the appended load of the weight apparatus to be released in the twinkling of an eye, but to decrease gradually. So the after-motion must prevail over the still active force of the latissimus. We might almost say that the force of the weight apparatus is severed by the force of the grasping apparatus which acts in the after-motion. This means that the muscles of the grasping apparatus often — in playing accented and "forte" tones — have to engender an enormous force.

K.:   I very much doubt, however, whether all the muscles of the grasping apparatus are capable of engendering such a force. I think the muscles of the large grasping unit could; but among the muscles of the small one, only the thumb muscles could do it, if any.

After-motion in large grasping unit

P.:   We gather from this that the after-motion is possible in both the small and the large grasping units when there is moderate weight, but that it is possible only in the large unit when there is great weight. In this case, a thumb-grasp comes into play, too, but we shall ignore this for the moment.

H.:   If we review the whole of the first-tone technique, we can say that there are three possibilities at the conclusion of the key-moving action:

1)   no after-motion at all, as with staccato;

2)   an after-motion in the small grasping unit — we shall consider later (p. 200) when to employ this;

3)   an after-motion in the large grasping unit — we need this after playing tones of great volume, intensity and brilliance, as with our chosen example of the intense isolated chord.

P.:   Which muscles make this after-motion?

W.:   Naturally, the wrist muscle that is on the underside at the time and has just intercepted the force of the weight apparatus. In the position of half-supination, which we consider as typical, it is the ulnar wrist-flexor (PL. B/23).

P.:   And what motion will it make?

W.:   It will lift the wrist around the supporting point of the finger on the key in an upward and forward circle.

P.: That's right, but this extensive wrist-movement in a circle around point B is not the only component of movement in the after-motion. We shall find a further typical component connected with it, which arises involuntarily if the after-motion is performed in the correct way, i.e., if it really occurs through the force of the grasping apparatus. Remember that during a good part of the after-motion, the force of the weight apparatus is still active. This causes a downward tendency in the head of the ulna, whereas the force of the grasping apparatus is impelling the wrist to rise; and this in turn means an upward tendency in the radius, since this forearm bone is the one that is connected with the wrist bones. Further, we must remember that this rising is not exclusively dependent upon the large grasping unit; the force of the thumb-grasp is active, too, and this also lifts the radial side of the wrist.

W.: Ulna downwards, radius upwards; that means supination. But since we have assumed that the hand is already in a supine position, the supination will increase somewhat.

P.: That's right; the raising of the wrist is associated with increasing supination. Besides this, however, we know (p. 100) that in our arm-chain — especially in playing a chord — supination is associated with a sideways swing of the wrist.

W.: Yes. This sideways swing comes towards the median plane of the body when the wrist is low, and away from the median plane of the body when the wrist is high.

H.: But since we carry out this supination movement while the wrist is rising, the direction of the wrist swing necessarily changes during this movement. At the beginning, the wrist is swung towards the median plane; but during the rise, there ensues an increasing swing of the wrist away from the median plane.

P.: It means that at the beginning of the after-motion, we can observe a slight supination with a slight wrist-swing towards the median plane, and then the wrist rises in such an oblique plane that the motion is directed towards the back of the hand. I am accustomed to express these three components of the movement in the form of short commands, which are usually understood by my pupils: "Rotate — swing — wrist up!"

H.: Our detailed analysis shows, though, that the first two of these three components, which the command has to give one after the other, actually take place simultaneously.

W.: To what degree must the extensive wrist motion around point B be carried out?

P.: A certain degree will be determined by the force of the preceding key-moving action, for which the after-motion is a safety valve. But we can exceed this minimum degree as much as we wish, and shall do so over and over again to the greatest possible extent while we are learning in order to bring about freedom in the playing apparatus. We can continue the after-motion to the utmost possible wrist-flexion, or we can make it with such force that the hand is thrown high over the keyboard. You will certainly also have seen mature pianists throwing their hands up in this way, by which they give free rein to the after-motion, making it with great impetus after an accent.

H.:   When learning, it is often profitable to make not just one but several after-motions after one key-moving action. The point is that during this whole series of motions we have the weight apparatus appended. Outwardly we see in these exercises that, after a key has been moved, the wrist is alternately raised and lowered around point B. I don't need to repeat that the raising must come from the force of the grasping apparatus. The lowering results when the grasping apparatus yields to the weight apparatus, which remains appended. In this way we achieve an enormous strengthening of the grasping apparatus and, in addition, greater independence between grasping apparatus and weight apparatus.

P.:   But let us suppose that in playing a piece of music we have made only one after-motion and that one so moderately that it did not throw the hand up from the keyboard. What situation are we faced with now?

Passive lifting from key-bottom

W.:   The key is still at key-bottom and is held there by the weight of the whole playing apparatus — and indeed by the weight alone, since we have assumed that the latissimus has gradually relaxed completely during the after-motion.

P.:   But now the tone shall end, i.e., the key shall rise from key-bottom. How can this come about?

K.:   It must be unburdened. This requires that not only the underside muscles of the weight apparatus be relaxed, but also that those on the upper side, which lift the upper arm, take over the weight of the arm, part of which had been carried by the key and the grasping apparatus.

P.:   How can a muscle which lifts the upper arm carry the weight of the whole arm, as long as the elbow is bent without being held in this position by flexor muscles?

K.:   You are right if you mean that the muscles that lift the upper arm can carry the weight of the upper arm only.

P.:   But that is enough, because the remaining weight of

forearm and hand is — as we know (p. 63) — so slight that the resiliency of the key prevails over it. So it is the resiliency of the key that brings key and hand to key-top, and this gives us the feeling in our hand that it is the key that provides the impulse for disuniting the finger from the key. Therefore, this feeling is the subjective proof that the movement has taken place in the right way, that the lifting has not been carried out by the muscles on the upper side of the grasping apparatus and not by elbow-flexors.

K.:   Do you mean to emphasize that it is only in the shoulder joint that the activity of the underside muscles, which do the lowering during the key-moving action, may be followed by the carrying activity of the upperside muscles?

P.:   No. Not even in the shoulder joint may the carrying activity of the upperside muscles follow the activity of the lowering muscles. The word "follow" implies that one event is succeeded immediately by another, but there is no immediate sequence here. In fact, it would be in direct contradiction to everything we have deduced so far. We have said that the tightening of the muscles that lower the upper arm normally begins to decrease in the first phase of the after-motion. The activity of the shoulder muscles that carry the upper arm, however, begins only at the end of the after-motion. So between these two events there is almost the entire after-motion, during which all the muscles controlling the shoulder joint are passive and the upper arm is controlled exclusively by the grasping apparatus. If the activity of the upper-arm-lifters were to begin earlier, i.e., during the after-motion, this movement around point A would push into the motion of the grasping apparatus around B and disturb it. Although this interval between the relaxation of the muscles that lower the upper arm and the activity of those that raise it is of enormous importance, it is of very short duration and can be expressed only in fractions of a second. How long it is in each special case depends upon the duration of the tone played, i.e., on note value and tempo.

H.:   This interval is manifested very clearly when the hand is thrown high in the after-motion, because this flinging-up happens only through the force of the grasping apparatus acting against the weight. Not until the hand is being lowered do the shoulder muscles that carry the upper arm take control, as we have already shown.

P.:   That's the way it should be. However, we very often see this movement imitated superficially without those conditions being observed. Then the lifting is done, not by the impetus from

Flinging up the arm

the grasping apparatus, but by lifting muscles. Of course, the imitation does not succeed entirely. If the hand is flung up correctly, the upper arm and ulna have fallen under the radius by outward rotation, the hand is spread and clasping towards the elbow, and the elbow is passively extended. All this we do not see if the arm is raised from point A. Above all, a bent elbow is always noticeable. A raising of the arm in such a way can, of course, never fulfill its purpose.

K.: I think we must turn back to the normal conclusion of the motion, in which the hand maintains contact with the keyboard.

Transition to next touch

P.: What more is there to say about it? If the next key-moving action is to occur on the same keys, the playing apparatus simply stays at rest — with spread hand, of course, and backward-clasping marginal fingers and the carrying of the upper arm from the back. Those are characteristics of a condition that should never cease. And in this condition the next key-moving action is made according to the first-tone technique as just described.

H.: If, however, other keys have to be touched next, the motion resulting from key resiliency goes over into a sliding on the keyboard to the tops of the keys which are to be played next.

P.: In any case, we do this as an immediate continuation of the resiliency motion, no matter whether the next touch has to occur right away or later, and especially when the second touch has to follow the first at some considerable distance. For if the hand is always "already there" early enough, the playing gains sureness of aim and freedom from anxiety.

H.: It goes without saying that the carrying of the upper arm must be maintained in sliding from key to key. The wrist joint is relaxed as the hand is carried at key-top by the keys.

P.: And in what condition is the hand?

W.: Of course, it is still spread.

Advantages of spreading

P.: That's right. When we speak of spreading, we think primarily of the spreading in the middle hand, which, with the exception of the spreading-away of the thumb, means only a dynamic condition, not a visible spreading. But we must also remember that with the spreading of the middle hand a certain finger-spreading is combined, which, if constantly maintained, leads eventually to increased possibility for actual spreading, important for chord playing. Thus we achieve a condition in which, even for small hands, the octave becomes a small interval, and so can be played with quite a strongly vaulted shape of the hand.

H.:   But even for the playing of single tones this increased possibility for actual spreading is beneficial, because in large jumps it is equivalent to reducing the distance by an octave.

P.:   Then we can more easily succeed in having the hand "already there" early enough.

H.:   Now we have learned to understand all the functions of the after-motion which we mentioned in the beginning (p. 157). For our observation of how to conclude it has taught us its significance for the preparation of the tone immediately following: The playing apparatus, which has been pulled to key-bottom during the key-moving action, rises again to key-top, from where the next key-moving action can be performed; but this rise is not the result of active lifting from point A.

W.:   And why should it not be permitted to originate from point A?

P.:   Certainly it is permitted to originate from point A; and in different kinds of playing without after-motion, which we shall discuss, it must be made in this way. But the ideal way, which gives us the least trouble in attaining great brilliance of tone, the only one whereby it is possible to let the tone resound, and which least of all leads to any mistakes whatsoever arising from the weight apparatus, is the raising of the head of the ulna from point B and not from point A. If it is raised from point A, the weight apparatus, which has just made the downward movement, must now make the opposite movement. That involves the danger that, already in the downward movement, allowance is made for the following upward movement in such a way that the end of the former is checked in order to prepare the latter. But we found at the very beginning (p. 26) that to retard the key-moving action in this way is forbidden by the nature of the piano.

H.:   It is quite different if the rise originates from point B. There the team-work between the separate parts of the playing apparatus is as follows: The weight apparatus directs the preparation for the key-moving action by controlled yielding and in its function as length-adjusting apparatus. It is during the key-moving action that the weight apparatus has to perform its chief task, but the grasping apparatus is already stepping in by virtue of the grasping tendency in the underside wrist-muscles, i.e., as a rule the ulnar wrist-flexor. In the after-motion this grasping apparatus takes over the main task of re-lifting the weight apparatus, which can again prepare the next key-moving action with the help of the length-adjusting apparatus. So the weight and the grasping

Advantages of
after-motion

apparatuses take turns in working: They throw the burden to each other like a ball. In this way the entire succession of movements returns to the beginning without any jerks.

K.: It reminds me of the activity of a blacksmith who saves part of the force necessary for lifting the hammer by the fact that in striking the anvil the hammer is resiliently thrown upwards. In the same way, the underside muscles of the grasping apparatus, which tighten during the key-moving action, throw the weight apparatus upwards after the key has been moved.

P.: If you are implying that the pianist should hammer at the piano like a blacksmith on his anvil, that is the direct opposite of what we are striving for. But insofar as the smith uses the force that becomes active at his point B for flinging up the hammer, he can very well serve as a model for many a pianist.

H.: If we leave the upward movement around point B to the grasping apparatus in this way, for the weight apparatus there is only one motion left for which strenth is needed. It is the downward and backward movement of the elbow away from the key, and the downward movement of the head of the ulna past the key. But it must never be a movement away from point A, as this would cause a push against the key, a pressure on the playing finger.

P.: Now we have completed our account of the playing of the intense isolated chord as an example of the first-tone technique. Later we shall have to analyse the characteristics of other types of this technique.

W.: Although we have dealt with the playing of a chord, the specific aspects of the chord have not been discussed.

Mechanical abutment of chord

K.: Are there specific attributes of chords in general or do considerable differences arise between chords, depending on the number of fingers used to play them?

P.: A chord is a chord. The use of two fingers of a hand gives it its abutment. Whether the other three fingers play or not is no doubt important for the individual case, but it brings no essential new element into the mechanical situation.

K.: Then there would be two fingers that are more important in playing a chord than others? Which are they?

P.: That varies, of course. If the chord has only two tones, the music could call for two adjoining fingers or two separated ones. When there are more than two tones, the two marginal playing fingers form the mechanical abutment for the chord. Of course, in the widely spread position, it is always the thumb and

Figure 12.   Franz Liszt, after lithograph of Josef Kriehuber.

the little finger that form the abutment for the chord. And this is so frequent and typical that we shall devote special attention to it. We must never forget, however, that what we shall have to say about the 1st and 5th fingers is equally applicable to any two other fingers and has to be practised with them too. That is why I have deliberately given those "obvious" facts about the two-toned chord first place in our considerations.

Vaulted hand

K.:   If you describe the marginal fingers as the mechanical abutment for the chord, do you mean that these two fingers would be more heavily burdened than the ones lying between?

P.:   Yes. This is again a situation where there is excellent agreement between the musical demands of our ear and the given possibilities of our hand. Our ear perceives it as harmonically sensible for the middle voices to recede between the melody tone and the bass. The fact, however, that by nature the marginal playing fingers are the most heavily burdened is immediately understandable if we consider what we have said about the hand being like a vault.

K.: I understand. The minute two fingers find a support on the keyboard or anywhere else, I can imagine an arched construction, the two pillars of which are these two fingers. It is the nature of an arch not to need an additional support between its two carrying pillars, and so the fingers lying between the marginal burdened fingers experience only a small weight.

P.: That is so. On this account, special skill is required in order to cope with situations in which accentuation is prescribed for one of the inner voices, e.g., because occasionally one has the value of a melody tone. In such exceptional cases the force of the conical grasping must be reduced to below the norm in the fingers playing outside the accentuated tone . . .

H.: Halt, Professor. You are beginning with the exceptional case, while we have not yet spoken of the typical playing of the chord.

P.: Good, we will begin systematically. Which part of the playing apparatus is most directly affected by the difference between playing a chord and playing a single tone?

W.: The hand.

P.: What general requirements have we established concerning the condition of the hand?

W.: The middle hand must be spread.

P.: Is that enough, since we know that in the chord a vault should come into being between the two carrying pillars?

W.: No. Now we must say: the middle hand must be spread and vaulted. The degree of vaulting depends upon the width of the chord.

P.: Right. And what have we said about the fingers?

W.: They must have the tendency to conical grasping in their basal joints.

P.: Spreading and vaulting of the middle hand and conical grasping of the fingers — these together connote a ball shape of the hand (pp. 92-93). Which point of the ball do the nail members approach by the conical grasping?

Squeezing the key-rod

W.: The South Pole, without ever reaching it.

P.: When you approach the South Pole, how does that affect the distances of the different nail members from each other? Before you answer, imagine that two men are standing on the equator, one in Central Africa, the other in South America. Now they start out for the South Pole in an exact southerly direction, each one keeping to his meridian. Will the distance between the two of them remain the same, decrease or increase?

W.:   Of course, they will come closer to each other, because all the meridians cross at the Pole.

P.:   Yes, they will come nearer each other, although they are not going towards each other but are both moving in the same direction, southwards. Now apply this to the nail members of the fingers.

W.:   They, too, will come nearer each other, although the fingers do not really grasp towards each other through the substance of the hollow ball, but remain spread.

P.:   Yes. How do we maintain complete spreading (cf. p. 94)?

W.:   By making the concial movement in the two playing fingers or in the two main carrying fingers of the chord, in opposite directions away from each other. If, for instance, I play with the 2nd and 3rd fingers, then the conical movement of the 2nd finger is towards the thumb, that of the 3rd finger towards the little finger.

P.:   The resulting nearing of the nail members comes from the flexing tendency contained in the conical movement.

H.:   The same naturally holds for any other pair of fingers, whether neighbouring or not. It is of special practical importance with the thumb and little finger, which in clasping-back towards the elbow, at first go apart but eventually approach each other.

P.:   And now let us remember what we have said (p. 156) about the position of our playing fingers on the surface of the keys. Let us consider the white keys; the application to the black keys takes care of itself.

W.:   We must play near the edge of the key, so that the finger has a support against the neighbouring key.

P.:   You say "neighbouring key". Do you mean the next higher or the next lower?

W.:   That probably depends on whether we play in pronation or supination.

P.:   It holds for the playing with one finger. But think of the tendency of the fingers to approach one another in chord playing.

W.:   In that case the two playing fingers or the two fingers holding the weight will naturally move towards the keys which lie between those being played.

P.:   Right. I call the group of keys lying between the keys being played the "key-rod", no matter how long this "rod" is. In an octave it will encompass six keys, in a third — only one. Because of the obligatory tendency of both grasping fingers to approach each other, the key-rod will actually be squeezed from both ends (cf. Fig. 13 opposite p. 173).

K.: Since the key-rod cannot yield to this squeeze, it is practically of no significance.

P.: On the contrary, it is significant just because of this. For

1) both fingers thereby find their lateral hold on the key-rod; and

2) since the existing tendency to movement cannot be effective in bringing the nail members nearer each other because of the solidity of the key-rod, then it will do the reverse and force the middle and basal knuckles apart. In this way the spreading which was already present in the hand is increased, and with it the firmness of the hand is enhanced.

After all that, you will easily understand why I refuse to start from one finger in teaching; because with only one finger, all these factors which give security in chord-playing are missing — i.e., the resting of the vault of the hand on two supporting pillars and the inner firmness of the vault arising from the resistance of the key-rod. With the one-finger touch the hand is really a vault resting on one pillar only. Of course, we have to learn to control such strange architecture, too, but not in the beginning.

K.: Was that the reason for your choosing the intense isolated chord as the ideal example for the technique of the first tone?

P.: It was one of the reasons. But now we want to consider in which phase of the playing procedure the key-rod is squeezed.

W.: Actually it cannot occur until we reach key-bottom. So it can affect only the after-motion.

After-motion following chord

P.: Quite right. Now let us remember that the essential component in the after-motion is the raising of the wrist in an arc over the playing finger. Where does the axis of this circular wrist-movement run?

W.: It corresponds exactly to the length of the keyboard.

P.: If the hand rests on two fingers, as we are now assuming, what is the relation of the axis of movement to these two points of support?

W.: It connects them. It runs through the key-rod length-wise, as a line connecting the two squeezing-points.

P.: Right. Therefore this axis is no longer a purely imaginary geometric line, but it has reality and substance in the key-rod. If we really do squeeze the key-rod, our grasping fingers cannot slip off during the after-motion once they have taken their stand, whereas they most certainly will if they do not have this guidance from point B, but make an aiming motion from point A.

K.: But an axis can connect only two arbitrarily chosen points. What if more than two fingers are playing?

P.: Haven't we said that in this case there are still only two fingers which are the main carrying fingers, and therefore they are those between which the key-rod is formed? Let us consider the typical case of a widespread chord to be played with four or five fingers, in which the thumb and the little finger clasp firmly back towards the elbow and thus function as the pillars for the playing of the chord. These two fingers will squeeze a long key-rod at the end of the key-moving action, and the points at which they squeeze the key-rod will now become the centres for the after-motion. The wrist rises around the connecting line between these two points. The pads of the thumb and little finger remain where they are, while those of the other fingers slide on their keys towards the piano lid (cf. Fig. 14 opposite p. 173). This and the return move-ment with sinking wrist cannot be practised too often. In this exercise the fact that the two main grasping fingers hold their position and the others slide is the best proof that the movements really are being made from point B.

H.: It is clear that during the whole of this exercise, in wrist-lowering as well as in wrist-raising, the spreading of the fingers and of the middle hand must be retained, since it is one of the conditions for the squeezing of the key-rod.

K.: Do I understand correctly that in the after-motion there is no difference between those fingers which have not played at all and those which have played, but are not the main carrying fingers?

P.: On the basis of the note value, which is usually the same for all tones to be played, we naturally require, in principle, that in the after-motion only fingers over keys that have not been played should slide at key-top, while those on the keys that have been played should slide at key-bottom. But in view of the smaller musical importance of the inner voices, it is no crime against the musical meaning if a player with small hands has all fingers, with the exception of the main carrying ones, at key-top during the after-motion and accomplishes the continuing vibration of the inner voices with the pedal.

K.: Good, I understand that. But one thing more: you have just called the circular raising of the wrist around the playing fingers "the most essential component" of the after-motion, but it seems to me that it is the only possible movement. If two bodies, in this case hand and keyboard, are connected at two points, namely, the two finger-key joints, then only one movement is possible; and that is the movement around the axis which connects the two joints. Any other movement in one of the two joints would release the contact in the other joint. If, for instance, in the given case a supination were carried out, the contact of the little finger with the key would remain while the thumb would be lifted from the keyboard.

P.:   That would be quite true if the hand with its fingers were an inflexible mass.

K.:   Oh yes! We must also consider that the hand is capable of changing its form.

P.:   Quite right. However, this changing the form of the hand does not permit an unlimited choice of movements. On the contrary, what we have said (p. 100) about the combination of pronation and supination with wrist-swinging applies to this very situation where the hand rests on two fingers, as you can easily see for yourself. Therefore, it applied particularly to the playing of the chord when we said (p. 160), speaking of the first tone in general, that at the beginning of the after-motion a supination occurs combined with wrist-swinging towards the median plane and followed by an oblique rise towards the back of the hand.

W.:   We keep speaking of an after-motion in connection with chords. Does this mean that the playing of each chord is followed by an after-motion?

P.:   As we agreed, we have concentrated on the intense isolated chord, which has the greatest possibility to continue sounding, and we have recognized that an after-motion in the large grasping unit is really necessary in this case. It is obvious that a staccato chord, for instance, will make quite different demands on us.

W.:   What demands?

P.:   There is a time for everything. Before dealing with that, we will take up the technique of the second tone tomorrow.

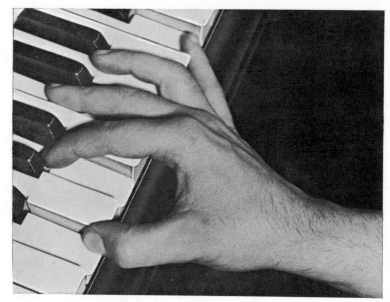

Figure 13. Squeezing the key-rod. Hand of Jörg Demus.

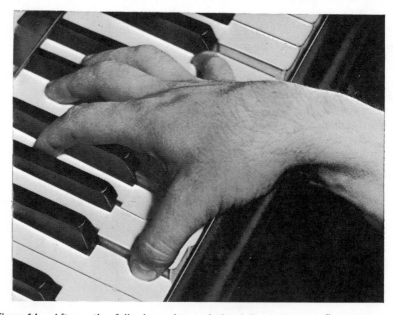

Figure 14. After-motion following an intense isolated chord. Hand of Jörg Demus.

DIALOGUE 8

The Technique of the Second Tone and the Cradle

H.:   Well then today we shall talk first of all about the technique of the second tone.

W.:   If I understand correctly it is the technique to be used in legato.

P.:   What do you understand by legato?

W.:   What any pianist understands, namely that the key about to be played moves down from key-top before the preceding key has begun to rise from key-bottom.

P.:   That we shall briefly call "binding from key-bottom to key-bottom". But we must be conscious of the fact that this sequence of events is only one aspect of binding, i.e., the purely temporal one, and that nothing has yet been done to create coherence in a musical idea.

W.:   Of course not; this musical coherence is really independent of legato, since coherence must be striven for not only in legato but can be just as necessary in staccato.

P.:   Quite right. And precisely for that reason our technique, which transmits the experience of musical coherence to the listener, has to be independent of the binding from key-bottom to key-bottom, because in staccato there is certainly no such binding.

K.:   If this problem of musical coherence is independent of legato, why do you bring it up in this context?

P.:   Because when I bind from key-bottom to key-bottom and when I try to make you feel a musical idea as a whole, I am in both cases striving for a kind of coherence. The first is the purely outer, the second — the essential inner coherence. If you allow me to make a comparison with high politics: Two countries can be bound by a treaty; this is an outer bond. Or they may be bound by sincere friendship between their peoples, by the same way of thinking, by reciprocal adjustment of their economic life; that is an inner bond. How many examples there are in history which show that a treaty is no more than a scrap of paper if it is not based upon an inner bond between the two peoples. Just so,

Binding from key-bottom to key-bottom and musical coherence

174

it is absolutely impossible to convey to the listener the real experience of legato simply by a binding from key-bottom to key-bottom,
if the playing has not achieved inner coherence.

K.:   Logically, this would mean that the experience of legato
can also be conveyed without any binding from key-bottom to
key-bottom, if the technique takes care of the inner coherence.

P.:   Quite so. And we shall come across cases in which the
legato effect has to be achieved without binding from key-bottom
to key-bottom.

K.:   To sum up what I have gathered from this, there are, in
principle, three possibilities for achieving coherence:

1)   the purely outer coherence by binding from key-bottom
to key-bottom — we have given our verdict against this already and
so we are interested in it only for its inadequacy;

2)   the purely inner musical coherence;

3)   the inner musical coherence combined with binding from
key-bottom to key-bottom.

P.:   That's right. The second and third possibilities will have
to be considered as techniques of equally full value.

K.:   But what do you mean when you speak of the "technique of the second tone"? Is it a question of achieving inner
musical coherence only, or this coherence combined with binding
from key-bottom to key-bottom?

P.:   The second tone relates to the latter, i.e., binding from
key-bottom to key-bottom, which must be carried out in a way
that will convey the experience of musical coherence. Of course,
we shall as far as possible strive for a union of outer and inner
coherence, just as countries with mutual understanding will
probably conclude an alliance by means of a treaty. And not
before we have fully understood this technique of the second tone
shall we be able to answer the question of how to achieve musical
coherence without binding from key-bottom to key-bottom.

K.:   And why can't the technique of the second tone always
be applied to the attainment of musical coherence?

P.:   Because there are natural limits to the applicability of
this technique. If you consider that we are concerned with binding
from key-bottom to key-bottom, you will understand right away
in which cases we cannot apply this technique.

W.:   First, when the interval between the two successive
tones is greater than the span of the hand, and, further, in cases
when both tones have to be played with the same finger.

P.:   When we apply the second limitation to chords, it means

Limits to applicability

that they can be connected by means of the technique of the second tone only if none of the fingers used in the first chord are to be used in the following chord. Therefore, chords with four or five tones are excluded from the technique of the second tone. But for sequences of two-toned chords, such as short runs in thirds or the inward resolution of the interval of the diminished fifth on the leading note — e.g., B–F to C–E — or the like, the technique of the second tone is applicable.

K.: You have just indicated some typical chord-sequences that have to be played according to the technique of the second tone. Are there any typical sequences of single tones that are played in this way?

W.: Well, probably scales and broken chords.

P.: Yes; but let me state expressly that the term "second-tone technique" must in no way be understood as synonymous with what we usually call "scale technique". The scale is only one of the many areas to which we may apply the second-tone technique. Because scales have special requirements, and also because they lack certain complications, e.g., there are no chords in them, scale technique is a special subtype of the technique of the second tone, and we shall often have to refer to it without using it as the model of the second tone in general. We shall consider primarily a technique in which any sequence of single tones or chords attains the greatest possible coherence and binding from key-bottom to key-bottom.

H.: Although for the sake of simplicity we choose our words as though we were dealing only with single tones connected from key-bottom, we must always remember that what we say refers equally to chords.

P.: Yes. And now let us consider how this binding can be brought about. We must start from the following situation: After we have moved a key, the arm-chain hangs between the breastbone-collarbone joint at one end and the finger resting on the key in key-bottom at the other end. Now another key is to be played by another finger. How can this come about?

Small grasping unit

W.: Since the answer must also suit a situation in which more than one finger is already resting in key-bottom — as was just stipulated — all one can say is that the next key can be played only by a finger movement.

P.: Quite right. Therefore, the technique of the second tone is a finger technique.

W.: It is, then, a technique of the small grasping unit,

whereas in our example of the first-tone technique we had to use the large grasping unit.

P.: Yes. But the difference is more far-reaching. Notice that here we meet the grasping movement right at the beginning, whereas in the case of the first tone we did not encounter it until the after-motion. With the first tone the centre for the key-moving action was in the shoulder or in the breastbone-collarbone joint — in short, at point A — whereas with the second tone this centre of motion is in the basal joint of the finger.

K.: Then point A is now in the basal joint of the finger.

P.: No, because for our definition of points A and B it is not enough that they are centres of motion; first and foremost they must be centres for the effect of force.

K.: That is just the situation here. For if the playing of the second tone comes about by finger movement, then it occurs by means of the force of this finger movement.

P.: This logic of yours seems so convincing that practically the whole world of piano playing is dominated by it. But if we make a certain comparison, you will immediately realise the rashness of your conclusion. To make it as graphic as possible, we shall suppose that the two fingers which play after each other are next to each other, such as the 2nd and 3rd. Just look at them a moment. Don't they have a certain similarity to two legs?

Comparison with walking

K.: Yes. The basal joints of the fingers would correspond to the two hip joints and the middle joints to the knees.

P.: The important thing is that the finger resting at point B has to carry part of the weight of the arm in its basal joint, just as the leg carries the weight of the trunk in the hip joint. Isn't that right?

K.: No doubt, although there is a difference in that the two hip joints are connected through the pelvis, whereas the two basal joints of neighbouring fingers lack such a transverse connection.

P.: It is true there is no bony bridge here like the pelvis. But don't forget, we require that the hand be in a constant condition of middle-hand spreading, by which we achieve a mechanical result similar to that given by the bony bridge, viz., firmness. Therefore, I feel absolutely justified in using the term "knuckle bridge" to express this mechanical unity of the spread basal knuckles, 2 to 5.

K.: Yes, admitted. I must further admit that the hip joint is the centre of motion for leg movements, as in stepping out, in the same way that the basal joint is the centre of motion for the finger movement which you just mentioned in relation to the second-tone technique.

P.:   Then we agree that the transition from one key-moving action to the next according to the technique of the second tone can in every respect be compared to the activity of walking.

K.:   Yes. I would then have to imagine that the floor consists of giant keys and that I am standing with one leg on one of those keys.

Supporting and playing fingers

P.:   That is the supporting leg. In the same way, the finger with which I have just played is the supporting finger. And what about the other finger — or in the comparison, the other leg?

K.:   At this moment, it is practically idle. But it won't be so for very long, since it is about to play.

P.:   Then let us speak of a "playing finger" and "playing leg" respectively. And now, how does the playing finger — or the playing leg — move the key? You have taken it as a matter of course that the force that moves the key down must come from the muscles of the finger, because there is a movement of the finger. Transfer this train of thought to the person standing on the giant keyboard.

K.:   Then I would have to say that the force with which the playing leg pushes down the next giant key must come from the muscles of the playing leg.

P.:   And would that be correct?

K.:   Only if I were to stamp with the playing leg instead of walking. But in walking, the muscles of the leg have nothing more to do than to bring the playing leg to the top of the giant key. The pressing-down would occur through body weight, which is carried over from one leg to the other.

P.:   Right. And what corresponds to this body weight in the real situation of playing the piano with the hand?

K.:   That again would be the weight apparatus, as we have said.

P.:   Then we can recapitulate: Although the second-tone technique is a finger technique, the force for playing does not originate in the finger movement but in the weight apparatus, just as in the first-tone technique. The finger movements, however, do serve to carry over the load of the weight apparatus from one key to the next.

W.:   But if it is the weight apparatus which actually moves the key in both first- and second-tone techniques, what is the great difference between the two?

Technique of point B

P.: Don't forget that in the first-tone technique point B appears during the key-moving action. Therefore, it cannot become a centre of motion before the after-motion. The key-moving action itself occurs around point A. The origin of force and the centre of motion were united at A. It is entirely different with the second tone. Just as the leg, in walking, guides the movements from its point of support on the floor, so the finger, standing on the finger-key joint, guides the movements of the playing apparatus. In short, the technique of the second tone is a technique of point B. In addition, point A remains constantly in the breastbone-collarbone joint, not as the centre of any movement in any direction whatsoever, but only as a centre for the vertically downward direction of the weight, which indeed must be constantly active so that it can be carried over from one finger to another. Whereas with the first-tone technique, the activity of the weight and length-adjusting apparatuses around point A alternates with the activity of the grasping apparatus around point B (pp. 164–165), in the case of the second-tone technique the grasping apparatus around B and weight apparatus around A must invariably be active simultaneously — one to produce movement, the other to provide force.

H.: Here lies the root of all mistakes. They arise when the separateness of the tasks of the two apparatuses is not observed, as when we try to obtain the force from the grasping apparatus or to direct movement from point A.

Aiming finger motion

K.: Aha! "Force from the grasping apparatus", that is what I thought was a logical outcome of the concept of a finger technique, but we have found it would mean stamping instead of walking.

P.: Yes, but in the case of the finger we had better say that it would mean aiming instead of grasping. And so many piano techniques are based on this aiming. What objections can we raise against such techniques?

W.: Chiefly, that the aiming implies a push against the key, which causes a noisy vibration — and all the other consequences that, as we know, run contrary to the demands of the piano.

P.: Yes; and besides this, let us consider whether it tallies with the requirement for an accelerated motion towards key-bottom.

K.: If I understand correctly, this aiming of the finger, which is comparable to stamping, is an extension in the middle and terminal joints of the finger combined with a simultaneous flexion in the basal joint. If the rate of extension at the angle is constant, a simple geometrical calculation tells us that the movement of the finger tip away from the basal knuckle is a retarded motion.

P.:   Would you reveal this "simple geometrical calculation" for us? I would like to have exact proof of this.

K.:   For exact proof we have to go into trigonometry.

H.:   For heaven's sake let us avoid that!

K.:   Then the following diagram (Fig. 15) will make these facts concrete and plausible. I have represented the finger here by straight lines, showing it in three different positions. In the first position, the angles at the middle and terminal joints are $120°$; in

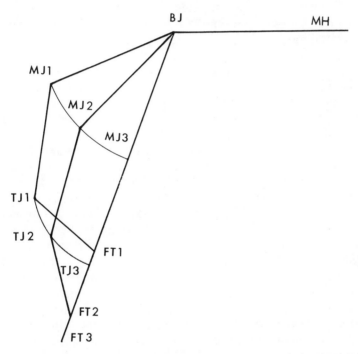

Figure 15.   The finger is moved in such a way that the combination of extension in the middle joint (MJ) and terminal joint (TJ) with flexion in the basal joint (BJ) caused the finger tip (FT) to move in a straight line away from the basal knuckle. Three positions are shown: in the first (BJ-MJ1-TJ1-FT1) middle and terminal joints are flexed at an angle of $120°$, in the second (BJ-MJ2-TJ2-FT2) — $150°$, and in the third (BJ-MJ3-TJ3-FT3) these joints are extended to $180°$. Consequently, the difference between two consecutive positions amounts to extension of $30°$ in the middle and terminal joints each time. As can be seen, the distance covered by the finger tip during the first extension of $30°$ (FT1-FT2) is more than double the distance it covers during the second extension (FT2-FT3).

the second — 150°; and in the third — 180°, i.e., completely extended. So in going over from the first to the second position and from the second to the third there is an extension of 30°. Further, I have assumed that in this movement the finger tip moves away from the basal knuckle in a straight line. You can see at a glance that in the first 30° extension the finger tip passes over more than double the distance of that in the second 30° extension. That means a retarded motion.

P.:   Q.E.D.

K.:   This retarded motion of the finger tip is a result of a constant rate of extension at the middle and terminal joints. You can imagine that the rate of extension would have to be greatly accelerated to move the finger tip with constant velocity, and an accelerated movement of the finger tip could hardly be achieved at all.

P.:   So for this reason, too, the force of the aiming finger-movement must not be used to move the key. We must also remember that the weight of the arm — which, in walking along with our fingers, we transfer from one finger to another — remains constant; and so it is possible that the volume of the tone can remain the same and can be regulated by the weight apparatus. On the contrary the force with which we can throw the separate aiming fingers into the keys differs with each finger, so that the volume of each tone is left to chance, i.e., to the strength of the separate fingers. You know how pianists are always trying to make the separate fingers equally strong, but the attempt goes against nature. The dear Lord has made the fingers of different strength, so it is ridiculous for man to try to make them equal in strength. No good can come of it, as Schumann learned when he completely ruined his hands for piano playing by such experiments. If we want to have equal force in fingers of different strength, then we must place at their disposal the weight of the arm, which works on all fingers equally and can be varied for each of them with the same precision.

H.:   Now that we very clearly understand the positive sides of the required technique by explaining the negative sides of the techniques we have rejected, it is high time to describe how the second tone is actually played.

P.:   By all means! Already in speaking of the first tone, we have said that the after-motion can be varied according to the role of the played tone in the musical context. So far we have only dealt with the possibility that an intense isolated chord is followed

Preparatory finger-grasp

by another intense isolated chord. Naturally, it is different when a first tone is followed not by another first tone, but by a second tone. So we must come in at that moment when the first tone has just been played but an after-motion has not yet been made, and we must ask ourselves how this after-motion must be made in preparation for the second tone.

K.:   You speak now as though a second tone always has to be preceded by a first tone. But didn't you say earlier that it can be preceded by a second tone as well?

P.:   Quite right. But since the binding of the second tone to the preceding first tone must be exactly like that to a preceding second tone, we have to create — by means of the after-motion following a preceding first tone — a situation as though a second tone had preceded.

K.:   And how can you do that?

P.:   We know how from what we have already said about the technique of the second tone, namely, that it is a technique of the small grasping unit. Accordingly, what kind of an after-motion must follow a first tone when a second tone succeeds it?

W.:   It must be a grasping with the small grasping unit.

P.:   Then please describe the after-motion in the small grasping unit, which we need here.

W.:   If it is the thumb which has played, it will grasp towards the basal hollow of the 4th finger (p. 96). If it was one of the fingers 2 – 5, it will grasp towards the wrist end of the thumb ball (p. 97).

P.:   And what is the result of this grasping movement?

W.:   The basal knuckles rise up and forward in a circle around point B. This naturally pulls the wrist and elbow forward, and they, too, rise from their former position. But the highest point is the basal knuckle, so that the hand hangs downward from the basal knuckle.

P.:   That's right. With this motion, the finger that has played the first tone becomes the first supporting finger for the subsequent playing of the second tone.

K.:   And now another finger can begin to play, can't it?

P.:   No. First we will have to make another preparatory motion. You will readily understand this from the comparison with walking. Imagine you want to walk eastwards, but you are standing so that you face north. Will you begin to walk immediately?

K.:   Of course not. Perhaps I could dance an "ecossaise"

Back of hand facing direction of stepping forward

like that, but not walk. First I must turn to the direction in which I want to walk.

P.:   We must do the same with the hand, then.

K.:   But what does it mean for the hand to turn in a certain direction?

P.:   Remember that the fingers are always more or less laterally weighted. Thus they differ from the legs, which are always weighted lengthwise in walking. The weight, affecting the finger from the side, will therefore be carried by the short lateral finger-muscles; and it is left to the long flexors and extensors to perform the fingers' weightless steps and thus accomplish motion along the keyboard. Every child, who uses his fingers to represent a little man running across the table top, realises that the natural way of making finger-steps is with the nail facing forward. In this position the weaker extensors have only to make the single fingers step forward from the basal joint, whereas the stronger flexors pull the hand along.

K.:   According to that, we are facing the stepping-off direction if we take a position of supination for a succession of notes moving away from the median plane, and a position of pronation for one moving towards it.

P.:   Yes, we'll keep to that rule in general.

K.:   Only in general? Why not always?

P.:   Notice that we have arrived at this rule from the idea of stepping forward. Now, when I step forward, not only do my legs move but my whole body moves onward. In the same way, stepping forward on the keyboard is not the concern of the fingers alone, but of the whole playing apparatus. For instance, if I play a scale over one or two octaves, not only do my fingers take seven or fourteen steps, but my hand, too, moves one or two octaves further. Therefore, in this case my hand must face the direction for stepping forward.

W.:   That means an ascending scale in the right hand or a descending scale in the left must be played in supination, whereas pronation must be used for descending in the right and ascending in the left.

P.:   Obviously. Now, in contrast, consider a broken chord. Notice that this term is not only a musical, but also a technical, statement. It is a chord the single tones of which are played in succession instead of together.

Broken chords

W.:   And just as the hand has a set position in playing the chord, it also keeps one position in breaking the chord and does not move up and down the keyboard. Hence, we need not change the hand position into the momentary direction of stepping forward, when in Alberti basses, for example, the sequence of tones is reversed after every three tones.

P.:   Yes. And even if the broken chord is so wide that we would be unable to play all the notes at once, thus necessitating a certain slight movement of the entire hand up and down the keyboard, we must not forget that some dancing steps can also be made in a different direction than forward — as the doctor just mentioned — and so in this instance we can keep our hand position unchanged in both up- and downward steps. What hand position would we choose in such cases?

W.:   Supination of course, since it is the more natural one and accords with the force of gravity and the structure of the arm.

P.:   Quite correct. At the same time we must always bear in mind that a supine position like this must not involve fixation in this position. On the contrary, here as always, there must be complete rotatory freedom to go over to any other chosen position.

H.:   So much for the exceptional case of broken chords. As a rule, however, it is necessary to face the direction for stepping forward. How is this position to be reached?

W.:   By means of a pronatory or supinatory movement.

P.:   Now let us remember that in the arm-chain which hangs freely between points A and B, and is directed from point B, pronatory and supinatory movements cannot usually be carried out in isolation (cf. p. 100).

W.:   But supination is associated with a wrist swing towards the median plane, and pronation with a swing away from the median plane.

P.:   That will happen here, too. However, we have established the limitation (pp. 100–101) that this combination of movements occurs in this way only with a low wrist.

Geometrically high and low wrist

W.:   Doesn't the wrist always have to be low?

P.:   Naturally, it must always be dynamically low, which means that no push against the key is allowed. Whether it is also geometrically low will depend upon what position results from the other conditions at the time. With the intense isolated chord, the heavy weight appended naturally produces a low wrist position, out of which a very extensive lifting can follow by means of the after-motion of the large grasping unit. But the technique of the second tone — in which it is never possible to append the greatest weight — is a technique of the small grasping unit, so that the movements in the large grasping unit are technically irrelevant; in principle, any position of the wrist can be taken.

W.: But which one is preferable?

P.: Here, too, the low position — if for no other reason than that there is a greater danger that a geometrically high wrist will become dynamically high, too. We shall mention a further advantage of the geometrically low wrist later (p. 196). Nevertheless, we must not neglect the high wrist-positions. Exercises for a clean touch with a high wrist produce a special freedom in controlling the whole playing apparatus.

W.: But shall we also use it when we are playing a piece of music?

P.: Yes. Consider that putting the thumb under a high hand is easier than under a low hand.

W.: That means we should play scales with a high wrist, since the thumb is continually being put under in scales.

P.: Yes. So how can we describe the position of the hand in scale playing?

W.: We can say that the wrist always precedes the fingers in the direction of movement. For in playing away from the median plane, the position of supination with a high wrist results in an inner wrist-triangle; in playing towards the median plane, the position of pronation with a high wrist results in an outer wrist-triangle (cf. p. 100).

P.: Yes. That is the situation resulting from a high wrist. You are perfectly at liberty to classify this hand position under the heading "scale technique", but you must keep in mind that this is just the most comfortable position for playing scales, and not the only one possible. We can play scales also with a geometrically low wrist, such as we prefer in other subtypes of the second-tone technique.

H.: This playing with low wrist brings us back to the combination of movements, characteristic of the second-tone technique, that consists of rotation, wrist swing and finger grasp. Finger-grasping is a combination of conical grasping with flexion, as we have repeatedly stated, and the wrist swing varies in direction according to whether the rotation is pronatory or supinatory.

P.: We hardly need to stress that all this refers to a movement around point B and that, therefore, this movement is directed by the grasping finger.

H.: By this movement the hand has at least come into a position from which the playing of a second tone can start. After all, that was the purpose of the movement.

P.: As we know, when this second tone is played, what happens is that the "playing finger" becomes a "supporting finger".
And just as in walking, this transformation cannot come about
suddenly. In walking, between the moment when one leg is still
completely unburdened and the other moment when it has to carry
the weight of the whole body alone, there is an intermediate stage
in which that leg and the former supporting leg carry the weight
of the body together. During this intermediate stage, the previously
unburdened leg gradually takes over more and more of the weight
of the body from the former supporting leg, and thus is gradually
transformed into a supporting leg. Accordingly, we must distinguish three phases for the playing finger.

W.: Naturally, in the first phase it still is completely unburdened; the second phase is that of metamorphosis; and in the
third phase it has become a supporting finger.

P.: Now let us observe the finger in the first phase, while it
is idle. What condition is it in?

W.: Completely relaxed as regards flexion and extension,
i.e., its terminal and middle joints must not be tensed.

P.: This condition of complete freedom from tension must,
of course, remain during the following phases even though loco-
motive force appears in them. What kind of movement will the
finger have to make?

W.: A grasp in the small grasping unit, i.e., a conical grasp.

P.: Which do you mean — the one towards the former supporting finger, or the one away from it?

W.: Since the grasping movement must be directed downwards, and because the back of the hand is facing the direction of
playing, it can only be a conical grasp directed away from the former
supporting finger; but in continuing the circumduction arc, it would
finally lead back to this finger.

P.: And which points have we learned to be the targets of
these grasping movements?

W.: With the thumb, the basal hollow of the 4th finger;
with the other four fingers, the wrist end of the thumb ball.

K.: But, of course, we do not reach either of the
targets.

H.: And even less in playing with a high wrist than in playing with a low wrist, because, as you can easily see, the grasping
movement can bring only the geometrically low wrist really close
to the key and to the finger which is supported there.

W.: According to what we have said the other day (p. 96),
this means that there is no flexion in the middle and terminal joints

of the finger when playing with a high wrist, whereas in playing with a low wrist slight flexion is necessary.

H.: Yes, you can see that at any time. But what matters is that any flexion necessary in the middle and terminal joints is made without antagonistic tensions.

P.: Correct. Through this grasping movement the playing finger is to become a supporting finger. When does the phase of metamorphosis begin? At the inception of the movement, at its end, or some time in between?

W.: Judging by what we've said about the firm key, i.e., the oppostion which the key sets up against its downward movement from the very beginning, the metamorphosis must begin at the moment the finger has reached the top of the key to be played and when it begins to move it downwards from key-top.

P.: That implies that already at key-top the finger begins to transfer a part of the weight of the playing apparatus to the new key which is to be played.

K.: Of course; and it is also in complete accordance with our original requirement that the force of the key-moving action must stem from the weight apparatus. If, on the other hand, the transference of weight should not occur until after key-bottom has been reached, it would come too late for the key-moving action, which would then have resulted not from the weight apparatus but from the force of the finger movement.

H.: The spatial arrangement of the fingers also favours a quick transfer of the weight from the finger which is giving up its supporting function to the finger which is about to take over this function. Since the back of the hand is facing the direction in which it is moving forward, the basal joint of the playing finger is lower than that of the former supporting finger, and so it can easily take over the weight from below.

P.: It is a similar situation when a stevedore takes over a load from the shoulders of his mate. He will bend his knees until his shoulders are lower than those of the other man in order to unburden him from below.

K.: We see from all this that the finger which is now becoming the support does everything itself in taking over the whole weight, so that the former supporting finger has to do hardly anything to get rid of the weight.

P.: Of course, the continuation of the grasping movement by the new supporting finger after it has reached key-bottom would suffice to lift the former supporting finger completely from

Unburdening
from below

the key. However, as the grasping movement proceeds, its vertical component becomes less and less, and thus the former supporting finger would be lifted gradually and hesitantly; therefore, the ending of the played tone would be undecided and blurred. But remember that the word "legato" expresses the binding together of two successive tones, not a vague fusion between them. So, on the contrary we must be most careful to avoid blurring them. In order to achieve clear articulation, we must actively jerk up the former supporting finger from the key.

H.:   By this jerk we mechanically gain a continual renewal of hand-spreading.

P.:   And the spreading of the middle hand is particularly important in the second-tone technique, because the knuckle-bridge thus formed at the basal knuckles enables the weight to be transferred from the supporting to the playing finger without wobbling, i.e., in a controlled manner. So from this point of view also, jerking up the former supporting finger contributes to clearness of articulation.

H.:   What we have described is the succession of movements in normal performance. But if, when practising, we make these movements in slow motion and can stop them at any desired moment, it will pay to glance at the situation in which both supporting fingers, the former and the new, find themselves at key-bottom.

W.:   At that moment it is the same as in playing a chord.

H.:   But, as a rule, there will be no similarity to the typical chord which is carried by the thumb and little finger, since any two fingers may be there at key-bottom. In the case of such chords, we have repeatedly stated that it is usually impossible to burden the fingers as far laterally as we normally strive to do in first-tone technique. The same will very often be the case in second-tone technique, and it is not too inconvenient: Because of the presence of two supporting fingers, the weight on one finger is not so great that an exclusively lateral weighting is absolutely necessary.

P.:   But since the two fingers have arrived at a chord situation at key-bottom, what must happen if the two played keys are not immediately adjacent?

W.:   The key-rod is squeezed, and by this means the vaulted hand achieves firmness.

P.:   I should hope that firmness of the hand would have been achieved before then. Haven't we just stressed the special importance of the firm knuckle-bridge — because of its effect on middle-hand spreading — for the second-tone technique? But it is entirely true that the firmness already there is enhanced by squeezing the key-rod.

H.: That, however, is not the only reason why it is important that the finger, grasping towards a white key in a conical grasp, should finally reach the side of the adjacent key, which is behind it in relation to the direction in which the hand is moving forward, and that here the finger should find its support. But by virtue of this, the turning of the hand towards the direction in which it is to move gains a further significance, because in this way the hand can be moved on in this direction by an after-flexion of the grasping finger. And so every grasp really becomes a stepping forward.

P.: That's true. Of course, on the black keys we attain lateral support by grasping against the margin of the key which we are playing.

H.: Yet we must not get the idea that forward movement occurs only by these finger steps. It also originates, to a great extent, from point A — especially in fast runs; i.e., the length-adjusting and direction-changing apparatus leads the wrist, and with it the fingers, laterally along the keyboard, just as it does when we slide the hand along the tops of the keys.

P.: That applies especially to scale playing, because then we cannot support the playing finger against the side of the adjacent key, since this key is still in key-bottom. So our former (p. 184) statement — that, geometrically speaking, the wrist leads in scale playing — now acquires significance in the dynamic respect, since in this case the forward movement is carried over from the wrist to the fingers and not the other way round.

W.: Now probably everything about the metamorphosis phase has been said; the playing finger has become a supporting finger at last. In this third phase is there also an after-motion, as there was for the technique of the first tone?

P.: If by after-motion you mean a new movement which has not yet started, certainly not. What would be the use of that? But just as in the technique of the first tone we learned that the after-motion is a run-off of the grasping intended during the key-moving action, so in the nature of things the grasping movement can continue here, too, when it has fulfilled its immediate task of moving the newly played key to key-bottom and lifting the previous supporting finger from its key.

W.: How far does this run-off go? If I understand correctly, it is a raising of the basal knuckle around point B.

Stepping forward

"Standing away from key"

P.: Here we are as little able to say exactly how far as we were in the case of the after-motion following the first tone. But much more important than the actual extent to which the basal knuckle is lifted, is the continuous existence of a tendency to lift it.

W.: How can there be a continuous tendency for a movement without it actually occurring?

P.: Let us remember what we said in general about the grasping movement in the small grasping unit.

W.: It consists of a conical movement in the basal joint combined with finger-flexion.

P.: And we know that the conical movement soon comes to a stop because of the construction of the basal joint, while the flexion can very well go on as far as you want. It is the conical movement that gives the finger firmness against the weight, while its contribution to the actual raising of the knuckle can be only slight, because the motion ends so soon. On the other hand, the knuckle can be raised as far as you like by finger-flexion.

W.: Now I understand. The flexion components of the grasping movement can be stopped in any position. But the tendency for conical movement must continue if the grasping finger is to retain its firmness. And that is absolutely necessary.

P.: Since this tendency for conical movement also implies a continuous tendency to raise the basal knuckle around point B, we can compare the ensuing relation between the supporting finger and the key to that between the supporting apparatus and the chair top. We refused to say, "I sit on the chair" — because of the continuously active tendency of the supporting apparatus to straighten up — and preferred to say, "I sit away from the chair"; just so, in this case, it is not, "The supporting finger stands on the key", but much more correctly, "The supporting finger stands away from the key".

H.: Moreover, in this connection we must remember what we have said (p. 163) about the part the middle and terminal joints of the finger play in the grasping movement.

W.: Since finger-flexion should occur, if possible, exclusively in the basal joint, the other two joints will not be flexed more than they were in the position of rest.

P.: But that means that the distance of the basal knuckle from the point of support on the key does not decrease. So although we cannot speak here of an active extension, yet we are concerned to prevent the finger from collapsing; and so from this point of view also, we find a tendency away from the key, a "standing-away-from-the-key".

H.: For the beginner it is, of course, important to check repeatedly whether all these force relationships actually exist; and, therefore, he will do well to stop the course of movement at this moment also and check the condition of his finger.

P.: He can test not only the condition of his supporting finger but also the overall condition of his playing apparatus and of his whole body. If necessary, he can correct himself by making some intermediate movements at this point. All this can be achieved if, without giving up the grasping tendency of the finger, one makes movements in the finger-key joint in the main directions of all three degrees of freedom in this joint.

W.: The first of these three movements is surely the same as the one we have already discussed as an exercise to follow the playing of the first tone.

P.: Yes; raising and lowering the wrist in a circle around the supporting finger by means of alternate tensing and relaxing of the underside wrist muscles. With these movements we check how far the elbow — and after playing a distant key, the shoulder blade, too — can be freely pulled forward, i.e., to what extent the length-adjusting apparatus is relaxed.

W.: The second movement would be that of the wrist to and away from the median plane around the vertical axis running through the supporting finger.

P.: It is obvious that in this lateral movement the lateral support of the finger against the adjacent key is particularly impor-tant; this support alternates between the lower and the higher adjacent key in inward and outward movements respectively.

H.: That means that if we perform these movements alter-nately in each direction, the finger tip slides alternately inwards and outwards on the played key.

K.: Before it can do so, the weight apparatus must be relaxed as much as possible, because otherwise the pressure would cause the finger tip to stick somewhere.

P.: Of course, we relax first to the extent that the weight of the arm alone remains operative, which suffices to keep the key at key-bottom. The same goes for the next movement.

W.: The third movement would be rotation around an axis corresponding to the lengthwise direction of the key.

P.: Yes, and since before the beginning of this rotation, we let the basal knuckle and wrist sink until the middle and nail members of the finger lie almost horizontally on the key, it is a rotation around the lengthwise axis of the finger itself.

W.:   And, therefore, around that of the hand and forearm, too.

P.:   Not at all, since in doing so we have not given up the grasp by flexion in the basal joint of the finger.

W.:   Oh, I see! So it is not a question of pure pronation and supination, but the wrist swings around the finger like a pendulum.

H.:   Nevertheless, pronation and supination are the most essential components of this movement.

P.:   Yes, and since we have relieved the finger of as much of its burden as possible, we can make the motion in such a way that the finger does not roll away sideways on the key like a wheel, but turns around its axis of length while staying in the same place at the side of an adjacent key, like a wheel turning on ice.

K.:   The purpose of this exercise, I suppose, is to test the pronatory and supinatory freedom of the whole playing apparatus.

P.:   Yes. With perfect freedom of rotation we should attain movement through the entire 360°, i.e., we must be able to supinate as well as pronate up to the point where the nail lies on the key (cf. Fig. 16).

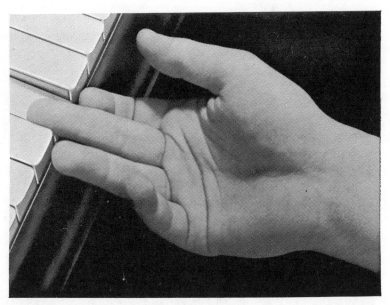

Figure 16.   Intermediate movement to ensure freedom of rotation. Hand of Jörg Demus.

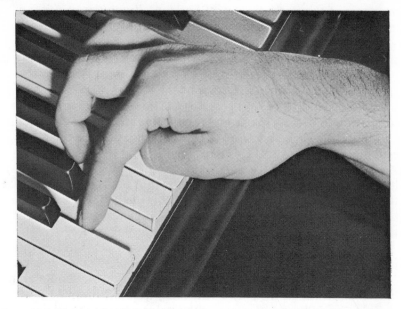

Figure 17. Scale playing. Putting the thumb under immediately after it has played. Hand of Jörg Dumus.

Figure 18. Inner cradle. Hand of Jörg Demus.

Figure 19.   Outer cradle.   Hand of Jörg Demus.

H.:   But don't let us forget that all these movements are pointless if the grasping tendency in the fingers does not continue to be active during them.

K.:   If I understand you correctly, these intermediate movements last for minutes. Would they, therefore, be totally eliminated in playing a piece of music?

P.:   Well, yes, but we sometimes find an opportunity when playing to make one or another of these movements to a limited degree, and thus to loosen a tension that has suddenly crept in. These exercises serve to bring about a physical condition that the performing pianist should really have permanently. When this condition has been achieved in the playing apparatus and in the body as a whole, the movements can be cut down to a minimum — although the ability to make them has risen to a maximum.

H.:   At the conclusion of all these intermediate movements, the supporting finger must, of course, make the movement that we already know as a combination of rotation and lateral wrist-swinging with grasping, by means of which the hand arrives in the position where the next finger can begin its grasping movement.

K.:   Now we have come full circle: We would be repeating ourselves if we were to describe the further course of movement.

P.:   Nevertheless, we must keep in mind that we have only five fingers on one hand, but the sequence of notes in one direction is often much longer.

W.: For that we have to put the thumb under the fingers or the fingers over the thumb, as every beginner knows from playing scales.

P.: It does not occur only in scale playing, though. Yet we shall use this typical case as a basis for our observations. Take an ascending scale with the right hand — in what position is the hand?

W.: In supination.

P.: Let it be a scale beginning on a white key, so that the thumb plays first. How does it grasp?

W.: With a tendency to move towards the basal hollow of the 4th finger, being spread away as far as possible from the basal knuckle of the 2nd finger.

P.: Good. Next the 2nd finger grasps. This grasp of the index finger lifts the thumb off the key. What do we do with it now? Do we leave it where it happens to be? Do we ignore it for the present, since we know that we shall not use it again until after the 3rd, or perhaps even after the 4th finger?

W.: No. Since we know how much fluency in playing is gained if a finger is beforehand at the spot where it is supposed to play later (cf. 163), we shall put the thumb under immediately (cf. Fig. 17).

P.: How do you to that?

W.: I need only to continue the typical grasping movement of the thumb until it is actually near the basal hollow of the 4th finger.

P.: If we picture to ourselves the path of the thumb's nail member throughout the movement, we see that the path forms an arc which intersects the plane of the keyboard twice. The path first drops below this plane — that was the key-moving action just completed — and then rises up over it again. And so we know already how the thumb makes its key-moving action once it has been put under.

W.: Yes. Now we only have to make this movement in reverse, i.e., a reposition. Right at the start the thumb's nail member will sink under the plane of the keyboard and thus move the key.

P.: But observe that in all these movements whereby the thumb is brought so near to the other fingers, its radial spreading from the basal knuckle of the 2nd finger must remain unchanged. And further note that in all these movements, its terminal joint must not be cramped, or else the whole hand and the whole arm will lose their natural position (p. 90).

H.:   Of course, the contrary situation arises in crossing the fingers over the thumb, as in playing a descending scale with the right hand.

P.:   It is the contrary in every way. First, in regard to the position of the hand. Since the sequence of notes is towards the median plane, it must be played in pronation.

W.:   And what about the movement of the thumb?

P.:   Whereas, when the thumb was put under, its movement of opposition was made in the air, now we must make this movement with the thumb resting in key-bottom, so that it lifts the rest of the hand over itself. The reposition, however, which moved the key when the thumb was put under, is now effected in sliding over the key-tops.

W.:   And this happens immediately after the key-moving action, so that the thumb at once finds itself over the next key to be played.

P.:   Of course. So in descending as well as in ascending scales the thumb, when it is not itself playing, is always ahead of the grasping fingers in the direction in which the hand is moving.

H.:   Of course, everything that has been said about playing scales applies equally to all other connected-note sequences in which thumb and fingers are put under and over respectively.

P.:   In this manner, we can continue any legato as far as we wish in one direction. We can also continue even if there is a change in direction — not simply by making a grasping movement on the key on which this change occurs, but by combining this finger-grasp with rotation and swinging of the wrist, which we have already described. So there is no technical necessity for interrupting the legato any sooner than the musical sense requires. But when the prescribed end has come, we can accomplish it technically by letting the movements of the small grasping unit, which we used in second-tone technique, run over into the wrist movement of the large grasping unit, which we know to be the most perfect means of technical separation from a following first tone.

H.:   Now we know how to play a second tone, but now how to play it with the desired volume.

Volume

P.:   It is clear (p. 117) that the force of the key-moving action depends on two factors: 1) the speed of the playing movement, and 2) the mass functioning in the movement. This is so obvious that, in speaking of the first-tone technique, it did not occur to anybondy to raise the question at all, because there it was self-evident that both factors could be found in our weight apparatus. The more the latissimus tensed, the greater was the speed of the key-moving action and also the greater was the appended mass. Now in second-tone technique it is more complicated; for although in this technique also, it is the mass of the weight apparatus that causes the moving of the key, it does so by means of a movement of the fingers.

W.: Then the volume can be influenced by both factors.

P.: Let us put it this way: Here, too, it is primarily dependent on the varying weight, which is effected by the latissimus and to which we have to adjust the grasping finger; but this adjustment can be made in different ways, i.e., the grasping finger can utilize more or less of the force of the latissimus for the key-moving action.

K.: Probably whether the wrist is held geometrically high or low also has some bearing on this, because the vertical component of the finger movement is much greater with a low wrist than with a high wrist (Fig. 20a and b), and this vertical component is the only effective one for moving the key.

H.: That is another reason why we prefer the low wrist position (p. 183); it makes possible a tone of greater intensity.

P.: However, we should under no circumstances overestimate the vertical component in finger movements. Even with the lowest

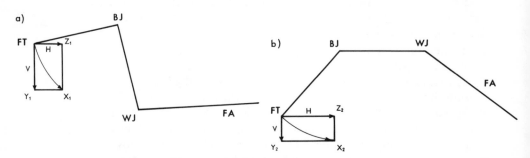

Figure 20. Position of the forearm (FA), wrist joint (WJ) and basal joint (BJ) of the finger in relation to the finger tip (FT)
   a)   with low wrist joint, and
   b)   with high wrist joint.
The arc described by the finger tip with its centre in the basal joint (FT-X1 and FT-X2) has been reduced to its key-moving vertical component (V) and its pulling horizontal component (H). As can be seen, with low wrist joint (a) the vertical component is the greater, and with a high wrist joint (b) — the horizontal component.

possible wrist-position, the horizontal component is still considerable and is quite manifest. Therefore, if you observe the fingers of
a pianist who plays correctly you have the impression that he is
stroking the surfaces of the keys horizontally with his fingers. It
might seem surprising that the keys are moved vertically downwards
by this horizontal stroking.

W.:   It is not contradictory if we remember that the downward movement of the keys is not caused principally by finger
grasping, but by the weight of the arm functioning vertically downwards.

H.:   Now that we have come to the end of our discussion of
the second-tone technique it will be useful to sum up briefly the
most important points:

1)   The second-tone technique involves binding from key-
bottom to key-bottom.

2)   It is a matter of finger technique, using the small grasping unit.

3)   Nevertheless, the force for playing comes from the weight
apparatus.

4)   As a rule, the back of the hand is turned to the direction
in which it is to move.

5)   The most important component in finger-grasping is the
conical movement.

6)   All aiming motions are to be avoided.

7)   The firmness of the knuckle-bridge must be ensured by
middle-hand spreading.

8)   The state of suspension that enables the appended weight
to be carried must be maintained from one key-moving action to
another.

9)   All the other general requirements, concerning the condition of the playing apparatus and the body as a whole, for piano
playing are to be observed.

P.:   Looking over this list, we realise that only the first of
these points, i.e., binding from key-bottom to key-bottom, is
common to all piano techniques; but for attaining real musical
coherence, it is comparatively unimportant. No matter how correctly the time relation between the new key-moving action and
the lifting of the finger that has just played is observed, the listener
will miss the experience of musical coherence if the other eight
essential points are not observed.

H.:   Then we have reached the point where we can answer
the question that was brought up at the beginning of today's

Inner and outer
cradle

discussion (p. 174); viz., how it is possible to achieve coherence without binding from key-bottom to key-bottom.

W.:   That would be in all cases of chord sequences where the musical sense demands coherence, but where it is impossible to use the technique of the second tone. We have recognized (p. 175) that all sequences of four- or five-note chords, or widely spread chords in which we have to use the same fingers again and again, are eliminated from the second-tone technique.

P.:   If we cannot use the second-tone technique in these cases, we must make use of the first-tone technique.

K.:   That is a task which seems paradoxical at first, playing a series of first tones which nevertheless are connected.

W.:   According to what we have said, they must be first tones; but at the same time must have the characteristics of the second tone in points two to nine.

P.:   It does sound a terrible paradox. But if we look at it more closely, we find that the most important points we have made in respect to the second tone apply also to the first tone — such as middle-hand spreading, conical grasping and avoidance of aiming motions. So actually only points two and three are left as special requirements for second-tone technique, i.e., the force originating in the weight apparatus must be guided by finger-grasping in the small grasping unit.

W.:   So it is only in the use of the small grasping unit that it differs from the technique of the first tone as we know it so far, where we found the weight apparatus interacting with the large grasping unit.

P.:   Quite right. I have invented the term "cradle technique" for this guiding of the weight apparatus by the small grasping unit, which is necessary for coherence.

K.:   Is this supposed to remind us of movements which are comparable to rocking a cradle?

P.:   Yes. We will start with having played a large chord with thumb and little finger. The wrist is still low. And now I begin a grasping movement with the thumb towards the basal hollow of the 4th finger, constantly spreading the thumb away from the basal knuckle of the 2nd finger, while the little finger yields more and more and so becomes passively hyper-extended. What position of the hand results from this (cf. Fig. 18, p. 192)?

W.:   The hand is supinated; the wrist rises with the root of the thumb and is brought towards the median plane. This is the same combination of movements that we associate with finger-grasping in second-tone technique. Now it has even stronger guidance, since in addition to the play of forces between the grasping finger and the weight, control is also exercised by the little finger resting at key-bottom. This guidance allows supination only in combination with a wrist movement towards the median plane, as we have repeatedly (pp. 100, 160, 183) stated.

P.:   I call the hand position arising in this way "inner cradle".

W.:   Then there is probably also an "outer cradle", which would arise from the reverse of these movements.

P.:   Describe these reverse movements which lead to an outer cradle.

W.:   The thumb must yield completely now, while the little finger grasps in the largest possible circle of circumduction towards the wrist end of the thumb ball (cf. Fig. 19, p. 193).

P.:   That's right. And what hand position does it give?

W.:   Now the hand is greatly pronated. The highly raised basal knuckle of the 5th finger has lifted the outer side of the wrist and brought it simultaneously away from the median plane.

K.:   If I now make a transition from the inner cradle by way of the intermediate position to the outer cradle and back again, it is actually comparable to rocking a cradle.

P.:   Of course, the movements you have just made — and every beginner makes — are in no way real cradle movements. It is true that outwardly your hand took approximately the positions that it would take in cradle movements, but your movements were guided from point A — whereas our first and foremost requirement is that the guidance should be from point B alone, by means of finger-grasping. Therefore, in this case, it must be only the alternating grasp of thumb and little finger that performs the cradle movement.

H.:   Only in this way can the weight apparatus remain appended with unchanged force, and a constant weighting of the keys thereby be achieved during this activity of the grasping apparatus.

P.:   Therefore, we are entitled to describe the cradle as the curve of constant pressure.

H.:   But only if it is a properly made cradle.

P.:   Obviously. We must give a warning about other possible misunderstandings. The pressure, which remains constant during the cradle curve, is, of course, the total burden my hand imposes on the keyboard, not the burden imposed on individual keys.

K.:   Certainly, the finger whose root is lower will receive a greater part of the load.

Cradle position and proportions of sound

W.:   In other words, the little finger will be more heavily burdened in the inner cradle, the thumb in the outer.

P.:   That's right. And from the standpoint of harmony, we must consider that in a chord the different voices have different degrees of importance. Melody and bass should predominate, and they are usually played by the little fingers of the right and left hand respectively. Since the little fingers are the most heavily burdened in the inner cradle, that is the position we should generally favour.

W.:   That is actually only a new formulation and new motivation for the well-known fact that the supine positions are by far the more important; for the inner cradle is a position of supination.

H.:   And now at last this new motivation tells us when we have to take positions of pronation, i.e., to adopt the outer cradle.

W.:   Yes. Above all, we shall have to do that in the exceptional case, when for instance, accompanying voices lie above the melody.

P.:   The lesser practical importance of the outer cradle, however, does not relieve the teacher of the obligation to practise the full extent of the cradle movement with his pupils and in this way to arrive at the complete freedom of the grasping apparatus from the weight apparatus.

Chord sequence in cradle-curve

K.:   Excuse me a moment. I am hearing about cradle positions in which key-moving actions can occur; I am hearing about cradle movements which, since they occur at key-bottom, can at best be after-motions. But in all this where is the key-moving action, which seems to me as a layman indispensable for playing the piano.

P.:   You yourself have told us just what we needed to answer that question. We already know that connecting chords by the cradle technique is a matter of first tones. We also remember that the term "first-tone technique" is a collective concept with many subtypes which differ from each other mainly in their after-motions. And now we have heard from you that the cradle movement is a kind of after-motion.

W.:   I understand. At one time (p. 159) we mentioned the theoretical possibility of an after-motion in the small grasping unit after a first tone, but we did not go into detail. So the cradle movement is this very after-motion in the small grasping unit.

P.:   That's true. Therefore, everything that we have said about the after-motion in general applies to the cradle as an after-motion — above all, that it is a safety valve for the moving tendencies that previously existed in the playing apparatus. Therefore, the after-motion following the playing of an accented chord will be more marked than that following a softer intermediate chord.

H.: Then the intermediate chords can be played with practically no after-motions.

P.: Everything that relates to the practical execution follows from that. Let's take a typical case of playing in an inner-cradle position and assume, furthermore, that the sequence of chords begins on an accented part of the measure.

W.: To begin at the beginning, the preparation of the key-moving action and the act itself must be made just as we have said for the technique of the first tone. During all this, the hand is moderately supine. But as soon as key-bottom has been reached, I begin a grasping movement with the thumb, by means of which the radial side of the wrist is raised high.

P.: So the thumb-grasp causes this lifting, because an accented chord has been played. The large appended weight that produced the accent must now, of course, be reduced in the same way that we described with reference to the resounding of the first tone. The only difference is that at that time we assumed the after-motion would be in the large grasping unit, while here the after-motion occurs in the small one.

W.: So now, too, the chord is ended as a result of my hand being raised to key-top by the buoyancy of the key.

P.: And, of course, we must follow this immediately by sliding over to the top of the keys to be played next.

W.: ... In order to be there as soon as possible for the next touch.

P.: No, the purpose of this now is not only to have the possibility for the next touch as soon as possible, but actually to make this next touch as soon as possible. Since it is impossible to bind from key-bottom to key-bottom, we must at least strive to keep the time interval between the end of the tone just played and the beginning of the next tone as short as possible.

W.: And now we can make the next key-moving action.

P.: Stop! First we settle another question. Shall we keep the cradle position which has resulted from the after-motion following the first key-moving action, or shall we change it while sliding over the keys?

W.: If I slide over a long stretch of the keyboard, a certain change of the cradle position — although not a great one — is bound to result, in that the supine position of my hand will be less marked over the further parts of the keyboard than over the middle section.

P.: That is unquestionably right. But of greater musical importance is another kind of change in the cradle position, which we shall arrive at from a simple technical consideration: If I wanted to maintain the pronounced inner-cradle position, which resulted at the end of the first accented chord, how could I make this cradle movement again after playing the next accented chord?

W.: I see. Of course, I must have my hand as near as possible to the middle position at the beginning of the next accented chord in order to be able to make as extensive a cradle movement as possible in the after-motion out of this position.

P.: Then you say we must lower the raised side of the wrist between the end of one accented chord and the beginning of the next. When shall we lower it? Immediately after the end of the first accent, or immediately before the second? Or lower it evenly over the interval of unaccented notes between the two accents, which — to translate a term of Rieman's — we shall call the "dead interval"?

W.: The last seems the most sensible course, since it alone avoids any abrupt change, which would impair the continuity of the sequence of touches, this continuity being so necesaary for coherence.

P.: The result is that during the series of unaccented chords the side of the wrist, which was lifted after the accent, is gradually lowered. The hand describes a cradle curve during this chord sequence. From a technical standpoint, the number of chords that can be included in such a cradle curve may be as large as you wish — and, therefore, can be whatever the music demands.

H.: If this change between accented and intermediate chords is repeated several times, the thumb side of the wrist makes a sort of wave motion as it rises and falls.

K.: But, of course, this is not what we think of when we use the term "wave" in mathematics or in physics — meaning a sine curve — but it is a real ocean wave with a weather side and a lee side, because the rise always occurs quickly after the accent, while the lowering occurs slowly during the series of intermediate chords.

H.: What we have said up to now about the inner-cradle position also applies, of course, to outer-cradle positions.

P.: Yes, and it is important that a cradle curve can never go over from an inner- to an outer-cradle position, or vice versa, but always comes to its end a little before the middle position.

H.: That is very significant, musically speaking. The inner cradle always signifies a certain ratio between the burdens imposed on the individual fingers and, therefore, a certain proportion between the volumes of the individual voices; and these proportions are different with the outer cradle. For instance, in the inner-cradle position of the right hand, the highest tone played by the little finger is always the loudest, the lowest tone played by the thumb softer, and the tones that may be played by the unburdened 2nd, 3rd and 4th fingers the softest. So the cradle position determines a certain proportion in the mixture of the individual voices and, therefore, a certain tone-character of the chord. Obviously this tone character remains the same in a chord-sequence played in the cradle curve.

K.: It can remain the same in principle, but not completely, because at the beginning of this cradle curve the little-finger side is rolled much further under the thumb side than at the end of the curve. Therefore, the volume of the highest voice must predominate over that of the lowest voice much more at the beginning of the cradle curve than towards the end. So the proportion in the mixture must change gradually during the sequence of chords.

P.: And that is exactly what we need. No doubt we agree that unpredictable changes in the proportion of the sounds within the chords would destroy any impression of unity and coherence. But complete uniformity of the chords would break the coherence, too, since it produces a sort of drum effect. We take advantage of this in staccato, where we are careful to keep the cradle position, once it is taken, completely unchanged during a sequence of chords in order to maintain complete uniformity of the tone character. Contrarily, the gradual regular change in the proportion of the sounds, which occurs during the cradle curve, conveys the feeling of coherence to the listener.

H.: But, of course, the drum effect, which breaks the coherence through absolute uniformity in the tone character, only comes about if chords of the same tone-quality follow each other immediately. If, on the contrary, there are intervals between chords of the same character, it is precisely this complete uniformity in their tone quality which creates coherence.

P.: We find such repetition of complete uniformity in tone quality across an interval in the relationship between the individual accents of several cradle curves in succession, each of which we shall play in exactly the same cradle position. Thus beyond the coherence within the individual cradle curves, a greater coherence from accent to accent can be created, and so a more extensive melodic unit can be held together.

204

H.:   At this point, it is important to realise that up to now
we have examined only one instance of musical phrasing, though a
very typical one — i.e., the extended arch of the musical meaning
with coherence from accent to accent, while the chords in the
intervals between the accents recede uniformly into the back-
ground. It is, of course, impossible here to discuss with the same
thoroughness all the other possibilities and requirements which
arise in musical interpretation.

P.:   Let us discuss only one more case, because it represents,
so to say, the other extreme from the one we have just observed.
I think we can consider a crescendo or decrescendo sequence of
chords as the opposite to the alternation of accent and dead interval.

W.:   In that case, of course, the most important thing is the
gradual increasing or decreasing of the appended weight from touch
to touch.

P.:   Right. The change caused by the varying weight suffices
in this case for the desired coherence, so that it is not necessary to
complement it with a gradual change in the cradle position. So we
can play the whole series of chords in a constant cradle position.

H.:   "Constant" here naturally means "dynamically constant", and it does not mean that a particular geometrical degree
of supination must be meticulously held to. On the contrary, we
know that this degree changes automatically with the distance
from the middle of the piano, if the cradle position is governed by
the grasping apparatus as it should be.

P.:   Whether we choose the inner- or the outer-cradle position, and what degree of the one or the other we choose, depends
upon the relationship in volume between the individual voices that
is necessary at the time.

H.:   We may take it for granted that in all other respects
everything we said about the cradle curve holds for such a series of
chords: playing without after-motion and sliding as quickly as possible over the tops of the keys to the next ones to be played.

P.:   When the last chord of the series has been played, we
shall add an after-motion, which will indicate the conclusion of the
sequence. We know from our discussion of the intense isolated
chord that the after-motion in the large grasping unit expresses
conclusion of this sort. It is important that it should be possible
to perform this after-motion from any cradle position.

H.:   But it cannot always be taken for granted. Generally,
the cradle technique is especially sensitive to the slightest mistakes
anywhere in the playing apparatus. Therefore, in the cradle

Chord sequence in
constant cradle position

technique more than in any other, we must pay particular attention to all the characteristics of a correctly adjusted playing apparatus — above all to the guidance of the weight apparatus by the grasping apparatus, the proper alternation between carrying and suspension, the lateral fall of the elbow, and to middle-hand spreading with conical grasping of the fingers. But since it is not at all easy for a pianist to observe all these conditions, the teacher cannot make the pupil practise the cradle movements too often.

P.:   Naturally, he will get the pupil, above all, to make these movements with grasping by the thumb and little finger, in the way we described at the beginning of this discussion. But is also possible to go beyond this by making the same movements using any two of the other fingers to direct them.

W.:   That is obvious, since we recognized right at the beginning that the cradle movement is similar to that resulting from finger-grasping combined with hand-turning in the technique of the second tone; and in second-tone technique, we can make these movements on any pair of fingers.

Cradle in
second-tone technique

P.:   Quite correct. I should only like to stress that the two movements are not only similar, but really are the same. It is true that we arrived at this movement in the second-tone technique on the assumption that only one finger is resting on the key, because first we observed it immediately following the playing of a single first tone. But if we make the same movement between two second tones, then the hand rests on at least two fingers, the former and the new supporting fingers — just as it does in the cradle movement.

H.:   To put it in a nutshell, the cradle plays just as large a part in the second-tone technique as it does for connecting chords played in the first-tone technique.

P.:   Yes, and everything in the second-tone technique that goes beyond the mere binding from key-bottom to key-bottom — i.e., the guidance of the entire playing apparatus by the small grasping unit — is in fact cradle technique.

H.:   That brings us back to where we started, because the cradle was defined in this way right at the beginning of the discussion.

P.:   Much as we realise the importance of cradle technique for achieving musical coherence, it would be a mistake to consider the cradle as the only means of expressing it. In fact, tomorrow we shall describe another method for achieving the same end, the technique of melody playing.

Melody Playing

H.:   In order to understand melody technique, which we will discuss today, we must first consider the role of melody in piano playing. We must remember above all that the piano is a poly-phonic instrument in which the melody hardly ever appears alone; sometimes it is accompanied by chords, sometimes it is supported by other voices. And all this can be divided between two hands in various ways.

What is a melody tone?

P.:   The melody is supposed to stand out from the chords and the accompanying voices as a differentiated unified whole. What must we require then of the melody tone?

W.:   For it to stand out like a singing voice, it must have carrying power, it must be full and of the greatest intensity.

H.:   You speak of the "greatest intensity". Let us be cautious about superlatives! Remember that within the melody there are still accents to be taken into consideration. How would these be able to stand out, if the greatest intensity were already being given to every tone?

P.:   But it is the accentuated melody tone only that we want to deal with under the heading "melody playing", and only when it occurs without a chord being played simultaneously by the same hand. We know already that we can achieve melodic coherence by means of the technique of the second tone, in chords — by means of the technique of the cradle curve. We can certainly achieve great intensity of tone with these techniques, but not the greatest intensity.

Necessity of first-tone technique

W.:   Why not?

P.:   Remember that tone intensity is dependent first of all on the force coming from the weight apparatus. Even in the technique of the first tone, it is only a part of this force that is carried over to the key by the playing finger, because the other part of the force is operative in the chain-like playing apparatus at the end near the body. What about the second tone? In this case, can the entire portion of the force that is left for the grasping apparatus be carried over by the new playing finger to the key that is about to be played?

W.:   No, because the former supporting finger still carries a part of this portion.

P.:   So we understand that because of the distribution of weight in the second-tone technique, we can never achieve the full volume of tone that is possible in the technique of the first tone. Moreover, we have also learned (p. 159) that grasping movements in the large grasping unit can be made more freely and amply and thus produce greater brilliance of tone than if we limit ourselves to the small grasping unit, as we do in the technique of the second tone and the cradle.

W.:   It means, then, that the intense melody tones of which we are speaking must be played according to the technique of the first tone.

H.:   And yet at the same time complete musical coherence must be achieved.

P.:   What must cohere with what?

W.:   Here again we have to take into consideration the two kinds of coherence, just as we did yesterday in discussing cradle technique, the one being coherence of accented tones with the subsequent unaccented tones, the other — coherence of accented tones with each other for forming a more extensive melodic unit.

P.:   Of course. And today's task is a bit easier than yesterday's. Whereas yesterday we spoke about coherence of chords, today it is about single tones.

W.:   Then we can attain coherence of the unaccented tones with each other and with the preceding accent by simply using the technique of the second tone.

P.:   Quite right. But what about the coherence of accents with one another? Yesterday we saw the possibility of achieving this by retaining the same tone quality in the accents, and we defined the tone quality as the proportion in volume of the separate tones in the chord. But what can be the common factor in the tone quality of several single tones?

W.:   All they can have in common is that they each have the distinguishing characteristic of a melody tone: They must have fulness of sound and the greatest intensity.

P.:   Yes. Therefore, our only problem now is the technical means by which we can attain this.

Extreme supination

K.:   Surely the transmission of force to the key must be as direct as possible for this. The more intermediate members there are, the greater the uncertainty and the loss of force.

P.:   Therefore, we must consider where the force for playing comes from.

W.:   From the weight apparatus.

P.:   And what part of the weight apparatus comes closest to the playing finger?

W.:   The head of the ulna on the little-finger side of the wrist. The head of this bone passes by the keyboard.

P.:   And so which part of the hand is moved down by the weight apparatus most directly?

W.:   The little-finger side. The thumb side is only pulled along so to say.

P.:   Anything that is pulled along remains behind, in respect to the direction of movement. And since the direction of movement here is downwards, "remaining behind" means "remaining above". If the thumb side of the hand remains above the little-finger side, what hand position is that?

W.:   It would be the most extreme position of supination that could be used at all in piano playing, the position in which the little-finger edge of the hand is directed downwards like a cutting edge, the same hand position as the one we see with Karate fighters.

P.:   Yes, for those fighters it is the hand, for us the fingers, which must be affected most directly by the weight apparatus. In both instances this is attained by extreme supination, with the little-finger edge of the hand taking the lead.

K.:   This hand position serves this purpose best because in every other position certain pronatory muscles are necessary for holding the chain on its underside between the nail member of the playing finger and the weight apparatus, whereas in extreme supination neither pronatory nor supinatory muscles have anything to do.

P.:   And the fewer muscles we have to depend upon, the surer and firmer is the guidance in our playing.

H.:   Moreover, the fingers are at their firmest in this position, because the purely lateral weighting works on the middle and terminal joints in the direction in which they cannot give way. So the task of catching up the playing force by the fingers is performed specifically by the short finger-muscles, which work only laterally; and the factor of uncertainty — stemming from the greater or lesser participation of the long finger-flexors, when the weighting is not purely lateral — is completely eliminated.

P.: Thus the finger becomes a very firm continuation of the hand — which now, mechanically speaking, reaches from wrist to fingertip — whereby the greatest security and precision in the transmission of force are made possible.

W.: Does this mean that melody playing is always to be executed in extreme supination?

H.: Let us be more cautious and say it is to be executed in as supine a position as possible for the particular key-moving action. Extreme supination obviously comes into question only in playing with the little finger. If other fingers were used in this position, the little finger and the ones between it and the playing finger would be in the way.

P.: Nevertheless, extreme supination plays an extraordinarily important part in melody technique because carrying melody tones are very often assigned to the little finger.

H.: Therefore, it will be advisable for us to start with the description of how the melody tone is played by the little finger.

W.: Actually, we know everything about it now. We have to use the technique of the first tone in maximum supination, and we have to append the heaviest weight — to support which the spreading of the middle hand and fingers must be especially strong.

P.: That is correct, although in this special case there is yet another means for attaining the firmness which is so needed in the hand: We can put fingers 2 – 5 side by side and so make the hand a solid block, with which we then move the key, little-finger edge downwards.

Hand as a block

H.: This block-like hand will be mainly used when several consecutive notes are to be played by the little finger, whereas when the little finger plays between notes played by other fingers, the spreading of the hand — indispensable to the other fingers — will not be given up for the sake of the block formation.

P.: That is so. Now we must consider whether it is only the hand in itself which has to withstand the appending of this heavy weight.

W.: No, naturally the wrist joint, too. With the hand in the position just described, the muscles which move the hand towards the little-finger side will be the ones which have to intercept the appended weight.

P.: Yes. And since the weight is very heavy, the wrist muscles will have to work very hard. Hence, according to the general principles for first-tone technique, a considerable rise of the wrist occurs in the after-motion — to such an extent that on completion, with the block-like hand, it is no longer the tip of the 5th finger which is in contact with the key, but that of the 4th, and finally that of the 3rd finger.

H.: Obviously, that is inevitable if we practise this movement.

P.: Since the activity of the muscles reinforcing the hand on the underside — i.e., in this case, on the little-finger side — is absolutely necessary at the moment the key is moved, in order that the whole force of the appended weight be transmitted to the key directly and in a controlled manner, we have these muscles begin their work immediately before the moment of contact with the key. This means that what we have just described as the after-motion by analogy to the normal procedure in first-tone technique, does not really follow the key-moving action, but takes place during it.

W.: That would be a procedure similar to that in the second-tone technique, where, too, the grasping effective during the key-moving action runs directly into the after-motion.

P.: The difference is, though, that in second-tone technique the small grasping unit has to be used, whereas here it is the large one. So the part played by the basal joint of the finger in second-tone technique is taken over by the wrist in melody tones.

W.: Of course, the basal joints are ruled out as joints here, since we use the hand as a block.

P.: Not only when we use the block-like hand, but with every sustained melody tone, the playing finger is united with the hand into a whole that is immovable in itself in the direction of weight. We know how to attain this.

W.: Yes. Firstly, the middle-hand spreading serves this purpose, and secondly, we must have previously carried out the conical movement of the playing finger to the absolute limit set by the joint.

P.: And there is a third point to be taken into consideration. What about the finger in itself?

W.: Of course, it must not be cramped in the middle and terminal joints.

P.: Certainly not. But what positions will these joints take?

W.: Since in playing with a block-like hand we fully extend the fingers in the act of moving the key, I might suppose the same would be done in this instance; but I can give no reasons for it.

K.: If the finger were bent in the middle and terminal joints, then the exclusively or almost exclusively lateral weighting of the nail member would cause a strong passive rotation of the finger in

Finger as a straight stick

the basal joint, which could not be entirely counteracted even by the most intensive lateral muscular support in the basal joint. And so the direct, controlled transmission of force would become unsure at this spot.

P.: If however, as required, the finger with the hand is to function like a lever all in one piece, then we must keep the middle and terminal joints extended. We must use our finger as though it were a straight stick governed from the wrist joint.

H.: Of course, these conclusions apply to melody playing with any finger. As we mentioned, in playing with fingers 1 to 4, somewhat lesser supination is indicated than with the little finger.

P.: But just the same, we should use the greatest degree of supination possible with those fingers, because only in this way can we attain the tone quality we have demanded at the beginning of today's discussion.

K.: Is great volume also an element in this tone quality?   Volume

P.: What we must have is the possibility for the greatest volume, but equally the possibility for the tenderest pianissimo. For exact control of the volume while retaining the richest timbre, it is necessary not to control the volume exclusively by means of the weight apparatus, as we did in the technique of the first tone, but through the interplay between weight and grasping apparatuses, as we did in the technique of the second tone. After all, we have stressed that in melody playing, just as in the technique of the second tone, the grasp comes about during the key-moving action and thus can influence the volume directly. From this point of view, we are justified in regarding the melody technique as a second-tone technique in which the wrist joint takes over the role of the basal joint of the finger.

H.: That is virtually all there is to say about melody technique, even though we have taken slow melody playing for the basis of our description up to now. It is obvious that quick melody playing would not permit the after-motions to the extent that we have described as ideal, and as we shall perform them when practising — for instance, to free the arm.

P.: If we now recapitulate, as we always do at the end of our discussions, we shall chiefly remember the definition which we have given for the melody tone: a tone of the greatest intensity and richest tone quality. So it is the last fulfillment of what we set as our aim for tone production at the beginning of our first discussion (p. 22). Now, just as every climber tarries a while after reaching the summit, we, too, shall stop at this point and break off our discussion for today, even though it was a short one.

DIALOGUE 10

Staccato and Related Techniques

What is staccato?

H.:   Yesterday and the day before, in dealing with the technique of the second tone, cradle technique and melody playing, we discussed those techniques that are used to attain musical coherence. Now it is time to consider the staccato ways of playing, which we have repeatedly contrasted to the binding techniques.

P.:   It is doubtless correct to regard "legato" and "staccato" as opposite concepts, meaning more or less "to bind" and "to separate", respectively. Yet let us not forget that there must also be a kind of separation in legato and a connection in staccato.

W.:   I understand. The separation in legato is the distinct articulation of each separate note, and the connection in staccato is the coherence of meaning that is also manifest in staccato sequences.

H.:   This coherence in staccato in spite of the gaps between separate notes can be compared to hemstitching, which also has gaps and yet retains unity.

P.:   What gives unity to the line of hemstitching is regularity. Likewise, we can be sure that the separation of notes in staccato playing must not involve irregularity, but that we need the utmost regularity here, too.

H.:   The principle of regularity should be applied first of all to the duration of the notes, but this is frequently neglected. Many pianists are inclined to give a staccato note no time-value whatsoever and simply give the key a sudden smack.

P.:   . . . Whereas half the duration of the given note-value is the only correct measure for the staccato note. If the composer had had in mind a still shorter duration, he could have shown it by shorter note-values and rests.

K.:   When a note is held for only half of its value and is followed by a rest of the same duration, this time-ration must surely be sufficient to separate the note from the following one.

P.:   But players hope to achieve clearer separation by making the note shorter and the rest longer, and they are naturally prone to cheat in this way if they do not command the means to separate the notes properly.

H.: A player who does this hopes to make a greater contrast to the other techniques which he has executed incorrectly: to the legato that has no true coherence, and to the intense isolated chords, which do not fully resound.

P.: It's good that you mentioned the contrast to the fully resounding chords. In speaking of them, we explained that full resonance is produced by means of the after-motion in the large grasping unit; at the same time (p. 158), we mentioned as a contrast the staccato note, which does not resound because it has no after-motion.

No after-motion

W.: The absence of an after-motion means that simultaneously with the release of the latissimus tension in the weight apparatus, there comes a release of the underside tension in the grasping apparatus.

P.: You are quite right to stress the element of release, the "staccare", in this; but you must remember that the playing of the key would not be concluded simply by this release of tensions, because the mere weight of the whole playing apparatus would be enough to keep the key at key-bottom.

W.: So we must also actively lift the playing apparatus to key-top after the time indicated by the note-value, or rather, after half of this time.

P.: And how do we do it?

W.: In the same way as with any first tone, i.e., by muscles which lift the upper arm around the shoulder joint.

P.: That is to say, by a motion directed from point A. We scarcely need mention that the key-moving action itself is directed from point A, too. And since no after-motion directed from point B comes between the moving of the key and the rising upwards, we must regard staccato as a pure point-A technique.

Elbow weights key

H.: In other words: every movement originates in the shoulder. In principle, the arm would need no joints. Since the shoulder is the only centre of motion, the elbow makes essentially the same movements as the finger. We can make this idea clearer to the pupil and thereby facilitate its execution if we tell him to imagine under his elbow a second keyboard on which he is to play with his elbow.

K.: If I understand correctly, in playing staccato, the arm is completely fixed in itself.

P.: Then you do not understand at all. It must still be a

freely hanging chain. This very downward movement of the elbow in the vertical plane, occurring every time a key is moved, implies that the elbow must have fallen into the vertical plane beforehand.

K.: Good. That is the lateral fall of the elbow. But how can the arm be like a chain hanging between two points of suspension if it has no distant point of suspension, i.e., point B?

P.: Has it always had this distant point of suspension in the ways of playing we have described so far? In the technique of the second tone, it had this point constantly; but in the types of the first-tone technique which we have so far considered, the arm has had this point of suspension only temporarily, losing it again temporarily between the playing of succeeding keys. Admittedly, in playing staccato, the length of time that this distant point of suspension exists is shorter than in the subtypes of first-tone technique which we have described hitherto, but it still exists for half the duration of the note-value. Throughout this period the arm is in a chain condition; and for the rest of the time the playing apparatus must be in a condition from which it can go over into the chain condition without hindrance, just as in every other subtype of first-tone technique. Staccato technique does not imply a different condition of the playing apparatus, but only a different time-relation in the sequence of events while the apparatus remains in absolutely the same condition that we constantly advocate in general: Middle-hand spreading, clasping-back towards the low elbow, carrying, suspension — all this applies to staccato as well as to any other way of playing.

H.: Above all, the joints of the arm, hand and fingers must not be antagonistically cramped.

K.: That general rule needs special explanation in this particular case, since the playing apparatus in itself would not need any joints for staccato, as you have just made clear.

P.: It is true that in playing staccato we could manage better than in any other way of playing with a rigid stick, without joints, in place of the arm. It would suffice for weighting and grasping, but what about adjusting the length?

K.: Beyond question, one needs freedom in the joints for that.

Types of staccato

P.: And the arm not being a jointless stick, we use the joints for additional functions, viz., to effect finer nuances in playing.

H.: And we use them both during the key-moving actions and in between succeeding ones.

P.: First let us consider their use during the key-moving

actions. It is clear that moving the key is essentially a function of the weight apparatus, proceeding from the shoulder. Now we know from second-tone technique that we can combine this activity of the weight apparatus with that of the grasping apparatus during the key-moving action and that we can gain a great deal for musical expression by modifications in the interplay of these two apparatuses.

W.:   Yes, and we were referring to the use of the small grasping unit.

P.:   That is to say, finger movements. But of course, we can also use the large grasping unit, i.e., wrist movements.

H.:   Accordingly, we can differentiate between:
1)   finger staccato,
2)   wrist staccato, and
3)   shoulder staccato.

K.:   Wouldn't it be more correct to designate the third as a pure shoulder-staccato? For from what you have said, every staccato is primarily a shoulder staccato, which may or may not be connected with activity in the fingers or wrist. In the case of "shoulder staccato" the grasping apparatus does not take part.

P.:   That is so. It is clear that each of these subtypes has a particular sphere of application.

H.:   If we remember what we said in discussing the second-tone technique, about the part taken by the small grasping unit in moving the key, we will understand that finger staccato can be used to obtain the clearest articulation.

Wiping the key in finger staccato

P.:   But only if we pay careful heed to the condition of the finger and hand, above all middle-hand spreading and conical grasping.

W.:   In one respect, however, the finger-grasp in staccato must differ from that in second-tone technique: It cannot give rise to a point B, around which an after-motion in the grasping apparatus would take place.

P.:   Obviously not. We excluded this possibility from the beginning. Now the finger only wipes the key, so to speak.

W.:   Do you mean that it just wipes the key superficially without moving it to key-bottom?

P.:   I mean just that. It is not hard to do if I hold the basal knuckle at the right height.

K.:   I understand. In the finger-grasp the finger tip moves in an arc around the basal knuckle. If the basal knuckle is low, the arc is intersected not only by the plane of the key-top, but also by that of the key-bottom, and thus the finger moves the key to key-bottom. If the basal knuckle is somewhat higher, the arc is intersected by the plane of the key-top, but that of the key-bottom misses the arc, and a plane lying somewhere between key-bottom and key-top becomes the tangent of the arc. Now the finger can move the key to this tangential plane and then grasp farther along the arc towards the wrist end of the thumb ball without occasioning a point B.

W.:   Good; but what is the point of moving the key downwards from key-top without coming to key-bottom? Does that produce a tone?

P.:   Yes, because the tone is produced not by the key, but by the hammer. We must give the key enough speed to fling the hammer against the string.

K.:   But how can you give the key this speed? The kind of finger movement you have described seems to me the least suited for making the key move with high speed. It does not even satisfy the condition which we generally recognize as essential, i.e., an accelerated movement of the key. The vertical component, which alone moves the key, decreases during a circular movement and so can only cause a retarded key-movement.

P.:   This retarding at the end of the key-movement is necessary if we do not want to get to key-bottom. Therefore, the acceleration at the beginning of the movement must be all the greater. It is obvious that great acceleration cannot be accomplished by means of the finger-grasp, since the plane of the key-top is already nearly tangential to the arc described by the finger. But we have never claimed that the sound-producing movement of the key was caused by finger movement. On the contrary, we know that each staccato, like any other key-moving action, comes from the shoulder. The movement of the weight apparatus, which becomes evident even at the elbow, is strong enough to give the key so much acceleration right at the beginning of the movement that the hammer is flung against the string. The finger-grasp serves only for exact regulation of the volume and for clear articulation.

W.:   And when do we use finger staccato?

P.:   Since we are always striving for the clearest articulation, we shall use it as often as possible. And understandably, it is possible in all staccato single tones.

Wrist staccato

W.:   So wrist and pure shoulder-staccati are left for chords.

P.:   Yes, and in deciding between these two we must consider the fact that participation of the wrist makes a fuller tone possible.

Therefore, we shall give preference to wrist staccato when playing chords in slow sequence.

H.: Naturally, in wrist staccato, too, we have to pay attention to middle-hand spreading and backward clasping of the fingers towards the elbow. Before playing, the fingers grasp the required chord span, and the hand — thus made firm in itself — now clasps back towards the elbow, which is sinking at the same time.

W.: Will the movement now be continued to key-bottom?

P.: Certainly, for even if a certain horizontal component comes into the grasping movement, a real tangential relation between the plane of the key and the grasping movement can never result.

H.: And in the same way, pure shoulder-staccato must be made down to key-bottom.

Shoulder staccato

W.: We must use this, then, in cases where neither finger nor wrist staccato can be used, i.e., in a quick sequence of chords.

P.: The way you put it, it sounds as though the shoulder staccato were a mere emergency solution to be used when for lack of time nothing better is possible. But that is not the case. Keep in mind that a quick sequence of staccato chords usually has a definite musical meaning, which we might express by the word "mysterious" or the like, and that this musical meaning would be destroyed by greater fulness of tone. Therefore, it is important from a musical point of view, that the shoulder staccato be really pure, i.e., free from all other components of motion.

H.: That is why we pay particular attention to it in practising, especially in its application to repeated octaves.

P.: It is obvious that in these repeated octaves the hand is kept firm in itself by means of middle-hand spreading and conical grasping of the two end-fingers in opposite directions. It is equally obvious that the firmness must not be attained by antagonistic tension of the long muscles, although there is a strong tendency to tense them. To avert this, we must always test the freedom of the wrist by moving it continually.

W.: That would mean wrist staccato again. But we are talking about shoulder staccato.

P.: In wrist staccato the movements of the wrist joint occur during the key-moving actions. Now it is a matter of wrist movements in between them, i.e., at key-top. We not only flex the wrist but also extend it in such a way that it alternately rises and falls during a long series of such octaves or other chords.

H.:   This rising and falling indicates freedom in the wrist joint and ensures the continuation of this freedom.

W.:   So now we have said everything of importance about staccato.

P.:   Only about what we would call pure staccato, because it does meet the definition which we made at the beginning of our discussion (p. 213), i.e., it has no after-motion and, therefore, does not fully resound. But we must not forget that also in a staccato passage there are usually accents, which have to stand out from the other notes not only by greater volume but also by resounding longer. This longer resounding produces the greater melodic curve from accent to accent, whereas in the intervals come the unaccented notes. We have already met this in our study of cradle technique and melody technique.

W.:   I see. It means a kind of compromise between opposites if we now try to achieve a resounding staccato. How can it be done?

P.:   There is no general rule; it depends on the particular musical requirement. Imagine, for instance, a series of staccato chords, among which at certain intervals a particular one is to stand out.

W.:   Certainly we would play the chords in the dead interval with shoulder staccato in order to make them recede.

P.:   But how do we play the accents? We could emphasize them with wrist staccato, but that would not be quite enough. We could use the technique of the intense, fully resounding chord with the extensive after-motion of the wrist, but that would be too much, because it would not be staccato at all. To compromise, we begin with wrist staccato but do not release the key after reaching key-bottom, continuing instead the wrist movement as an after-motion in the large grasping unit, just as we do for the intense, fully resounding chord. This after-motion does not have the full extent which would otherwise be possible, because part of the wrist movement has already been used for playing.

H.:   Anyway, the wrist rises a good deal while all this is happening. It falls during the following shoulder-staccato in the dead interval and rises again at the next accent.

W.:   So the wrist makes a wave movement similar to the one we described before in the cradle curve (p. 202), quickly rising at the accents and slowly falling between them.

K.:   Except that now in staccato the wrist as a whole describes this wave line without changing its degree of supination

Accent in staccato

or pronation; in the cradle curve only one side of the wrist, mostly the thumb side, rose and fell.

H.:   Of course, this difference of movement implies a musical difference: When the degree of supination or pronation remains unchanged, the weight is distributed in the same proportion every time between the different keys which are played, resulting in a constant tone-quality and thus also in the separating drum-effect; however, in the cradle curve the tone quality changes continually, but regularly, and so produces coherence even of the chords in the dead interval.

K.:   The staccato effect in the one case, and the legato effect in the other, are naturally reinforced by their different time-ratios — by which I mean the ratio between the time spent by the hand in sliding over the key-tops and the time it spends resting at key-bottom. Whereas in staccato we can express this ratio in numbers as 1 : 1, in the cradle curve the time spent at key-tops should be as short as possible and so the value of the fraction should come as close to zero as possible.

P.:   Naturally. But now we have had enough of this. Let us observe another particularly important modification of staccato technique. There is the possibility that in a series of staccato chords one line in the chord series has to predominate as a melody voice.

Melody voice in staccato

H.:   In the nature of things, we can get this effect by including a grasp by a particular finger in the shoulder staccato which we use for the whole chord.

W.:   You mean a combination of pure shoulder-staccato with finger staccato.

P.:   Of course, you can put it like that, but it is not accurate. We do not reach key-bottom with finger staccato, but we do with shoulder staccato; and, therefore, we do it all the more if we include a grasp of the finger in the shoulder staccato. Thus a finger-key joint, a point B, is formed at key-bottom, around which an after-motion, i.e., a raising of the basal knuckle, occurs in the small grasping unit.

H.:   In this case there cannot be a complete raising either, since it happens during a staccato key-moving action of the whole hand. So here again we have a compromise between full resounding and staccato effect.

P.:   We could go into a few more such modifications, but the technique necessary at the time will be evident to the understanding and sensitive pianist from what we have already said.

H.:   In all the modifications we have examined up to now, the mixture of a staccato character with other elements is not expressed in the score. The composer simply puts the staccato dot there.

P.:   But there are still other cases that can be understood as mixtures of staccato and other musical elements, and these are indicated by expression marks of their own. The most important of them are portamento and leggiero.

H.:   The term "portamento" tells us that we are dealing with carrying tones, which have a fullness of sound almost like melody tones.

P.:   Therefore, appropriately enough, we do use the technique of the melody tone to a great extent. We go into extreme supination and play with the finger fully extended in the terminal and middle joints, as with a straight stick. The simultaneous staccato effect, however, is produced by our letting go after we have reached key-bottom — before the wrist movement, which is contained in the key-moving action, has continued into a complete after-motion.

H.:   It is entirely different with the leggiero; the pearly quality expressed by its name can only be attained if it is something in between staccato and legato, as its usual definition says.

P.:   Since leggiero always deals with single tones, we have to consider it as a mixture of finger staccato and second-tone technique.

W.:   That is hardly possible. How can I combine wiping through with binding from key-bottom to key-bottom?

P.:   By wiping the key without wiping through, and by forming a finger-key joint at the moment when the deepest point has been reached.

K.:   Don't forget that the wiping does not move the key to key-bottom and that firmness at key-bottom is necessary for forming a finger-key joint!

P.:   It is not firmness at key-bottom which is necessary, but a firm key. We have stressed (p. 27) that from the beginning of its downward movement the key offers resistance and is therefore a "firm key". Granted that halfway down it is not as firm as at key-bottom, but this firmness is enough for a correctly carried playing apparatus to go over into suspension with the slightest weight and to carry out the technique of the second tone on the point B which is thus created.

H.:   All the seeming contradictions which have complicated

Portamento

Leggiero

the theoretical analysis of leggiero make themselves even more conspicuous when it is put into practice. The pianist who, during the after-motion, has to carry part of the weight of the arm from point A naturally feels a great temptation to do this by means of a general fixation in the playing apparatus. The elbow rises laterally, the shoulder is pulled forward, and all the other bad consequences follow.

P.: Accordingly, a perfect "jeu perle" is a height of the pianist's art that we very seldom experience.

W.: If we have already dealt with the height of piano technique, such a height as goes beyond the aim which was originally set and which we achieved yesterday, there is scarcely anything left to say.

P.: Oh, no. There is very much more. Let us look back. The first six days we discussed the prerequisites of piano technique and the factors that can upset it. Then we applied this knowledge to the practical execution of different types of playing, and in doing so we always called to mind in each case what hindrances might arise to our attainment of the demands made. Now there remains the extremely important question of how these hindrances — the nature of which we have learned theoretically — are to be combatted practically. This will be tomorrow's task.

Muscular Tensions and Their Relief

Tensions and
tension systems

W.:   No doubt the hindrances — whose elimination we want to discuss today — are mutually antagonistic tensions.

P.:   Yes. We are interested in tensions anywhere in the body, whether they concern the playing apparatus directly or a distant part of the body such as the supporting apparatus, head or foot. These tensions in remote parts interest us for two reasons: firstly, because they hinder the freedom of movement in the part of the body where they exist — for instance, they restrict the movability of the supporting apparatus in the three degrees of freedom, which are required for freedom in playing; and secondly, because tensions localized far from the hand can be part of a tension system (p. 56) to which muscles of the arm also belong, so that the existence and relief of these remote tensions can affect the hand.

W.:   That's understandable. Just as in a machine the movement of each wheel depends on that of every other wheel, so in the human body the hand is connected with the supporting apparatus by a sort of driving belt, so that the condition in one place forms an inseparable whole with the condition in the other place.

P.:   Quite right. Only we cannot be satisfied with the general statement that everything is connected with everything else; but using the results of many years of experience as a teacher, I want to discuss more specifically which tensions can be considered as one system of tensions because they appear and they disappear together. That would be a real step forward in answering the important practical question of how these tensions can be relieved — not only singly, but to go one better, as whole systems.

H.:   The task of releasing tensions can only be accomplished by constant cooperation between pupil and teacher. We must not forget that a cramped pupil is not conscious of the tensions in his muscles. Again and again he must be made aware of them by the teacher; indeed, in the beginning, he will probably flatly deny that there is any unwanted activity in his muscles, until it is brought home to him by the teacher.

P.:   There are two situations in which the teacher has to combat tension — at the piano, and away from it. We shall see the necessity of both when we consider that antagonistic tensions are a matter of habit, and so this condition of our muscles exists in every other activity as well as piano playing. I have invented numerous exercises which will help to overcome this condition. The pupil needs the most varied postures and the most varied aids for these exercises, and so he must do them independently of the piano. Even when a considerable freeing of the muscles has been accomplished by means of these gymnastic exercises, tension will still creep in repeatedly at various points and become noticeable in piano playing. Now it is the teacher's task to intervene during the playing, to order the pupil, "Let go here", "Let fall there!"; and in this way to correct again and again the condition of the body, and with it the quality of the tone, to which the pupil — since he is too busy with notes, rhythm and expression marks — pays no attention. From observation of the pupil while he is playing, the teacher can find out to which tensions he is particularly inclined, and, therefore, which gymnastic exercises should be prescribed first of all.

Relief of tensions at the piano and by gymnastic exercises

W.:   But what are the signs by which the teacher recognizes tensions in the pupil?

P.:   There is a general sign for all sorts of tensions: the dullness of tone. But beside this, there are dozens of special signs indicating tension at particular points. We shall now pick out the most important of them. If we understand the nature of the tensions correctly, we shall always find the way to free ourselves of them, and to do so instantaneously without more or less interrupting the playing. Later we shall discuss the gymnastic exercises all together.

H.:   And as in all our discussions we now begin with the fingers.

Tension systems involving fingers

W.:   We have described various types of tensions in the fingers (p. 84). There is the cramped terminal joint; there is the terminal joint which has collapsed, and behind which the middle joint protrudes at a sharp angle; and there is the claw hand.

P.:   And in addition, there is the finger that looks almost as we said it should, but has less freedom of flexion in the basal joint and is found to be cramped from the general shape of the arm. One thing is common to all finger tensions: The elbow has been more or less raised laterally.

W.:   How is it possible that there are so many different kinds of finger tension? Don't they all arise basically from the same situation, viz., antagonistic tension of the long flexor against the long extensor?

K.:   Certainly. But this basic situation can be modified in many ways; e.g., it is affected by the fact that on each finger there is not just one long-flexor sinew, but two, so that the condition of the finger is dependent on two long-flexor muscles. Furthermore, the long muscles can tighten not only against the opposition of other long muscles, but against the short muscles as well, and in this way can hinder their free action. Finally, the tension of a long flexor can function largely against the outside resistance of the key.

P.:   This means that although long flexors and long extensors have a share in every finger cramp, we can speak of a predominance of flexor tension or of extensor tension. We can consider the cramped terminal joint and the collapsed terminal joint as chiefly flexor tensions; whereas for the finger that has almost the right shape, but is restricted in flexion of the basal joint, tension of the extensor against the short muscles is probably responsible. In the claw hand, flexors and extensors are equally involved.

H.:   Aren't we going too far into theory?

P.:   No, for here we see typical instances of tension systems. Extensor tensions are always combined with tensions of the muscles that fix the ribs and shoulder blade upwards and forward-upwards respectively; so we shall find the head-turner (PL. B/3 and C/29) tensed under the ear, in the lower-jaw and tongue-bone muscles (PL. B/1, B/31 and B/30) as well, and finally in the greater breast-muscle in the anterior axillary fold (PL. C/3). Therefore, we can try to free the fingers from all these points, if the simple order to let the elbow fall laterally has no effect.

W.:   How do you find out that the head-turner, for instance, is tensed?

P.:   Very simply. I touch it under the ear and feel that it is hard. And when I tell the pupil to turn his head the movement is limited. The same can be done for all muscle tensions. Touching has the additional advantage that often by means of strong pressure I can make the pupil release the tension; for instance, firm pressure against the anterior axillary fold can work wonders.

W.:   Then that is the tension system of the finger extensors. And to which system do the finger flexors belong?

P.:   Here what I notice in the first place is a connection with the hamstring muscles (PL. B/13), which tip the pelvis in such a way that it rests on the chair with the back part of the sitting knobs.

Moreover, the calf muscles (PL. B/16) are tensed, whereby the tip of the foot presses against the floor.

W.:   Then I suppose correction is possible from the lower half of the body?

P.:   Certainly. Tilting of the pelvis, by which the sitting knobs shift backwards so that they are burdened more in front, often helps immediately.

H.:   But of course what we have just learned about the relationship of the finger extensors to the muscles of the neck and the finger flexors to the muscles of the thigh emphasizes only the most important relationships. Over and above these, finger tensions can be connected with all the other stiffenings in the whole body which are still to be discussed. Indeed the main reason for discussing all these other tensions is that they ultimately affect the fingers.

P.:   But in speaking of the relationships of the fingers to the remotest parts of the body, we must not forget their immediate vicinity. Indeed we must remember that with the lateral tilting of the fingers, which results automatically from the lateral fall of the elbow, a great temptation to cramp the fingers is eliminated. Therefore, whenever a tendency to finger tension of any kind shows itself, we should immediately take a more supine position of the hand and fingers than would otherwise be necessary in an uncramped arm.

W.:   And finally we must remember that the thumb plays a special part among the fingers.

Thumb tension

P.:   Yes, indeed! We have already mentioned that tensions in the thumb are particularly liable to hinder the lateral fall of the elbow. When the tendons of the thumb extensors are greatly tensed, they can be seen (PL. C/14 and C/16) on the back of the hand, running from the wrist towards the thumb as two plainly protruding strands, between which the skin forms a hollow, the "anatomical snuffbox" (PL. C/15).

W.:   This "snuffbox" cannot be seen in an uncramped hand, can it?

P.:   No. Moreover, we must take note that tension of its extensors not only impairs the freedom of the thumb in flexion and opposition — which is immediately obvious — but also that the long thumb-extensor (PL. C/16) because it runs obliquely, influences the rotatory freedom of the thumb in such a way that the thumbnail cannot be completely turned away from the other fingers as it ought to be (cf. p. 88).

H.:   If we remember how this same muscle influences the

position of the elbow, we see that the lateral rise of the elbow is related to the hampered thumb-rotation. Therefore we can eliminate both evils at the same time. We can often cause the elbow to fall laterally if we strive for the most extensive rotation of the thumb in opposition.

W.:   Does the thumb belong to a special tension system different from those of the other fingers?

P.:   I am struck by the fact that tensions of the thumb are usually related to tensions in the other side of the body. Tension in the left leg is connected with tension in the right thumb and vice versa. The free outward movement of the opposite leg in a double cone around the hip-heel axis — as well as the relief of tension in the toes — is of the greatest importance for freeing the thumb.

H.:   Although we have mentioned only the most important relationships of the thumb, we can conclude our discussion of finger tensions and turn next to the wrist joint.

P.:   Since we know that wrist tension is largely caused by the long finger-muscles which pass over the wrist, we have hardly anything to add to what we have just said about the fingers. Again, it is mainly a question of the lateral fall of the elbow. Now we shall choose as points of suspension the shoulder at one end and the basal knuckle of a finger, supported at key-bottom, at the other.

H.:   If the arm really sags freely like a chain between these two points, then the wrist joint will be free in all directions, i.e., for flexion and extension, as well as for movements towards the thumb and little-finger sides. It means that all these movements can be made up to the limit imposed by the joint itself.

P.:   The next joint to concern us is the elbow. Tension of the elbow flexors and extensors against each other hinders the length-adjusting apparatus most directly.

W.:   Does that mean that we cannot reach the keys we want to reach?

P.:   No. Even the most tensed-up person manages to reach the keys. But how does he reach them? Don't forget that the length-adjusting apparatus is the bridge between the supporting apparatus and the hand. If this bridge hangs like a chain, then the two systems are independent of one another; then a free after-motion is possible; then, too, the three degrees of freedom of the supporting apparatus in respect to the chair are present — without having the playing disturbed by the movements of the supporting apparatus. None of this is possible when the length-adjusting apparatus is cramped.

Tension of arm muscles

W.:   From that I can gather which movement we must make to relieve these tensions. We described it the other day (p. 106) as follows. The wrist is pulled forward by strong wrist-flexion after we have reached key-bottom; and at the same time the supporting apparatus is tilted far backward, so that all parts of the length-adjusting apparatus are stretched to the utmost.

P.:   That's right. Of course, this exercise stretches the flexor muscles of the elbow, above all the biceps (PL. B/27 and C/5) — tension of which, moreover, hinders rotatory freedom of the fore-arm. Further, we must think of the tension of the elbow extensor (PL. B/28 and C/19). In order to loosen this we must, of course, flex the elbow.

W.:   So now we must activate the biceps, which we have just relaxed, and perhaps make it begin to tense again.

P.:   Not at all. Notice that we did not accomplish the stretching of the elbow flexor by means of activity in the elbow extensor either, but we used comparatively remote muscles, namely, wrist flexors and hip and trunk muscles. We shall use a similar method now. While the hand is resting on the keys, we must repeatedly bring the shoulder towards the hand and away from it by alternately bending forward and backward.

H.:   Now we have said the most important things about the tension of muscles within the arm, and we can pass on to the muscles connecting the arm with the trunk.

Tension of breast muscles

P.:   Here our first concern is the greater breast-muscle (PL. C/3 and C/4), situated in the anterior axillary fold. You can easily convince yourself how firmly it tightens, if you feel the anterior axillary fold of the pupil.

W.:   If I remember correctly, the shoulder is pulled forward by the tension of the greater breast-muscle.

P.:   Yes, and the whole frontside becomes tensed. If you press against the pupil's chest and try to force him backwards you will meet with unbelievable opposition. These frontal tensions naturally reach down to the legs. Here again we notice that the tension system is disposed diagonally across the body — in that muscles on the inside of the left thigh tense together with the right breast-muscle, and in this way hinder both the left leg from sinking freely to the side and also the trunk from turning to the right. Of course, the opposite happens with the left breast-muscle.

W.:   What can we do against this?

P.:   It is implied in what we have said. We must oppose frontside tensions by straightening up the trunk as much as possible. Strong pressure against the breast muscle can affect it directly and, being a push against the trunk, can also initiate a loosening of the whole frontside. And we shall have to place particular emphasis on the free double-conical movement of the leg around the hip-heel axis.

H.:   It is similar in the case of tension of the upper part of the hood muscle (PL. B/4 and C/1), which always works together with the breast muscle in the fixation of the shoulder girdle (p. 106).

P.:   The only difference is that in cases where mainly the upper part of the hood muscle tenses, we hardly have to consider the possibility that it does so only on one side. Here everything happens symmetrically on the frontside of the trunk down to the front of the legs, which in the region of the groin are firmly connected with the front of the trunk.

H.:   In this case it is extremely important to bring the pupil to the point where he has the courage to let his trunk fall freely backwards — with the released legs representing a free counter-weight, so to say.

P.:   But we must not forget the direct influence on the upper part of the hood muscle.

W.:   In order to stretch it, we must lower the shoulder blade properly and, beyond that, actively push it strongly downwards.

P.:   That's right. It will be obvious that we can feel the tension of the hood muscle at the side of the neck above the shoulder. On the othe hand, the hard swelling that we can occa-sionally feel in the nape of the neck immediately below the skull corresponds to the long nape-muscles, which are partly covered by the hood muscle (PL. B/2). These muscles are actually only the counterforce to the tension at the front and will, therefore, be loosened with it. In less extreme cases, it is enough to straighten up the supporting apparatus and push back the buttocks for this purpose.

H.:   It will not be enough in those cases where tension at the front extends by way of the throat to the lower jaw, which is then pressed against the upper jaw with grinding of the teeth.

P.:   Then we shall have to move the lower jaw extensively in all directions, i.e., not only by opening and closing the mouth, but also by moving the chin to the right and left, like a cow chew-ing the cud. Moreover, we should throw the head back, as shown in the picture of Liszt (Fig. 12, p. 166).

H.:   In this way the head and neck can be kept out of the play of forces in the body altogether. Of course, it is quite different

letting fall each side of the body. The swelling of the lateral hip-muscles can be felt below the iliac crest.

W.: Then, if I remember rightly, there are still the inner thigh muscles.

P.: Tension of these is shown in pressing the knees together. The result, as we know, is to make free lateral turning of the supporting apparatus impossible. But, of course, the double-conical movement of the legs is hindered, too. It is clear that by making this movement energetically we can relieve this tension.

W.: Now we still have the hamstring muscles (PL. B/13) to consider. Since they pull the sitting knobs forward, we have found them to be considerable obstacles to straightening-up freely.

P.: The protrusion of their tendons at the knee hollow is the clearest outer sign of their tension. But they are also noticeable by the tendency to scrape the feet backwards or to tip the chair forward. Moreover, they cause a distinct pressure of the sitting knobs (PL. A/10) against the chair top because of the changed distribution of weight at the supporting surfaces (cf. Fig. 10, p. 145).

H.: If we here repeat that in order to counteract this the supporting apparatus must be properly straightened up and moved forward and backwards after letting fall both sides of the body, while the double-conical movement of the legs must be made to the sides, it may seem very boring; but it cannot be said often enough.

P.: If we finally consider the muscles of the shank and foot, too, we will begin with the tension of the calf muscles that tends to push the knee upwards.

Tensions in shank and foot

W.: So it has the same effect as the tension of the front hip-muscles?

P.: Yes. The two groups of muscles usually work together. Against this we must naturally look to the free sinking of the thigh.

W.: Isn't the free movability in the ankle joint affected by tension of the calf muscles?

P.: Of course, and this is a question of freedom in lifting and lowering the foot. At the same time we can often observe a lack of freedom in tipping the foot sideways, which is manifest as a hindrance to the double-conical movement of the leg. Finally, we must not forget cramping of the toes, which we have often mentioned — above all, of the big toe. To relieve the tension here we can do nothing but call the pupil's attention to it and tell him to let go.

H.:   That concludes our quick survey of the most important tensions and tension systems.

P.:   It provides a certain basis for the second part of today's considerations, namely, the question of what gymnastic exercises independent of the piano are best for relieving these tensions.

W.:   Isn't it peculiar that we need gymnastic exercises for relaxing the muscles? We generally think of gymnastic exercises, on the contrary, as having the purpose of strengthening the muscles.

K.:   I believe that even as far as sport alone is concerned it would be wrong to stress the strengthening of the muscles to the exclusion of everything else. Great sporting achievements can be made only if attention is paid to properly co-ordinating the muscles, not only to strengthening them. And as far as I know, some importance is given now even in gymnastic instruction to relaxing exercises.

P.:   This standpoint is all the more valid for us — though I must admit that even we must not altogether neglect muscle-strengthening in our exercises, e.g., for the short finger-muscles. But our main aim must be to get rid of mutually antagonistic tensions.

H.:   And we must always concentrate on this purpose in our exercises. Even though we may perform them over and over again, we shall be unsuccessful unless we are continuously conscious in every movement of what we are striving for and unless we constantly think of this aim.

P.:   If you can achieve this concentration in working, you often find out various things, which I perhaps have not even mentioned — but these details that one discovers for oneself are often the most valuable. So you can gain much more from short but concentrated periods of practice than from long stretches of thoughtless activity.

K.:   You are asking for concentration on a certain aim — without, however, saying more about this aim than the general remark about eliminating mutually antagonistic tensions.

P.:   Your dissatisfaction with this general character of the remark is only partially justified; because in each of our exercises we shall be striving for a general, as well as for a local, success. We want to achieve the circumscribed local success by virtue of the special nature of the individual exercise, which particularly affects a certain group of muscles. To what must we pay special attention in the area of the body directly affected?

W.:   In the individual joint, we must pay attention to whether the movements can be carried out to the limit imposed by the joint or whether they are restricted beforehand by muscle tension; and in a whole limb, to whether it is heavy or light, i.e., whether the weight is an essential factor in the course of movement or whether its effect is cancelled out by tension. In the supporting apparatus, we must pay attention to completely free straightening-up, which is to be combined with the downward tendency of the shoulder girdle, thus creating firmness and sure control of the playing apparatus from the trunk.

H.: Much of this can not only be checked inwardly by the feeling in the muscles, but can also be perceived outwardly. We can see the extent of movability in a joint and can feel hardened parts of muscles as swellings when they are tensed. The teacher must pay attention to those facts and can thus help the pupil during the exercises, but the pupil must contribute perseverance and concentration, which are much more essential than anything the teacher can do for him.

P.: We must not limit such localized observations to the part of the body directly affected by the exercise at the time, but now and then we must check one or another part of the body farther away, especially those parts that we know are the points where there is likely to be countertension in the tension systems.

H.: If we really pay careful attention to all this, we shall unexpectedly be led from local to general success. Then sooner or later in the course of some attempt the body will take on a new general condition which the pupil has not hitherto experienced. Suddenly one discovers how, by means of relaxation, the natural weight is entering into the interplay of forces. One has learned to trust gravity and to react positively to it — in an active yielding, so to say. And although this new condition has been only partly achieved, it produces an extraordinarily pleasant feeling in the body, as though one were stripping off one's chains.

P.: Then the further attempt must be made to keep this condition — which can in the beginning be lost again very easily — and to build upon the initial success in proceeding to further liberation. Now it is easier; now you can replace your hitherto purely theoretical ideas about muscle tension with bodily sensations which can be renewed again and again, and the release of tensions becomes an actual practical experience. In this way automatic co-ordination arises between the intelligence and refined body-feeling, and the exercises will remain interesting for you.

W.: But we cannot expect complete success until all the

exercises which are still to be discussed have been successfully accomplished, can we?

P.: Perhaps that's saying too much. You must remember that not every person has all the tensions we have discussed, or at least not all to the greatest degree. One person has one tension more strongly developed, and another a different one. For this reason I must use different exercises serving different purposes with my different pupils. I do not intend to describe here all the exercises which I use with my pupils from time to time, but I should like to give a selection of the most important ones; from among them something useful can be found for every type of tension. You will understand that it is not absolutely necessary for every pianist to do all the exercises which we shall now cite. But in any case I recommend that one should not limit oneself to too few exercises, because there is more prospect of success if one attacks the fortress from many sides.

H.: Now we know enough in general to be able to begin with the individual exercises.

P.: Yes, and first we shall take the exercises directly affecting the supporting apparatus, i.e., trunk and legs.

W.: Here I suppose you are thinking primarily of the standing position adopted by Paganini, as we described it the other day (pp. 141–142).

Standing up

P.: The achievement of the "Paganini exercise" will be the ultimate object of our efforts. But we shall begin with simpler ones. The first thing we will practise is standing up from a chair.

W.: I should think anybody can do that.

P.: But how? Observe the person who sits slumping on his chair with rigid knees. In order to get his buttocks loose from the chair he must lean very far forward, possibly bracing himself with his hands on his knees.

W.: Good, now I know how not to do it; but how should I do it?

P.: If your trunk is straightened up and your hip and knee joints are relaxed, it happens automatically. The straightened-up trunk has its line of gravity further forward than the trunk which sags, and therefore it can be raised from the chair directly by hip-extension without leaning forward. While the buttocks are leaving the chair, a slight forward movement of the knees in an arc around the ankle joint occurs, whereby the line of gravity is shifted slightly more forward, so that it now passes through the supporting surface of the feet. Now you can raise yourself completely by a continuation of hip-extension and by knee-extension.

H.: Of course, that was an analysis in slow motion. Actually it goes much faster, each part of the movement flowing over into the next.

W.: Sure enough, it is possible that way.

P.: When you have practised this normal rising to a standing position enough, we shall modify it somewhat by supporting ourselves in doing it.

W.: So we are going to do what we have just scolded the person who slumps in his chair for doing.

P.: The same thing done by two people is not the same thing at all. When he supports himself with his arm, he does it by pushing, so that his weight burdens his arm in the direction of length. We, however, in this exercise will use the peripheral movement of the arm in an arc around the shoulder. In this movement the little-finger ball of the circling arm meets the resistance of the piano lid and the continued arm-movement helps the legs to lift the trunk. If we use only one arm, we raise ourselves on three legs, so to speak.

W.: In rising in this way the trunk turns away from the supporting hand.

P.: Very good. If this turning-away occurs, it is proof that the correct freedom to turn is present in the body.

H.: Let us not forget to observe the condition of the supporting arm. The hand with the fingers remains loose, the wrist is low, the elbow is laterally fallen during the movement, the shoulder is pulled far down by the back muscles so that it does not rise from the trunk towards the head, but the whole side of the body is lifted. What rises most distinctly forward and upwards is the rib cage in the vicinity of this shoulder.

P.: After we have done this exercise, first with the right and then with the left arm, we shall finally use both arms at the same time. It is obvious that now there will be no sideways turning while rising.

W.: In doing this last exercise we are really completing the movement the tendency for which arises in strong accents with both hands (p. 116).

P.: Yes; or to express it from a different viewpoint, we now rise on all fours.

W.: Since these two ways of expressing ourselves refer to the same thing, we realise that the technique of the first tone and the four-legged stance have something in common.

Walking on all fours

P.: They have the same muscle condition and movement processes. Therefore, the next exercise is walking on all fours.

W.:   Do you really mean that we should simply crawl on the floor like little children?

P.:   Yes, we crawl on the balls of our hands and on the knees. In doing so we must see that fingers and hands are relaxed and that the trunk is allowed to sag freely with a broad chest beneath the supporting shoulders.

K.:   This sagging indicates that the trunk is free of tension.

P.:   Experience has taught us, though, that the teacher often has difficulties in getting his pupils to consent to doing this exercise. For instance, there are some people who feel too superior to animals to creep around on the floor on all fours.

H.:   In such cases it is best to leave out this exercise, valuable as it is for putting the body in the correct condition. What is done unwillingly can do more harm than good.

P.:   Another reason for opposition to it is that nobody is ready to believe that an exercise in this position, which has not the remotest concern with piano playing, can be of advantage for playing the piano.

W.:   But we have just this minute learned its mechanical analogy to the technique of the first tone.

P.:   And even if this were not the case we must remember that mutually antagonistic muscle tensions are mostly constant conditions, which we encounter in all positions of the body and which, therefore, we can combat in all positions, even in lying down.

W.:   But haven't we stated (p. 51) that one needs no muscles at all while reclining?

P.:   It's true that we don't need them, but many people do use their muscles even in a lying position.

W.:   Oh yes, that may be the reason why one is often so tired after lying down.

P.:   However, lying-down is a condition in which we don't have to worry at all about balance and, therefore, one where muscle tensions are especially superfluous. So in recumbent position it is particularly easy to relieve the remaining tensions.

The three degrees of freedom in relation to chair

H.:   But now we return to the chair and remain sitting on it, but of course not like a sack of potatoes.

W.:   No, we must have movability on the chair according to the three degrees of freedom.

P.:   It is this movability with which we are now concerned. Remember that a movement cannot really be described as free until we are able to make it far beyond the extent to which we need it practically. So in the exercises our movements have to have a much greater compass than actual movements at the piano.

K.: In the forward- and backward-bending exercises this will be difficult, since the back of the chair will soon stop the backward movement.

P.: Therefore, in doing the exercise which serves to acquire this freedom, we should sit sideways on the chair with the back of the chair at our side. And now with the head hanging freely I simply let my trunk fall backwards. The legs, hanging too, form the counterweight.

W.: When I do it I feel an extraordinary tug in the front of my body.

P.: This tug is doubly important: First, it occurs only when the front of your body and your legs are not completely cramped, because if they were the fall of the upper and lower halves of your body in opposite directions would be prevented; secondly, this tug will do away with the tensions which are still there.

H.: That exercise was mainly for freedom in bending forward and backwards. Now what about lateral tilting?

W.: We have already considered it in the greatest detail (pp. 135 and 140). The main thing is that the side of the body from which I am tilting away should fall as completely as possible.

P.: Yes. If I simplify the geometry and think of the trunk as a rectangle with the corners at the two shoulders and the two hips, the lateral tilting must not be a tilting of the rectangle onto one of its lower corners, but the rectangle must be distorted into a rhomboid.

W.: And the transition from rectangle to rhomboid is made by letting one side fall.

P.: Yes, and above all you must not forget about letting fall the shoulder.

H.: It is obvious that the straightened-up condition of the spinal column must not be lost in this movement.

P.: Now let us proceed to the third degree of freedom, i.e., sideways turning. Freedom in making this movement is naturally only possible if the sitting knobs are unburdened, and therefore do not press into the chair, and if the legs neither scrape the floor, nor clamp together, nor press upwards, but passively follow the movement of the trunk.

H.: So now we are turning our attention from the trunk to the legs.

Leg exercises

P.: Yes. We shall now add several specific exercises for the legs and feet. The first exercise is this: Lift the tips of your feet and turn them outwards at the same time.

W.: What eventually happens is that the thighs fall out-wardly by the force of gravity alone.

P.: Yes, because in this exercise the muscles on the inner side of the thigh relax.

K.: But naturally when the tips of the feet are lifted the calf muscles are stretched also.

P.: . . . And thereby freed from tensions. The areas of the calf muscles and inner thigh-muscles are the ones to which we must pay attention in this exercise.

W.: Is this the only exercise for the legs?

P.: No. In the next one we shift our weight in sitting alter-nately on the right and the left sides, pushing backwards the knee and thigh of the side which is unburdened at the time.

W.: In this exercise the lumbar lordosis is increased a little each time.

H.: Yes, and it is important that the lumbar region remains untightened during the exercise.

P.: For the following exercise we shall leave the sitting position and lie face downwards. In this position we spread one leg away laterally. I have observed that this has a good influence on frontal relaxation and loosening in the lumbar region.

W.: I think I feel it, too.

P.: And now let us do the same exercise while standing. Now we are standing on the leg and spreading the other one away to the side.

K.: It seems to me that this exercise would actually induce anyone to tense his muscles in order to keep his balance, which in this position is very much endangered.

P.: I don't doubt that that is the case with you. But our aim must be, even under the most unfavorable conditions for maintaining equilibrium, to trust natural balance and to relieve tensions.

Letting fall one side of the body

W.: Since we have arrived at the aim of our exercises for the supporting apparatus, we can now try standing according to Paganini's example, which we have recognized as expressing the perfect condition of the supporting apparatus (Fig. 11, p. 157).

P.: Yes. You cannot practise standing like this often enough. You must stand on one leg, from which the support rises through the whole side of the body, then pull the other side of the body up, only to let it fall again as far as possible. This fall has its run-off in the turning outward of the foot. Paganini, being a violinist, always used his left leg as the supporting leg, but we will do this exercise using the right and left leg alternately as the supporting leg.

W.:   But as pianists we are only indirectly interested in standing.

P.:   For that reason we shall now do the same thing while seated. We shift the weight of the body temporarily to one side and lift up the buttock of the other side, and then let it fall together with the whole raised side, as far as the chair top allows.

H.:   Don't make the objection that we have already spoken about this exercise today. It is so basically important for the whole condition of the body that we cannot return to it too often.

P.:   Before we leave the supporting apparatus to direct our main attention to the playing apparatus, we will try an exercise that shows the co-ordination between the two and paves the way for the guidance of the supporting apparatus by the playing apparatus, which is what we are striving for, and not the reverse. We stand at the side of the piano, having opened the top as for a concert, grasp the edge of the piano with both hands and, fully stretched, let ourselves fall backward. The hand is spread but not cramped, the thumb grasps downwards on the outside. If the rest of the body is properly relaxed, the whole body yields easily to the movements made in the wrist joints.

Guiding the supporting apparatus with the hand

H.:   We must keep in mind the unity of the supporting and playing apparatuses that appears so plainly in this exercise, when we are doing the following exercises for the playing apparatus, because these exercises would be pointless if we were to pay no heed to the condition of the supporting apparatus.

P.:   Above all the trunk must be completely straightened up in these exercises, because otherwise arm movements can never be made freely. This applies to movements around the shoulder as well as to those in which the hand takes the lead, although it will be particularly noticeable in the first group because of the shoulder resting on the chest.

H.:   Of course, we cannot go again into the details of what we mean by a straightened-up trunk. Only the most distinct external sign may be mentioned, which is that the middle of the thoracic section of the spine must not protrude.

P.:   Yes. And with the trunk in this condition we shall now make movements of the shoulder, upper arm and forearm.

Freeing the weight apparatus

W.:   That means the weight apparatus is now the main subject.

P.:   Yes, but it does not mean that we can ignore the grasping apparatus at the same time. We must be careful to spread the hand, to have rotatory freedom and freedom from other tensions in these exercises, too.

W.:   It is practically the same as in the exercises for the supporting apparatus.

P.:   These fundamental requirements are always the same. The first exercise now is simply to circle the arm past the side of the trunk, like the vane of a windmill. We will do this movement slowly at first and then with ever increasing speed until we feel a tingling in the fingers as the result of centrifugal force.

K.:   Outwardly this movement appears to be made only in the shoulder joint, but you can convince yourself that the shoulder-girdle joints are working with it, since the shoulder itself is continually changing position.

P.:   Certainly the shoulder will move up and down, but the important thing is that it should always take the lowest position possible in accordance with the position of the arm at the time.

W.:   So we have to take heed for a low shoulder here, too.

P.:   Yes. Our next exercise is especially aimed at this low shoulder. But we must acquire it step by step. On the first beat we raise the shoulder, on the second let it fall freely, and on the third push it down forcefully.

H.:   In doing this you can recite in 3/4 time: "High — dead — push down!"

P.:   Here again we must remember the relation of the shoulder movements to the supporting apparatus. The fixations which may hinder these movements can best be relieved by turning the feet radically outwards.

W.:   Sure enough! When I do this I feel a loosening of the muscles at the back over the pelvis, and then I can push the shoulder down behind the protruding rib cage much more freely.

P.:   Now we will move the shoulder in a circle.

W.:   Haven't we just done that?

P.:   No. We circled the arm around the shoulder; now we circle the shoulder around the breastbone-collarbone joint, while the arm hangs freely from the shoulder. We make the circle in both directions, first up and forward, then up and backwards.

W.:   I am surprised that this is the second exercise in which the shoulder is repeatedly raised, in spite of the fact that we are striving for a low shoulder.

P.:   What disturbs us is not the temporary high position of the shoulder, but its upward fixation. In our exercises this fixation is combatted by the immediate change from a high position to a low one again and again.

W.: So even the raising of the shoulder serves to achieve as deep a shoulder as possible. As a matter of fact, I think I can already feel the exercise is having this effect.

P.: Never believe you can get lightning effects from the exercises. Now in the following ones we want to influence the weight apparatus in its interplay with the grasping apparatus.

Rotatory freedom of the arm

W.: Here I suppose we must pay particular attention to the freedom of rotation between the two.

P.: Yes, the next exercise helps this rotatory freedom. We make the hand into a hollow ball, as already previously (p. 93) described, and then in quick succession make pronatory and supinatory movements to the greatest extent possible between the forearm bones, i.e., through 180 degrees.

W.: If we restrict ourselves to forearm rotation, the elbow probably stays bent.

P.: We start with a bent elbow, but while moving the hand we slowly extend and flex the elbow alternately, so that the ball-shaped hand, rotating on its axis, is in turn brought towards and taken away from the body.

H.: We scarcely need to be reminded that the lateral fall of the elbow must be maintained in doing this.

W.: When I do this exercise, there is a slight tingling in my fingers, just as there was in circling the arm.

P.: That's a sign that you have done it fast enough and extensively enough.

H.: It also proves that, at least for the moment, you have the necessary rotatory freedom between the weight and grasping apparatuses.

P.: These two apparatuses, however, must not only be free in relation to each other, but must also work together correctly. This co-ordination is fostered by exercises that to a great extent correspond to the actual situation in playing the piano. At least we will sit at the piano to do them.

Exercises in which keys are touched

W.: And do we play, too?

P.: Yes. The first exercise consists in playing a sequence of chords, using the technique of the first tone, according to the detailed description we have given. We shall choose the type of after-motion in which, by means of wrist-flexion, the arm is thrown high up each time to about eye level.

W.: So this is really an exercise for the grasping apparatus.

P.: That's right, but it is almost more important as an exercise for the weight apparatus, since it depends on the latter being free to the extent of not hindering the flinging-up of the arm, and since it helps to give the weight apparatus this freedom. However, we must be careful that the flinging action does not originate in the shoulder.

W.: Now I remember (cf. pp. 161–162). If the arm in falling were bent at the elbow and the elbow were raised laterally, that would be a sign that the movement came from the shoulder.

H.: Quite correct. The most important criteria for the general condition of arm and hand may be called to mind again here: The arm is supine and the outer fingers clasp towards the low elbow.

P.: Next we combine this exercise with arm circling, i.e., we fling the arm up and continue this movement in a circular movement around the shoulder so that the arm describes one and a quarter circles each time before it falls back to the keyboard.

W.: But we would never do that when actually playing the piano.

P.: Granted. Neither shall we use the next exercise in actual playing, although it relates to an extremely important event in actual playing, i.e., the downward movement of the weight apparatus past the piano.

W.: In proper playing, this downward movement is caught up by the grasping apparatus.

P.: But in the exercise we shall leave out the element of catching up. We do use the small grasping unit, but it alone, in order to play keys with 2nd and 4th or 1st and 3rd fingers. Since the wrist joint offers no resistance, it is passively hyperextended and the fingers slide away from the keys just played.

W.: In that case the arm movement continues downwards until the arm is approximately perpendicular.

P.: Yes; first we shall do this exercise in this way, but afterwards we shall add the arm circling again, and so continue the arm movement until the hand slaps down again on the keyboard.

W.: Now, of course, the arm is swung in the opposite direction to the one in which we moved it after flinging it up.

H.: During this arm-swinging the hand should not be allowed to relax completely at the wrist but should retain a moderate extension.

Exercises with winch

P.: In the following exercises we shall devote ourselves principally to the grasping apparatus.

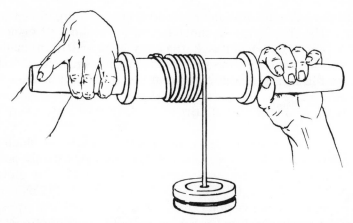

Figure 21. Winch. The most suitable dimensions are as follows. Middle part: diameter 2", length 6", perforation for the string in the middle. Handpieces: slightly conical with greatest diameter 1.5", length of each 5"; a raised rim, about 1/3" high, between the middle part and each of the handpieces is advantageous. Length of the string, 3'; appended weight, 2 lb.

W.: We shall certainly need the keyboard as point B for this.

P.: No. First we shall take substitutes for it — namely, bodies that are not static, as the keyboard is, and therefore cannot function as real points B, but that are something to grasp and are real enough to represent points B in our imagination and for our sense of touch. We could use a stick, perhaps an ordinary walking stick, even one with a crook. Or sometimes I use a short thick piece of wood on which I wind a string carrying a weight, so that the piece of wood becomes a winch (Fig. 21).

W.: What is the purpose of this artificial point B?

P.: As you know, we always want to attain more in our exercises than we actually need. If we actually need the ability to direct the movements of the whole playing apparatus from an im-movable point B, then it is an extra achievement if, in our exercises, we direct the movements from a movable grasping-point. Besides, we can make more extensive movements around the latter than we need for playing the piano, and so we can be sure that the move-ments are free to the extent necessary for us.

H.: In fact, by means of exercises with the stick and winch we can reach the point where the reciprocal tensions in the body are totally eradicated. Of course, in order to reach this point it is important that during these exercises we observe the whole body and its possible tensions.

P.: And moreover, care should be taken that the arms and

244

the supporting apparatus are in the correct condition. So let us repeat: The elbow must be fallen laterally, the shoulder blades must be pulled down and back, the body must be straightened up. The most advantageous posture for the legs is a slight straddling. We raise the arms forward to about eye level without bending the elbows.

W.:   And now we hold the winch with the hands raised forward, do we?

P.:   Yes, on both sides of the middle part around which the string is wound. However, the winch is really held by only one hand at a time, while the other hand serves as a fork to support the handle of the winch. But of course even in the holding hand only so much force must be exerted as is necessary for grasping, which means that each finger can be easily lifted at any time to show that it is not tensely pressed around the handle.

W.:   I think I am now holding the winch correctly.

P.:   Not yet. The thumb must be spread away from the 2nd finger as far as possible, and the winch must be as deep as possible in the fork formed by these two fingers so that you feel a strong pull in the web-skin between thumb and index finger.

W.:   Now I can feel it. What shall I do now?

P.:   Since the string is completely unwound, we shall wind it up, and so, gradually lift the weight. We can conceivably do this in two ways, by winding towards or away from ourselves.

W.:   Which way do we choose?

P.:   Both, of course. But first we roll away from ourselves so that the string hangs down on the side of the winch toward us.

W.:   That is done by means of flexions in the wrist joints.

P.:   Quite right. Since the starting position of the wrist joints is an extreme, but absolutely uncramped, hyperextension, the movements of flexion can be very extensive. We shall begin by flexing the grasping right hand in this way so that the winch turns freely in the fork of the left hand and the weight is raised a little.

W.:   I've done that. What next?

P.:   Now hold the winch with your left hand, and the right hand passively sinks back into the starting position of hyperextension.

W.:   I understand. Now I flex the grasping left hand and thus raise the weight a little more. And this is repeated by alternate hands until the string is completely wound up.

P.:   That's right. Having done this much, let us observe how the string is wound up, whether it is any old way or as neatly as a winding machine would do it. Precision of winding is a very useful indication of the condition of your playing apparatus.

H.:   For the moment, however, let us not be discouraged by the confused way the string has been wound up and let us begin to unwind it, or rather, we shall leave this job to the heaviness of the weight.

W.:   To do this I simply have to loosen my grasp and immediately the string will be completely unwound.

P.:   There wouldn't be any use in that. We gain a great deal, on the contrary, if we allow the unwinding to proceed step by step, whereby the hand is carried along a little each time.

W.:   This results simply in a reversal of the movements we have just made for winding up.

P.:   Except that it is not the muscles but the heaviness of the weight which provides the motive force. My arms are entirely passive.

W.:   That results in much stricter guidance from point B for each arm than we ever achieve in playing the piano.

P.:   Yes. Actually what happens is that in the grasping hand, let's say the right hand, we start from extreme flexion of the wrist joint and loosen the grasp of the left hand, while the right wrist yields to the pull of the weight until there is maximum hyperextension. Then the left hand slides upwards loosely around the winch, grasps it there, and is turned downwards by and with the winch, which rests in the loosening right hand.

H.:   And so, alternately, until the weight is at the bottom again.

W.:   Now we can wind up the string on the other side.

P.:   Naturally. And in doing so we can retain the initial extreme flexion of the wrist joint in the hand that is grasping at the time (cf. Fig. 21). Only, this hand is now hyperextended actively.

W.:   The fourth part of the procedure will be to let the string, which is now hanging down at the side of the winch away from us, be unwound by the heaviness of the weight again.

P.:   You understand that perfectly. And I hope you understand, too, that in doing this the wrist joint of the grasping hand must again take a hyperextended starting position, from which the transition to extreme flexion occurs again passively.

W.:   That would logically be followed by the first exercise with the winch, in which the wrist is actively flexed.

Exercises with stick

H.: In this way we can repeat the exercises again and again in a continuous sequence without getting too much of them.

P.: But for the moment, unfortunately, we must interrupt these beneficial exercises in order to discuss others. The next will be exercises with a stick or cane. In the case of these, however, I must stress right at the beginning that you can have too much of them. One of them consists in swinging the cane until its impetus carries the hand into extreme positions, whereby the tensions in the muscles are torn apart. Though it has this highly desirable effect, the exercise involves the risk, in the case of very tightly tensed muscles, of inflammation of the tendon sheaths, especially in the region of the wrist on the thumb side. We avoid this danger by choosing as light a cane as possible, so that its impetus cannot be too great. Nevertheless caution is advisable. The moment there is any feeling of discomfort in these exercises, it is best to stop them instead of heroically continuing.

H.: These precautionary measures are of course superfluous if we do not swing the cane, as when we simply use it as a substitute for the winch. Since in this case we do not have to raise or lower a weight it is simply a question of turning the cane around its axis of length by means of flexion or extension of the wrist joints.

W.: So wrist flexion will serve to rotate the cane away from me and extension to rotate it towards me.

P.: Of course, here we do not have four different exercises as we did with the winch, but only two.

H.: It is obvious that now all wrist movements that turn the cane are active ones.

P.: But now we shall proceed to the swinging exercise. We grasp the middle of the cane with uncramped fingers, let the upper arm hang down freely and flex the elbow to a right angle while it rests on the hip.

W.: Now I am holding the cane almost vertically in front of the right side of my body.

H.: Yes. Of course, while we are doing this, the body must be kept straightened up to the utmost, and the shoulder blade pulled far down behind.

P.: Now we begin pronatory and supinatory movements of the forearm.

W.: When I do that the cane swings in a vertical plane.

H.: It swings through 180 degrees.

P.: Yes. But next, while continuing to rotate the forearm,

remove the elbow from its support at the hip and raise it slowly forward. At the same time, slowly extend the elbow joint so that the cane continues to swing uninterruptedly in a vertical plane.

W.: When the elbow is completely extended, I can increase the rotatory movement even up to 360 degrees.

P.: And this we want to do, too. We should always let the swing of the cane run its full course, and not make the supinatory movement immediately at the conclusion of the pronatory one or vice versa. If we follow this rule, the cane will really whizz through the air. The greater the sound it makes, the more correctly the exercise is being performed; so the sound is an audible indication of the correct condition of the body.

H.: We can make this exercise a little easier for ourselves if we support the wrist of the rotating hand on a fork formed by the thumb and index finger of the other hand.

W.: And how long should I practise this?

P.: As long as you feel safe, as I have said.

H.: In brief periods this exercise can never do any harm. It can be used to great advantage as a relaxation between other exercises.

P.: The next exercise, although not completely harmless, is much less dangerous, since the cane does not receive any impetus in it. It is simply alternate flexion and extension of the wrist, and the main purpose of the cane is to give the hand something to grasp.

W.: I expect the cane will be held at the middle again. I know that attention must be paid to the correct condition of the grasping apparatus and of the whole body.

P.: That's right. The movements are simply back and forth, and not to be done in 2/4 time, but in 3/4 time.

W.: So one bar includes flexion — extension — flexion, the next one extension — flexion — extension.

P.: And just as in regular musical performance, we should always give the movement corresponding to the first beat of the bar an accent — which means that we make this movement very strong, while the two following ones are only aftereffects.

W.: So the accent changes from bar to bar: First it is on flexion and then on extension.

P.: That's just what we want. With reference to the position in space we will do this exercise in four different ways:

1) with the back of the hand facing upwards,
2) with the back of the hand outwards,

3)   with the back of the hand beneath, and

4)   with the back of the hand facing inwards.

H.:   The next exercise is very similar: Instead of flexing and extending the wrist, we move the hand alternately towards the thumb side and little-finger side.

W.:   I suppose that this also is done in 3/4 time and with the four different positions of the back of the hand.

P.:   Yes, it is. In the last exercise with the cane, we shall combine the movements of the two preceding ones. We move the hand from extreme hyperextension towards the little-finger side, then in extreme flexion on towards the thumb side and finally back into hyperextension or vice versa.

W.:   What we are doing is circumduction.

P.:   Right. And without pronation or supination.

W.:   In this exercise the tip of the cane describes something between a circle and a square.

P.:   That's about it. Don't be frightened if now and then there is a creaking in your wrist when you do this.

W.:   Then it is not a sign of danger, like the discomfort in swinging the cane, is it?

Exercises with pencil

P.:   No. Now we lay aside the cane and take a smaller object: a pencil. We grasp it loosely with the 1st, 2nd and 3rd fingers.

W.:   That's simply the way we learned to hold the pencil at school.

H.:   No, we grasp the pencil transversely so that the tip does not point away from us as in writing, but points to the left or right.

P.:   The thing to pay attention to here is the intense spreading of the middle hand. The outward sign of this is the great distance between the basal knuckles of the index finger and thumb.

W.:   I suppose we combine this with as much contrary rotation as possible so that the thumbnail is turned downwards.

P.:   That's right. We extend the 5th finger and, to a slighter degree, the 4th finger and spread them away from the other fingers.

K.:   Actually the hand looks like that of a person who picks up an object in an affected way.

H.:   Except that there will be no middle-hand spreading in the affected person's hand.

P.:   Now with the hand holding the pencil in this way, we make movements in all directions.

W.:   You mean flexion and extension, movements towards the little-finger side and the thumb side and finally circumduction, don't you?

P.:   Yes indeed. But beyond this we will combine these
wrist movements with movements in the other joints of the arm,
i.e., flexion and extension in the elbow and arm movements in all
directions around the shoulder joint.

H.:   Of course, in all this the elbow must remain laterally
fallen, and the supporting apparatus must be in the correct condition.

P.:   This exercise aims at enabling the moving hand to grasp
while it is loose but spread.

W.:   Do we need the pencil anymore?

P.:   No. Now we are going to get along with our fingers
alone. Two fingers are brought to meet each other, let's say the
2nd and 4th. We do this alternately over and under the 3rd finger.

Finger exercises
without piano

W.:   That's not hard at all.

P.:   Anybody can do it somehow. But it is important to see
that the elbow does not rise laterally while you do it — as it did
with you. Let it fall.

W.:   I understand.

P.:   Next bring the 3rd and 5th fingers to meet each other
above and below the 4th finger.

H.:   You can think up similar exercises yourself. What you
must always watch out for is the effect of the exercise on the arm,
which must always remain in such a condition that it hangs freely.

P.:   Another very important finger exercise is active rotation
of individual fingers in their basal joints inwardly as well as outwardly.

W.:   Are these the exercises in which the tendons of the long
extensors finally slip off the basal knuckles?

P.:   Yes, that's what I mean. Whereas the finger muscles
were active in these last exercises, the middle hand and fingers are
passive in the next one. Our purpose is now to destroy restricting
tensions by means of external force, and we shall use the forearm
of the opposite side as an aid. We place this as deep as possible
between the 2nd and 3rd fingers right to the web-skin. Now we
turn the hand, thus passively spread, back and forth in pronation
and supination.

H.:   In doing this, as always, we must see that the elbow is
laterally fallen.

W.:   In such exercises, I really have the feeling that the two
fingers are properly separated from each other.

P.:   In order to get this feeling not only between the 2nd
and 3rd fingers, let us continue by placing the forearm between

3rd and 4th and finally between 4th and 5th fingers, making the same rotatory movements.

H.:   Of course, the same has to be done with the other hand, as all exercises are important for both arms and both hands.

P.:   Finally, we will devote ourselves to the arm as a chain. It is good for the teacher to co-operate in achieving this condition. He takes hold of the nail member of one of the pupil's fingers and, standing quite near the pupil, alternately raises the arm high and lowers it again. If the pupil's arm is really a chain, the teacher has to raise and lower the weight of the arm — neither more nor less than this weight.

W.:   And what has the pupil to do, besides simply yielding?

P.:   He must concentrate on the condition of the arm and picture to himself intensively the following process:
Under the nail member, the rest of the finger falls; then
under the finger, the hand falls; then
under the hand, the radius falls; then
under the radius, the ulna falls; then —
W.:   I know:
Under the ulna, the upper arm falls; then
under the upper arm, the shoulder blade falls; then
under the shoulder blade —
K.:   Stop! Here we are at the end of the chain, insofar as a link can fall below another.

P.:   And here we are at the end of those gymnastic exercises, which I wanted to discuss with you.

K.:   What is more, we have reached the end of the whole discussion.

H.:   Oh no! To finish, we want to find our way back to our instrument and say something about exercises at the piano.

P.:   That will be tomorrow's task.

DIALOGUE 12

Exercises at the Piano

W.:   At least we have piano exercises on our programme.

P.:   But we will limit ourselves to exercises concerning basic problems of the touch, the same problems with which we have been dealing the whole time. . And we must keep this limitation in mind. Nobody is to get the idea that I am creating a new school of velocity. There are plenty of those already, and some of them are even quite useful. The task I have set for myself is one step more basic. The purpose is to get the playing apparatus into a condition in which velocity is possible without causing harm. The ability for velocity will come by itself in this way and the player can then choose whichever school of velocity he wants for his training.

Significance of the exercises

W.:   And there are no schools in which the exercises you want are to be found?

P.:   Closest to my intentions come Wiehmayer, Tausig and Pischna; and it is beneficial to transpose the exercises given by these authors into as many keys as possible. But you will imme-diately see that the exercises I consider most necessary are so primitive that anybody would be ashamed to write them down, just as the most vital and elementary facts are always subjects for shame.

W.:   So we are actually dealing only with the principles of first- and second-tone techniques, aren't we?

P.:   Quite right. The hollow form of the hand should be developed, and from here — i.e., from the periphery — the condi-tion of the whole body is to be influenced.

H.:   Since exercises which are particularly simple from a musical standpoint have been chosen, all our attention can be con-centrated on the condition of the playing apparatus. We need not repeat here in detail the points to which we must pay attention as indicating the condition of both the playing and supporting appa-ratus. As a rule, it will be evident in the particular exercises.

P.:   Since in all the exercises we shall be dealing essentially with the same condition of the body, the various groups of exercises can be chosen at random, and it is not necessary to finish one group conscientiously before starting the next.

W.:   What do you mean by groups of exercises?

P.:   Well, one group relates to the first-tone technique, a second to the second-tone technique, a third to the cradle technique, a fourth to scale playing and a fifth to octave playing.

H.:   Then let us begin with the first-tone technique.

Exercises in first-tone technique

P.:   Yes, and we shall not begin with the playing of single tones, but of chords in closed and open positions, as we have already mentioned (p. 151).

W.:   Is it all the same, no matter which chords?

P.:   Yes. It is more important to work out carefully each particular phase of the touch in its various modifications:

1)   preparation at key-top,
2)   moving the wrist down past the keyboard,
3)   catching the motion by the backward-clasping fingers,
4)   raising the wrist in the after-motion
    a)   in closed position,
    b)   in open position, where attention must be paid to the free sliding forward of the non-carrying fingers,
    c)   starting from various cradle-positions,
5)   free rising of the playing apparatus to key-top as a result of key resiliency, with subsequent sliding at key-tops, or
6)   flinging up the arm by means of strong wrist-flexion,
7)   suspension adapted to a heavier or lighter appended weight.

W.:   If I have understood correctly, first I am to practise preparing the key-moving action for a while without playing at all, is that so?

H.:   No, of course we always combine the different phases with one another in practising, but we do it in as slow a motion as possible so that we can concentrate our attention on each phase.

Exercises in second-tone technique

P.:   That's enough about the first tone. In the exercises for the second-tone technique the first problem is to develop the hollow form of the hand and the grasping movement in the small grasping unit, but not yet the actual binding from key-bottom to key-bottom.

W.:   I understand. First we make the grasping movement of the finger simply as an after-flexion following the playing of a first tone, and in doing so take care to spread and vault the hand and also to use the right combination of movements — raising the basal knuckle, swinging the wrist and rotation.

H.: In all this the main thing is that this combination of movements should be guided by the grasping finger and not by point A.

P.: When, as a result, the finger has become a real supporting finger, we shall make movements of the playing apparatus around point B according to the three degrees of freedom.

H.: It is hardly necessary to speak again in detail about this exercise, since we dealt with it so thoroughly the other day (p. 190); but it would be very bad for the pupil if he skimmed over it as we are doing today.

P.: I have found still another kind of preparatory exercises for playing the second tone to be very useful. I usually call them the tethering exercises, because in doing them all five fingers rest closely bound together on the keys.

W.: Then I must first play a chord, something like c d e f g. But how can I add anything to it using the second-tone technique?

P.: You certainly can't. But you can raise one finger, perhaps the thumb.

K.: This then becomes negative piano playing, so to say. Instead of putting the fingers into the keys, you are taking them away from the keys.

P.: Yes. However, at the next moment we go into key-bottom with the finger which was just raised, in this case the thumb. But at the same time we lift a different finger, let's say the middle finger. And the important thing now is that at this moment your attention should be concentrated on the finger which is about to be raised and not on the playing finger. For this purpose I ask my pupils to say which finger they are raising, so now the pupil would have to say "three".

K.: What's the sense of turning the attention in this topsy-turvy manner?

P.: At the moment of moving the key the pupil tends to cramp the playing finger, but if his attention is directed away from this finger the danger of cramping is greatly reduced.

H.: Of course, we can continue this exercise as long as we wish. I think we understand that after the third finger has been raised it is used to play the next key. And at the same moment we must raise a different finger, e.g., the second, and so on. If we present this exercise diagrammatically by indicating the tops of the keys with a straight line and by writing the fingers in key-bottom below the line and the raised ones above it, it would look something like this:

12345	1 2345	3 12 45	2 1 345	4 123 5	3 12 45	5 1234
4 123 5	2 1 345	3 12 45	1 2345	12345		

P.: But it is also important to do these tethering exercises over various widths, not only as we first assumed over a fifth, but over an octave as well, i.e., c e g a c.

H.: In doing so, the thumb-grasp must always be directed towards the basal hollow of the 4th finger and the grasp of the 2nd to the 5th fingers inclusive towards the wrist end of the thumb ball — although this should hardly need to be mentioned again.

P.: Only when all this has been successfully accomplished with the right hand as well as with the left do we really practise a series of tones according to second-tone technique with binding from key-bottom to key-bottom. Of course, now, too, we must keep in mind all the conditions we had to observe in the preparatory exercises.

W.: You mean spreading and vaulting of the hand and the correct combination of basal-joint-raising, wrist-swinging and rotation.

H.: Moreover, we must now see to it that the after-flexing finger does not lose contact with the key before the finger that is to play next has become a supporting finger.

P.: Above all, we must not forget to make the after-flexion as extensive as possible after every key-moving action, because this is the best means for freeing the finger that is to play next from tension.

H.: It is of lesser importance in which sequence we play the notes of the five-note row in this exercise. But here, too, we must not forget to practise sequences in closed positions as well as open ones and towards the median plane as well as away from it.

W.: ... In order to practise pronatory positions as well as supinatory ones. I understand that. The limitation to the row of five notes means that we omit crossing the fingers over and putting the thumb under.

P.: Yes. And from time to time we should introduce between two key-moving actions the movements for practising the three degrees of freedom in the finger-key joint in order to test the freedom of the whole body and the chain condition of the playing apparatus.

H.:   Here again let us remember that the chain condition finds its visible manifestation in the lateral fall of the elbow — although only in supinatory positions can the elbow hang truly vertically under the line connecting shoulder and hand.

P.:   As to the cradle technique, we will first practise the cradle movement that is a changing over from the inner cradle to the outer cradle and back by means of alternate grasping with the thumb and little finger.

Exercises in cradle technique

H.:   We already know it is not enough that the movement seems outwardly correct; what matters is that it should be controlled by the grasping and yielding fingers.

P.:   We must also see that the grasping movements are always aimed at the correct point, i.e., the basal hollow of the 4th finger in thumb-grasping, and the wrist end of the thumb ball in grasping by the little finger.

H.:   After we have attained sufficient precision in these movements with the 1st and 5th fingers, we shall practise them with other pairs of fingers as well.

P.:   Finally, we shall play sequences of chords in the cradle curve in order to get to know the practical application of cradle technique, too.

H.:   In doing so, we will play the same sequence of chords in inner and outer cradle-positions, then with heavier and lighter appended weights and finally varying the weight in order to produce crescendo and decrescendo effects.

P.:   If now we practise scale playing our first problem is crossing the fingers over the thumb and putting the thumb under. We will begin with the following exercise for putting the thumb under because it is the simplest: While the 2nd finger is resting on a key at key-bottom, the thumb alternately plays a lower and a higher neighbouring key.

Exercises in scale playing

H.:   In doing this, of course, we must have the supporting index finger and the grasping thumb both in the correct condition.

W.:   I know; both fingers must be free of tension, especially in the terminal joint. The thumb must be spread away and move with a spiral grasp.

P.:   While the thumb is moving from one place to another, the supporting index finger makes an after-flexion in order to lift the thumb for the next touch. But this after-flexion must not cause the back of the hand to change its position.

H.:   It is advantageous to pause between each two thumb touches, yet the thumb must be put under immediately after finishing the previous touch to wait throughout the pause over the next key to be played.

P.: Now we shall vary this exercise — first of all by using the thumb on keys at different distances, next by using, instead of the 2nd finger, the 3rd and then the 4th as supporting fingers. With each new supporting finger, we can change the width of the grasp.

H.: But let us not forget that we can also use two of these fingers at once as supporting fingers and finally all three. The thumb is always put under and brought back over shorter and longer distances.

P.: The exercises for crossing the fingers over are analogous.

W.: I understand. Now we use the thumb as supporting finger, e.g., on c', and with the index finger we play d' and b alternately, then e' and a, and so on.

P.: But it is important that the thumb should be the chief motor of these movements.

H.: It is obvious that these crossing-over exercises are to be done not only with the 2nd finger, but with the 3rd and 4th fingers as well.

P.: The next thing we can do is to play continuous sequences of notes, in which we cross the fingers over and put the thumb under. In doing this we watch particularly that the thumb is always ahead in respect to the direction of playing.

W.: That means that the thumb is put under or reposed immediately after it has played.

P.: Yes, but instead of being satisfied with letting it slip through under the other fingers to any old position, we must bring it immediately over the key it is to play next. For this I should recommend the following exercise. In the stave, we have indicated over which key the thumb has to be at the time.

H.: We know, of course, that in doing all this attention must be paid to middle-hand spreading and extensive after-flexion of the finger that is supporting at the time.

P.: Another good exercise for correct crossing over and putting under is the so-called "transporting" exercise, in which the thumb alternately plays with 2 or 3 other fingers. The written notes explain best what is meant by this.

W.: In this exercise we really have the whole scale, except that several notes are played together instead of after each other.

P.: So we are not far from actually playing a scale. In doing this we shall start with our old friend C major, two octaves ascending and descending, right and left. Since we do not care about velocity but only about discharging the movements correctly, we shall play them slowly and with one hand only.

W.: When you talk about discharging the movements correctly, I suppose you mean the complete metamorphosis of each playing finger into a supporting finger.

P.: Yes, because only in this way will the following playing finger be really free. We do not need to list again all the other requirements which we always have of the grasping apparatus, weight apparatus and supporting apparatus.

H.: Nor should it be necessary to say that after C major all the other scales should follow.

W.: And shall we quicken the tempo eventually?

P.: "Quicken" is perhaps not the right word. Let us go on straightaway to what I call the "fast scale". But we shall work on it slowly, step by step, always testing the three degrees of freedom of the finger-key joint at the first note of the scale.

W.: What does that mean I have to do?

P.: Well, we play the first note of the scale and make movements around the key in all three main directions. When these go freely, we fling the arm high by means of a strong flexion of the wrist joint.

W.: Never in the world will that become a scale.

P.: No. But at least it was the basic note. Then we begin in the same way, i.e., we play the first note of the scale again and we make intermediate movements again, but now shorter ones, since we hope that the playing apparatus has already been completely freed of tension by means of the previous movements. This time we do not fling the playing apparatus immediately but proceed quickly to the second note of the scale and only after this do we make the strong flexion of the wrist.

W.: I understand. Next we go from the tonic over the second to the third note, then to the fourth, and so on.

H.: Yes, until we reach the octave — or better, two octaves.

P.: But what matters is that the whole sequence of notes,

from the basic note to the last one played on each occasion,
should always be at the greatest possible tempo, so that we can
represent the scale in written notes something like this:

H.:   In spite of the speed, each finger must naturally make a
proper grasping movement in playing.

P.:   Because of the brevity of the touch, finger-grasping as a
rule does not continue into an after-flexion. However, we should
make an after-flexion, even if only a slight one, after each last note
before the after-motion in the large grasping unit, by which the
hand is flung high from the keyboard.

H.:   As we see from the written exercise, fast scales are to be
played descending as well as ascending. Naturally we have to practise them with the left hand as well as with the right. It is hardly
necessary to stress again that in runs away from the median plane
a supinatory position must be taken, and in runs toward the
median plane — a pronatory one.

P.:   And now we shall follow the C major scale with the
others, paying particular attention to those where the basic note
is not played by the thumb or little finger.

H.:   Now only the exercises for playing octaves remain to
be discussed.

P.:   Of the many possibilities here three interest us particularly:

  1)   repeated octaves,
  2)   octaves as intense isolated chords, and
  3)   sequences of octaves played according to the cradle
technique.

W.:   If I remember rightly, we mentioned repeated octaves
in connection with staccato technique (p. 217). The thing is to
grasp an octave with thumb and little finger and repeatedly to play
the same pair of notes staccato, a typical instance of which can be
found in the accompaniment to Schubert's "Erlkönig". In order
to be sure of the freedom of the wrist, we continually make wrist

Exercises in playing
octaves

movements, not while moving the keys, but in between times, i.e., at key-top. During such a sequence of touches, the wrist is successively low, moderately high, high, moderately high, low — and so on. And, of course, there are as many intermediate levels as you want.

P.: You have described quite correctly what we perceive outwardly. Don't forget the middle-hand spreading and chain condition of the arm. Furthermore, the thumb, as it clasps towards the elbow, takes over the guidance of the whole sequence of touches. We have chosen such a simple sequence of chords because we want to concentrate our attention on all these factors and above all on the freedom of the wrist joint.

H.: We have already treated the other possibilities in octave playing. In the intense isolated chord, we should pay special attention to letting the movement continue into the well-known after-motion of the wrist. The successive use of these two different techniques — namely, those of repeated octaves and of the intense isolated chord — will help us to adapt our playing apparatus quickly to the most varied demands. But it also shows us that basically the same condition of the arm is necessary for everything.

P.: Finally, let us not neglect to add a sequence of octaves played according to the cradle technique, even though we have just referred to them in the cradle exercises.

H.: Yes, it can't do any harm to come back to it often, because of the importance of the cradle for the condition of the whole body. We know from experience that the conscientious teacher will again and again find something wrong whenever the cradle technique is being practised.

P.: That holds not only for the cradle technique but for all the other techniques we have discussed in the past few days. There is always something wrong, and the teacher would be doing his pupil a disservice by generously ignoring these mistakes. Even if the pupil says a thousand times: "Now I can't let anything more go", or "But I am doing everything just as you showed me", the teacher must not give in as long as he can see, hear or feel a mistake. Tenacity like this is not recommended for teachers whose main idea is to earn money by having a large flock of pupils, because any pupil who is not really seriously striving for artistic perfection and who does not have complete trust in his teacher will be put off by such methods and will look for a more accommodating teacher.

W.: Whoever can endure it, Professor, must be particularly

Per aspera ad astra

grateful to you for precisely this tenacity of yours. Without it, I would have been satisfied halfway through — if not sooner — and would never have known the wonderful feeling of freedom and calmness which comes after the tensions disappear.

H.:   Only after this condition has been attained is it possible for the player at last to forget about technique and to devote himself entirely to the music. He is no longer distracted by technical difficulties and so is all the more receptive to the purely musical aspect. The conscious or unconscious anxiety that the sound he produces will not turn out an adequate representation of his inner concept has disappeared. Instead, he feels that he can depend on his hands, which now easily and without tiring obey even the subtlest musical impulses.

P.:   Yes, that's the way it ought to be. Let us hope that very many pianists will get to know this feeling.

Key to Plates

All three plates are numbered from the top left anti-clockwise.

Plate A.

1.	Jaw joint	26.	Wrist bones
2.	Neck vertebrae	27.	Ulna
3.	Ridge of the shoulder blade	28.	Radius
4.	Thoracic vertebrae	29.	Head of the ulna
5.	Iliac crest	30.	Middle-hand bones
6.	Lumbar vertebrae	31.	Basal joint of the finger
7.	Hip bones	32.	Basal member of the finger
8.	Sacrum	33.	Middle joint of the finger
9.	Coccyx	34.	Middle member of the finger
10.	Sitting knob	35.	Terminal joint of the finger
11.	Greater trochanter	36.	Nail member of the finger
12.	Ankle joint	37.	Wrist joint
13.	Heel bone	38.	Elbow joint
14.	Middle-foot bones	39.	Upper-arm bone
15.	Toe members	40.	Lower corner of the shoulder blade
16.	Ankle bones		
17.	Splinter bone	41.	Breast bone
18.	Shin bone	42.	Shoulder blade
19.	Knee joint	43.	Shoulder joint
20.	Kneecap	44.	Shoulder-top
21.	Thigh bone	45.	Collar bone
22.	Thick neck	46.	Ribs
23.	Hip joint	47.	Thyroid cartilage
24.	Upper front iliac spur	48.	Tongue bone
25.	Ulna hook	49.	Lower jaw

Plate B.

1. Chewing muscles
2. Nape muscles
3. Head-turner
4. Upper part of the hood muscle
5. Lower part of the hood muscle
6. Posterior axillary fold, formed by the latissimus
7. Anterior saw-muscle
8. The broadest muscle of the back, the latissimus
9. Back muscles in the lumbar region, covered by a flat tendon
10. Lateral trunk muscles
11. Lateral hip muscles
12. Buttock muscles
13. Hamstring muscles
14. Front shank-muscles
15. Lateral shank-muscles
16. Calf muscles
17. Straight thigh-muscle
18. Radial wrist-flexor
19. Long finger-flexors
20. Pea bone
21. Thumb ball
22. Ulnar wrist-extensor
23. Ulnar wrist-flexor
24. Little-finger ball
25. Tendons of the long finger-extensor
26. Two radial wrist-extensors
27. Biceps
28. Elbow-extensor
29. Deltoid muscle
30. Strap muscles
31. Muscular floor of the mouth cavity

Plate C.

1. Upper part of the hood muscle
2. Deltoid muscle
3. Anterior axillary fold, formed by the greater breast-muscle
4. Greater breast-muscle
5. Biceps
6. Two radial wrist-extensors
7. Little-finger ball
8. Basal joint of the finger
9. Basal member of the finger
10. Middle joint of the finger
11. Middle member of the finger
12. Terminal joint of the finger
13. Nail member of the finger
14. Tendon of the short thumb-extensor
15. Anatomical snuff-box
16. Long thumb-extensor
17. Long finger-flexors
18. Radial wrist-flexor
19. Elbow-extensor
20. Upper-arm bone
21. Ribs
22. Breast bone
23. Shoulder joint
24. Shoulder-top
25. Ridge of the shoulder blade
26. Collar bone
27. Breastbone-collarbone joint
28. Rib-supporters
29. Head-turner
30. Strap muscles